MANHUNT

MANHUNT

HOW I BROUGHT SERIAL KILLER
LEVI BELLFIELD TO JUSTICE

FORMER DETECTIVE CHIEF INSPECTOR
COLIN SUTTON

JOHN BLAKE

Published by John Blake Publishing,
2.25, The Plaza,
535 Kings Road,
Chelsea Harbour,
London SW10 0SZ

www.johnblakebooks.com

www.facebook.com/johnblakebooks ∎
twitter.com/jblakebooks ∎

First published in paperback in 2018

ISBN: 978 1 78606 571 1

A catalo ....

Printe ....

The right ....

been asserted by him in accordance with the Copyright, Designs and Patents Act 1988.

Papers used by John Blake Publishing are natural, recyclable products made from wood grown in sustainable forests. The manufacturing processes conform to the environmental regulations of the country of origin.

Every reasonable effort has been made to trace copyright-holders of material reproduced in this book, but if any have been inadvertently overlooked the publishers would be glad to hear from them.

John Blake Publishing is an imprint of Bonnier Books UK
www.bonnierbooks.co.uk

CONTENTS

PROLOGUE

The third week in August 1979. The sun was shining, school was out and life, though really just beginning, was perfect. A good set of A-levels, a place to read law at a decent university, a career in prospect, great friends, family and a lovely girlfriend.

Yes, life was fantastic and, unlike my schoolmates, I wasn't cleaning hospital wards or lugging roof tiles to earn some money before going up to university. I was 'outdoor-clerking' for a firm of solicitors, sitting behind counsel in court, assisting, wearing a suit even and learning what life as a lawyer was going to be like.

Yet that stuffy afternoon at Snaresbrook Crown Court was the beginning of the end of a long-charted course. The defendant, our client, was a member of a local family I knew well and avoided as much as possible. He was, in the north-London vernacular of the time, a jobber – rough and ready in speech and manner, no stranger by appearance to the serious violence of which he stood accused. His face bore many scars of encounters past, and his suit, though expensive and modern, was just too much; cheeky rather than chic, an outfit in which he was clearly uncomfortable.

His story was implausible – even my sheltered eighteen-year-old view of the world told me that. Beer glasses didn't find their way into faces without some considerable help. He had done it; it was as plain as the flattened nose on his patchwork face.

Our counsel was much like me, but 25 years older – a grammar-school boy, red-brick university followed by the Criminal Bar. He was quick in thought, articulate and confident as he presented the defendant's fairy story. It was, he assured the court, quite understandable that, as a brawl broke out, the defendant had rushed to get away, tripped on the carpet and the pint of Whitbread Trophy just flew from his grasp. And, members of the jury, it was obviously an unfortunate coincidence that the glass landed, and broke, on the head of a complete stranger – who just happened to have the defendant's brother in a headlock at the time.

Incredibly, it worked, and the jury came back with a not-guilty verdict in short order. Vice-like handshakes and backslaps having been exchanged, counsel and I retired across the road to the Eagle. 'Well,' I thought, 'I'm here to learn, so I'll ask . . .'

'How did you do that?'

'Confidence, my boy. Look them straight in the eye and give them both barrels,' was the satisfied, almost smug reply. He leaned back on the pub bench, lit a cigar and exhaled expansively.

'No, that's not what I meant . . . sir,' I said, adding the polite title quickly lest my sharpness appeared disrespectful. 'How can you work so hard, apply all your skill, learning and experience to help a thug like that get away with glassing someone?'

PROLOGUE

'That's the game, isn't it? The only game. Whatever you think, whatever bollocks they tell you, you do your best to make it true. Convince the jury, use whatever parts of the system you can, get them off. And watch the briefs come rolling in.'

'But, well, what about the truth? What about what's right?'

A smile creeped across his face and more Castella smoke poured out.

'Ah, you have ideals. Ideals are fine. I had them at your age, believed in them too. Until I realised that ideals are fine but can't pay the mortgage like the Legal Aid fund.'

It was at that very moment that my life changed; that I realised I simply could not and would not be a part of keeping undesirables like our client at liberty. I was going to pull as hard as I could in the other direction. I was going to join the good guys.

*

The first week in January, 2003. Cold, grey and threatening snow. Four of us stood in the spacious but shabby kitchen of the million-pound mansion flat in Seymour Street, just down from Marble Arch. With me were the local Detective Inspector, my number two, Tony McKeown, and Michael the Lodger. Michael was a young barrister who had just returned to his digs after spending the Christmas break with his family and, so far as we police officers were concerned, he couldn't have arrived any sooner.

Bridie Skehan, the ninety-three-year-old owner of the flat, had been missing since Christmas Eve 2002, when she was seen departing the midnight mass at Westminster Cathedral. She had been on foot, her age had forced her to give up her large American cars a few years ago, unwillingly because she cherished them and the memories of her socialite years in the fifties and sixties, from her time working at the US Embassy to being a sought-after interior designer for the moneyed residents of Mayfair.

No trace of Bridie existed thereafter. It wasn't even certain she had made it home from her devotions. Her friend and neighbour Molly had reported her missing on Boxing Day; Molly had a key and had let herself in when she received no answer at Bridie's door. She had told the local police that Michael and another lodger, John the accountant, had gone home and were not expected back until the first week of 2003, but also that there were two other lodgers, a couple, who were foreign and as far as she knew were still meant to be in residence.

Paddington Green CID had contacted the Homicide Command for assistance on the morning of Tuesday, 3 January 2003. It was my first day with my team at Barnes, one which I had intended to spend looking over outstanding investigations and meeting the officers I now commanded. But by 4pm we had been called out and, rather than learning the team's strengths and weaknesses theoretically from the supervisors, I was about to see them in action in a real, live, investigation.

While we were talking Michael through his movements and what he knew of Bridie for the third or fourth time, his attention wandered from our patient questions and he stared at a row of hooks screwed into the bottom of a wall-mounted cupboard. Instinctively, the three detectives followed his gaze.

'Wait a minute. Something's missing – have you moved the key to the shed?' Michael asked us, not accusingly but more seeking reassurance.

I looked at my colleagues and we shook our heads in unison.

'I don't think we realised there was a shed,' I said, looking at the local DI and getting a confirmatory shrug.

'There is a row of them in the back alley, more like outhouses than sheds,' Michael explained.

We asked Michael to show us and he led us out through the front of the building, along to a dark and freezing alley at its west end, which arced back round behind the block. We arrived at a small terrace of brick-built sheds, each about ten feet by six with a solid door and a small window. Michael indicated Bridie's shed and carefully with a gloved hand I tried the door. It was locked. At that very moment it began to snow, huge clumps of flakes driving down into our faces as our eyes met in worried glances.

I summoned DC Dave Leach, nominated as our exhibits officer. He produced a powerful torch and we peered in through the dusty window. As his beam flicked around the tiny, cluttered space it picked out a large cardboard carton in the corner. On its side was printed 'Sony', it looked like it had once contained a television set, probably a large and bulky one, pre-dating flat screens and plasmas by several years.

'Does Bridie have a big Sony telly?' I asked Michael, knowing we could go and look but not relishing the walk round in the blizzard.

'Yes, she does, she got it last year,' Michael replied.

So, the box should be empty. The shed door succumbed to firm pressure from Dave Leach's shoulder and we were in. An unshaded bulb hanging from the ceiling gave a little illumination but then Leach's torch let us see the Sony box properly. Tightly wedged in the far corner of the shed, it had been haphazardly covered with rags and smaller boxes but its sides were plainly visible. And in the bottom right corner was an obvious wet patch, radiating out from where the box rested on the concrete floor, a dark quadrant that shouted trouble.

Leach went to his large kitbag and donned a paper examination suit, latex gloves and a mask. This was real now, quite probably a crime scene and the correct precautions were needed. He entered the grimy shed and set the torch down, so it flooded the corner of the carton with white light. This showed us, even those of us watching silently from ten feet away, that whatever was staining the box had also leaked on to the floor. And it had an ominous red-brown tint.

Leach's paper suit rustled as he shuffled deliberately back to the door and took a scalpel from his bag. Returning to the carton, he knelt and began a sort of commentary for us.

'I am going to cut the stained part away and bag it so that it can be analysed. That should also give us an idea of what is inside without disturbing the flaps on the top of the box, which is where we might get some fingerprints or DNA back.'

I wasn't sure if this talking us through his actions was normal or especially designed to explain what he was doing to me as his new boss. Either way, I was impressed, both that he was doing absolutely the right things and that by talking us through it, he was allowing us to confirm or discuss before he took any action.

'Yes, crack on – sounds like a plan,' I gabbled, wanting to reassure him that I approved.

'I'm being very careful not to press too hard, not to let the blade touch anything inside,' Leach continued – and he was being careful. It took a good three or four minutes for him to remove a quadrant of damp cardboard with a diameter of about ten centimetres. As Leach sealed it carefully in an evidence bag, we craned from the doorway to try to see what had been revealed. It looked a bit like the fake fur you see on cheap cuddly toys, the things won by children at fairground stalls. Long, fine and silver-white. As Leach positioned his torch much closer to the hole in the carton it was obvious the base beneath the silver strands was a dark pink. What we could see was Bridie's head.

By 2am on Wednesday, 4 January 2003, we had arrested both Bridie's 'missing' lodgers, Iranian Ahmed Al Haddad and his much older Filipino lover, Nympha Ong. Al Haddad blamed her and told us, chapter and verse, how they had planned to steal the deeds for the flat, thinking they could use them as security to raise a large sum of money to elope with. How they had battered her to death with her own walking stick and hidden her in the TV box after failing to remove her body in a borrowed suitcase. He was horribly crestfallen when we told him our search of the flat had revealed Bridie had £42,000 cash in a carrier-bag behind her sofa.

Ong, predictably, blamed Al Haddad for the hare-brained plot but, equally predictably, a jury convicted them both of murder and they received life sentences later in the year.

As first days in a new job go it was a spectacularly memorable one. As exciting as it had been to find a body, solve a horrible murder and arrest the perpetrators, what was more important to me was the way in which the team had worked. Each and every member knew his or her job, had made the correct decisions and between them brought about success. I was overjoyed at the prospect of working with these talented and dedicated people for the foreseeable future. I got the feeling we could take on anything together and, a year later, my biggest case was to prove just that.

CHAPTER ONE

CALL OUT – OPERATION YEADDISS

The third week in August 2004. The sun was shining and life – with luck, only just about halfway through – was perfect. I had the job I'd craved for so long – Senior Investigating Officer in charge of one of the Metropolitan Police murder teams – two brilliant children, a move to a new home just a week away, great friends and a lovely wife.

My career in the police, though certainly not as lucrative as one at the Bar might have been, had been satisfying. Relatively quick promotion to Inspector, then the opportunity to achieve my long-standing desire to investigate murders. I had served in the Met, West Yorkshire and Surrey before returning to the Met in September 2002. I had held the rank of Detective Chief Inspector since 1996 and was fully trained as a Senior Investigating Officer – the coveted SIO role, responsible for running the most serious investigations, almost exclusively murders.

The Met murder command at that time consisted of twenty-seven teams, each headed by an SIO. These were divided into three groups of nine, each allocated to a rough third of London. My team was based at Barnes, a wealthy and fashionable suburb by the Thames in south-west London. However, our area included much north of the river, including the tough boroughs of Camden, Brent and Ealing, as well as Westminster in the centre. It was almost inevitably in these areas that most of our inquiries began; while we also had responsibility for Richmond and Heathrow in the west and Barnet in the north, murders were so rare in these places that we could sometimes forget they existed.

Each murder team spent one week in nine 'on call', where it would be responsible for the first response to suspicious deaths. Occasionally, this would result in the team taking on a new investigation but, more usually, it would be handed over to the team designated 'in frame'. This status meant the team was to take on the next investigation that arose in its area and was determined by senior officers, having regard to their capacity available in the light of existing investigations. While 'on call' was restricted to one week in nine, 'in frame' was open-ended, in that, if nothing happened in your area for several weeks or (most rarely) months, your entire team could be waiting to react any moment to a call, and thus found their private lives severely restricted.

Happily, being neither on call nor in frame on 20 August 2004, I was simply dozing at about 7am, thinking not of murder but of our impending house move, which was now but a week away. When the home phone suddenly dragged me into full consciousness, I was completely confused. Work always used the mobile and, in any case, why would they be ringing me this early when not on call or in frame? In fact, everyone used my mobile, so I only just resisted the temptation to let the wrong number or the double-glazing salesman or whoever it was take it out on the answer phone. But my virtual obsession with always being contactable took over and I made it to the phone before the answer machine cut in:

'Hello, sir, it's Brent.'

I recognised immediately the distinctive tone of Brent Hyatt, one of my team Detective Inspectors. So it must have been work. My first thought was that some catastrophe must have befallen one of the team but he said, 'Your mobile's off and Nigel Counsell's trying to get you to take a job. Can you give him a ring?'

I was even more confused – I wasn't expecting a job, and why was my mobile off? I solved the latter quite quickly, realising that the charger had failed and the battery had died. But the job? I rang Nigel, a fellow SIO who was 'acting up' – standing in to cover as on-call Superintendent – and he quickly ran through the barest facts. A young French girl, Amélie Delagrange, battered about the head and found dying in the middle of Twickenham Green.

So by 9am, I was at Twickenham Police Station for a handover briefing with acting Superintendent Nigel Counsell and the on-call SIO, DCI Dave Cobb. Nigel was a man I respected and liked, with a reputation for attention to detail. Dave, before promotion, had been the deputy to the SIO on Operation Upwey – the investigation into the very similar murder of Marsha McDonnell in nearby Hampton in February 2003. So I was confident that whatever I was given would be both properly done, so far, and helpful. I knew, just from the talk between colleagues, that the suspect for Marsha's shocking murder was a local sixteen-year-old, whom I shall call Sharpe. There was some circumstantial evidence, to which weight was added by the opinion of some highly regarded psychological profilers, that Sharpe was responsible. His mental state was such, though, that he had not been charged but instead detained under the Mental Health Act. I made a note to ensure that the first action should be to ensure he was safely locked up the previous night – which, it transpired, he was, in a secure facility somewhere in County Durham.

The first information imparted was the operation name. All major investigations in the Met are randomly allocated a name, not so much for secrecy but so that officers may have a neutral, short-hand label by which they can refer to the investigation. These names were taken from a gazetteer of place names, each calendar year's operations having the same initial letter. Usually at that time, British place names were used but, since 2004 was the year for places beginning with 'Y', there were not enough British locations to go round and so the USA gazetteer was brought into use. Hence, the investigation into Amélie's murder became Operation Yeaddiss, named after a small town in Kentucky about a hundred and fifty miles south-east of Lexington. Not that I suppose a British murder investigation would be its inhabitants' first choice for a civic twinning. Like all the best operation names, though, it did have sufficient potential for misspelling to cause some frustration, if not confusion. 'Two Ds and two Ss' became a new mantra for me for a short while.

The briefing was much wider than I expected. Dave Cobb took up the story first and I typed up copious notes thus:

CALL OUT – OPERATION YEADDISS

Operation Upwey was the investigation into three linked assaults in the area between Twickenham Green and Hampton.

Marsha McDonnell was murdered in Hampton on 4 February 2003; this led to an incident one month earlier being viewed as an assault rather than an accident. That had involved sixteen-year-old Jesse Wilson, who had sustained massive head and facial injuries close to her home in Strawberry Hill. It had been believed by her family and doctors that she had slipped on the icy pavement, but Marsha's murder had thrown a new light on this and it was now firmly believed that she, too, had been the victim of an horrific assault. Like Marsha [and, as we were shortly to find out, like Amélie Delagrange, the murdered French girl], she had been struck a mighty blow to the back of her head with a blunt and heavy instrument – in all probability, some sort of hammer. Her facial injuries were probably caused by her falling forwards on to the paving slabs.

All the evidence pointed towards Sharpe, who had been in secure accommodation in the north-east since March 2003. The original team and experts were sure that he was responsible but there was never enough evidence to charge him. The links between the attacks were seen as the victim profiles – age, gender and appearance; the proximity of the locations and that all were wearing dark coats, with hoods, and had Walkman or iPod headphones in at the time.

The next to speak was Detective Inspector Tim Dobson, from the local Richmond Borough CID. He immediately gave the impression of a calm, patient and detailed investigator in outlining the facts around the third assault:

On Sunday, 14 April 2004, Edel Harbison, an accountant in her early thirties, left a restaurant on the north side of Twickenham Green. She was walking to her home, about a quarter of a mile away. Her usual route would have been across the base of Twickenham Green, but she was unable to remember anything after leaving her friends at the restaurant at about 10pm. She was found nearby by a passing motorist, with the familiar massive wound to the back of her head and facial injuries severe enough to require reconstructive surgery.

Detailed examination of her injuries had revealed three or four wounds resulting from heavy blows. It wasn't until the following day, when her bags were found in a pool of blood in a nearby street, that the actual scene of her assault was identified. Her mobile phone, keys, handbag and shopping were intact; nothing had been stolen, save for the possibility that somebody had opened and drunk from a carton of orange juice among her groceries. This had been seized for forensic examination, but then an over-enthusiastic tidy-up of the property store by a Richmond sergeant the next day had resulted in its destruction and the opportunity had been lost.

It was felt unlikely that the offences were linked, though the possibility of a 'copycat' attack could not be excluded. There was no evidence against any individual, and very little CCTV footage – just the restaurant and the local buses.

The orange-juice carton was to be the most recent (but thankfully last) in a series of missed opportunities that I was to uncover as the investigation proceeded. At this stage, though, I just put it out of my mind. What interested me more was the assertion that it was unlikely that the offences were linked. The fact is, happily, that attacks like this, where a stranger commits a murderous assault in the street, are extremely rare. Here we had three very similar attacks in very similar circumstances on very similar victims, and all in a small, very suburban and safe corner of London. And now there was a fourth. To me, there was every reason to think that they might be the work of one person, but then I had no baggage from the original Marsha investigation. It seemed that there were some officers who, having been sure that Sharpe was Marsha's murderer, now found it uncomfortable – almost inconvenient – that, contrary to their firmly held belief, two further attacks had taken place while he was locked up three-hundred miles away.

To me, although the possibilities within the whole situation were immediately apparent, they were also irrelevant. The other offences had been investigated before, unsuccessfully. My first task was the new one, an offence where I could start from the beginning and where there would be new opportunities. Once we had found Amélie Delagrange's killer, then and only then might it be worth revisiting the older attacks. And it was to Amélie that Dave Cobb turned as he took over the briefing once more.

CHAPTER TWO

AMÉLIE DELAGRANGE

Amélie Delagrange was born on the edge of Paris on 8 February 1982. Jean-François, her father, was an architect, Dominique, her mother, a personal assistant. They gave her the middle names Martine and Josette, after her grandmothers. She was their first child and her arrival prompted them to put into action a long-held desire to move away from the city. Jean-François designed a house for them in a small village called Hanvoile, lying in the beautiful Picardy countryside. Young Amélie grew into an intelligent child, as loving a daughter as one could wish for but also with a streak of independence and a quick sense of humour. Among a strong academic performance across the board, she particularly excelled at languages and, with the prospect of becoming fluent in both English and Spanish, she intended to follow a career as a tri-lingual secretary or PA.

Amélie had spent time in Spain and also in Manchester but,

when intending again to go to work abroad to improve one of her languages, she chose to return to England. She preferred the way of life there, she had said; she felt comfortable, even safe. So, in April 2004, the pretty blonde French twenty-two-year-old with the beaming smile and the wicked sense of humour came to London. Not, of course, to central London, with its hustle and bustle and crime. She found work waitressing in Le Maison Blanc, a French coffee shop adjacent to the railway station in the lively but solid middle-class suburb of Richmond upon Thames. Having secured a room at 66, Gould Road in nearby Twickenham, she set about her work with her usual good humour and efficiency. She found some French friends through work and even started a romance with a young Frenchman, Olivier Lenfant. She was happy, settled and enjoying herself but never forgot those at home, speaking to her parents and Veronique, her sister, almost daily using her French mobile phone. Having found that quite expensive for keeping in contact with her friends in England, though, she eventually bought an English T-Mobile SIM card and used that in a borrowed Sony Ericsson handset too. That was possibly the first stroke of luck we were to have when investigating how Amélie had met her death.

Friday, 19 August 2004 was a fine day in an unremarkable summer. Amélie had been working at Maison Blanc, then had done a bit of shopping in Richmond before meeting up with a few French friends in Crystalz, a wine bar on the main street in Twickenham, just a few doors down from the police station. At about eight thirty in the evening, she had called Olivier and invited him to come over, as her landlady was away and she was going to be alone in the house. Naturally unaware of the effect it was going to have, Olivier turned down the invitation – he was tired after work and, instead, they arranged to meet up at the weekend.

Her friends told us later that, having had perhaps four glasses of wine and not being a heavy drinker, an hour or so later Amélie decided it was time to go home. She crossed the road to the bus stop outside The Sorting Rooms, a large pub formed in the old post office, to wait for any of a number of buses that would take her the mile or so to Twickenham Green. That was the last time anyone who knew Amélie saw her, and so we must take up her story from my notes of the handover from DCI Dave Cobb in the briefing at Twickenham Police Station the next morning:

22:20 approximately last night, Twickenham Green, Tristram Beasley-Suffolk was wandering around the edge of the Green, when he sees her by the cricket pitch. She is face down, alive and in the 'recovery' position. He goes across to the wine bar and restaurants and calls for help. The girl is taken to the West Middlesex hospital, she is found to have one huge wound to the back of her head and dies shortly after arriving there.

She was dressed as if she was on a night out. She had nothing on her; she was lying immediately underneath the rope which protects the cricket wickets. There is a black top there, which Mr Beasley-Suffolk had placed over her. Also there was a plastic carrier bag and in it a piece of paper with two phone numbers written on it. Nothing else, nothing to help identify her.

MANHUNT

The on-call officers attending had called the phone numbers and spoken to a French man who said a girl had called him that evening, said she was in Twickenham and asked him round to her house. Her mobile phone was not found, it is still missing and the Telephone Intelligence Unit have been informed and are working to trace it. He gave her first name as Amélie, and said she worked in a French delicatessen in Richmond. A woman from there has given her full details as:

Amélie Martine Josette Delagrange

born 08/02/82 so 22 years

from Paris suburbs

In UK 2 months, working at the deli in Richmond – Maison Blanc.

Visual identification has been made by the shop proprietor, and we have a photo from her boyfriend. Her parents are in Paris; she speaks to them 3 or 4 times a week. Home address is 66, Gould Road, Twickenham (2 streets north of the Green).

There will be a post-mortem examination this afternoon at Kingston Hospital, by Dr Rob Chapman.

The scene preserved so far is the Green and First Cross Road.

Other possible considerations are-

- A pool of blood, it is believed, has been found in the street at Cross Deep, about half a mile away.
- The Green was still pretty lively and busy at 1am when Dave Cobb arrived there.

- Some house to house enquiries have been done by the local uniform officers.
- There may be CCTV at the wine bar and other local businesses.
- 2 POLSA [specialist search teams] have been briefed for the Green.
- Vanessa, a friend, was probably with Amélie last night.

I will be lent four officers from Operation Upwey, the Marsha McDonnell investigation; the psychological profiler Dr Adrian West who had helped on Marsha's case had been informed and was considering the facts, and a Press Officer was on his way to me.

And that was it, really. The sum total of knowledge as to who she was and what had happened to her, as it stood about twelve hours after someone had quite literally caved her skull in. A good idea of my initial thoughts can be gleaned from the notes I made immediately after this briefing – those starting 'P-' are things I wanted to record in the policy file, a document where SIOs enter their important decisions, and the reasoning supporting them; those beginning 'A-' are those actions I wanted the team to start getting on with as soon as possible.

P- Second scene (Cross Deep) – SOCO to swab blood for DNA
P- PDFs [Personal Descriptive Forms – officers would be required to note the physical description of everyone they spoke to on the inquiry]

A- *Phone data from T-Mobile – ask TIU to get the data for
   calls and cell-sites, not just billing*
A- *Check banks, ATMs etc. – preserve their data and CCTV
   for victim or suspects in the area*
A- *DC Neil Jones to be the CCTV officer*

A list of steps that immediately presented themselves to me
as I considered where we went next – perhaps informed by a
combination of training, past experience and simple intuition.
However, hindsight was to prove that two of them, relating to
the mobile-phone data and DC Jones and the CCTV role, while
not revolutionary, were absolutely crucial to how things were to
turn out.

Though I was itching to get down to the scene and have a
look, the next hour or so was spent first sending out a few officers
on the very urgent actions that needed doing: speaking to Olivier,
Vanessa and the people at Maison Blanc, and then sitting down
with the boss, Detective Chief Superintendent Andy Murphy, to
sort staffing, roles and the structure of how we would work.

CHAPTER THREE

THE FIRST DAY

Andy Murphy and I went back a long way. Not in the bosom-buddies or even drinking-partner sense, but we had worked together in the early 1990s at Islington, we knew a bit about each other and there was a mutual understanding, which could only help. Importantly, too, he had experience of being an SIO for a high-profile serial investigation and so brought some first-hand knowledge of the issues that were likely to arise, which others could only guess at.

First on the agenda was staffing. I needed a deputy but my first choice – Detective Inspector Tony McKeown – was on leave and so unavailable. My other DI, Brent Hyatt, who had woken me that morning, was busy with other cases and, additionally, Andy Murphy had doubts about his experience and suitability for such a high-profile investigation, which was likely to be very fast-moving. I had another acting DI on attachment with me at the time but he was untrained and untested in the environment. So it was that DI Richard Ambrose was seconded to me from a Hendon-based murder team. Richard had been the office manager as a detective sergeant on the original Marsha investigation and so would bring an in-depth knowledge of that case. His first words on the subject were that he was never convinced that Sharpe was responsible; the cynic in me thought that he had no choice but to say that. However, as I grew to know him, I realised that he was far too straightforward for that. I came to like Richard immensely; his attitude, his manner and his sense of humour were just what we needed at times – and what he needed, given his daily sixty-five-mile round trip to our office in Barnes. His unswerving loyalty to me, and his being a Tottenham Hotspur season-ticket holder, helped too.

Mickey Singh, the temporarily attached acting DI on my team was to head the intelligence side of things. Thereafter, at the lower ranks, I was promised assistance from all over – Flying Squad, Kidnap and Hostage Squad and, of course, from other murder teams. Even the hardened, sometimes fearsome, Flying Squad officers – who spent their usual working days chasing the very worst armed robbers – were happy to lend a hand. 'Proper work, this, Guvnor – we've all got wives, sisters or daughters,' was what one Flying Squad DC said to me. They also had a legendary reputation for exploiting overtime budgets and showed they had lost none of their skill in that regard, but I cared not a jot. The quality of their work was first-rate.

Two days into the inquiry, my team numbered more than seventy – about twice its normal size. But it was recognised very early on that this was to be no normal investigation; the senior officers at Scotland Yard appreciated the risks in what had been and what might happen, and resources were not to be a problem. For the first few weeks, at least, if I needed something, I asked for it and I got it.

There were two other very important officers lent to me that day, both of whom formally transferred to my team very shortly afterwards and were with me every step of the way, to the very end. Clive Grace was a Borough constable, who had been the liaison officer for Edel Harbison after her attack in April 2004. He was a man of huge experience, great attention to detail and was, as he proudly would say, 'Old School.' Drafted in to bring knowledge of Edel's case, his commitment and skill quickly impressed me and he became firmly ensconced in my intelligence unit. He was to complete some of the most difficult and painstaking work in the whole investigation, outstandingly, across all the different cases. If he were crucial to the investigative processes, the other officer was just as crucial to me and my management of it.

Detective Sergeant Jo Brunt was Detective Superintendent Sue Hill's staff officer and, on the day Amélie's case broke, Sue was abroad. Typically, Jo thought she would offer her services, as she didn't have much else on and, as she put it, 'I thought you might be a bit busy.' From her first role as my scribe over the first few days, making notes for me at the scene and in meetings and briefings, she then took on the role of a case officer – preparing the submission of files and papers to the Crown Prosecution Service – and then, additionally, acted as my deputy when the role became vacant. Jo had an undeserved reputation for being negative, cold and intolerant but was also regarded as an excellent, caring detective. As we worked together, it became clear that the caring side was actually her dominant and driving factor. She has an ability to understand the dynamics of a team beyond any officer I have encountered before; she is most thorough and perceptive of all the implications of any action to be taken. She, too, was absolutely loyal and supportive of me all the way through the investigation, even in our worst and darkest moments. I told her many, many times that I could never have done it without her, but I am still not sure she believes me.

The team having been shaped, Andy Murphy then discussed how he could best support me, particularly in the coming week while Sue Hill, my line manager, was away. He emphasised that he would not interfere with my operational decisions – 'You are the SIO' was an oft-repeated phrase. He would, though, try to take some pressures from me by dealing upwards with the very senior officers, who would undoubtedly take a keen interest in the progress of the case, and he would deal, for the first few days at least, with the media. I was happy, naturally, with the first offer. The second, I confess, I was slightly suspicious of. I had often seen officers more senior to the SIO doing interviews and statements in the wake of high-profile cases. Since I had always done this for myself and felt it part of my job, it had made me wonder why – was it as simple as the boss muscling in on the glory? Yet now, knowing Andy Murphy and knowing that would never be his aim, I had to consider that there might be some merit in allowing me the space in which to manage the investigation without the constant demands from the media. It took about twelve hours for me to realise this was, indeed, a very good reason. Seeing the regularity with which Andy was called upon by the press, radio and TV, I knew that I just could not have done it for myself in the midst of everything else that was going on, so I was hugely grateful for his taking it on. And Andy got it exactly right, not only in what he was saying but in his quick meetings with me before he did so, ensuring I knew what he was planning to say and giving me the opportunity to influence it as I saw necessary from the investigative perspective.

At about 1pm on Friday, 20 August, some fifteen hours after Amélie had been attacked, I arrived at the scene. Twickenham is world famous for its eponymous rugby stadium, but less than half a mile away is the Green. A triangular oasis of grass in the suburban sprawl, it funnels two A-roads towards the town centre. Across its centre, roughly north to south, runs a footpath; to the western, wider side is a cricket pitch, complete with sightscreens and a pavilion. Such is the good order of the locals that the ropes protecting the wickets are largely observed by all, excepting the odd inquisitive dog. The area around the sightscreens is frequented by a small group who like to drink strong cider in the open air – the nearest, it seems, that the Green got to disorder prior to the attacks. To the right of the footpath, there is no formal purpose to the grass until, at the eastern apex, one reaches Arthur's. This is a small bistro, obviously popular, despite there having been no attempt whatsoever to disguise its previous incarnation as a public lavatory.

On Staines Road across the north side are a few small businesses – a curry house, a wine bar and a motorcycle shop being the obvious attractions, as well as a shop with a slightly incongruous display of *Star Wars* costumes. A few side streets run up to the north into a small estate of Victorian terraces, which includes Gould Road, where Amélie was lodging. The western boundary of the Green is First Cross Road, where the houses overlooking the cricket field are smarter, and, along the south, where the Green runs into Hampton Road, there are large detached houses, a church and a primary school. Buses from Twickenham to Hampton, Hounslow and beyond run along both sides.

It was, on a bright August afternoon, a scene of suburban tranquillity, the cricket screens and pavilion adding an essentially British quality. Virtually the last place one would imagine a series of murderous assaults to be effected on young women. But the white scene-of-crime tent placed roughly at short mid-on by the cricket square, and the plastic cordon tape fluttering in the summer breeze, quickly reminded me of my awful purpose in being there. From where I stood, within the distance of a lusty knock from a Sunday slogger with his eye in, at least three young women had been battered on the head, for fun. One was dead and the other two would never be the same again. And less than two miles away, Marsha McDonnell, too, had lost her short life in the same way. Taking in the scene, the phrase 'unlikely to be linked' sprung to mind again and seemed ever less sensible an appraisal.

As I walked around, my phone was ringing constantly. Information, snippets, suggestions. The local community – shocked, frightened and desperate to help – were coming forward in droves. Much of it made little sense but, somewhere within the deluge of detail which always follows such outrages, the key might be hidden. So every phone call, every visit to the mobile police station situated just down from Arthur's restaurant, was logged, recorded and considered.

One of the first apparent leads was a sighting of a man hanging around and smoking roll-ups by one of the cricket sightscreens at about 10pm. The witness said he resembled Diego Maradona, the disgraced Argentinian footballer. This made a welcome change from looking like Phil Mitchell from *EastEnders*, the description that seemed to arise in most major investigations at the time. So, as well as collecting all the fag-butts from around the area for DNA analysis, I needed the sightscreen examined for fingerprints. Nobody could say whether 'Maradona' was our man but, at this stage, I needed to at least preserve any means of identifying him, just in case. Practical problem number one: cricket sightscreens are very large, at least when compared to police vans. Since one of the most sensitive ways of disclosing latent finger-marks is to 'fume' the object with vaporised Superglue, a detailed examination *in situ* was not an option either. It was time for some lateral thinking. Towing it to the laboratory was considered but discounted, on the grounds that, not only might the unsprung iron wheels not be up to the trip, but that the effect on London's traffic of a police car dragging a sightscreen 10 miles at 4 mph might quickly dissipate the massive public support we were enjoying. Finding a suitable low-loader was proving difficult, so the local fire brigade was summoned. Using their equipment normally reserved for cutting casualties out of wrecked cars, the screens were disassembled with care untypical of the brigade, carefully wrapped for transit and taken away. Whether batting then became more difficult for the rest of the summer I am not sure; but I know that the Metropolitan Police did eventually buy the club a lovely set of new screens in time for the following season. We never did find any prints on the screens, nor, for that matter, the true identity of 'Maradona'.

The POLSA teams had arrived. In the somewhat strained and pointless police-speak desire for snappy acronyms, POLSA is as good as anyone could come up with for the specialist search teams. It stands for, nearly, Police Search Advisor, which should strictly mean the inspector in charge, rather than the whole team. The teams consist of ordinary constables from boroughs who have been trained to conduct minute, intrusive and sometimes destructive searches, and were originally formed to ensure that venues used for State visits and similar potential terrorist targets were clear of suspicious devices.

In August 2004, it was relatively easy to get the services of two such teams for a case like Amélie's; in the London post 7 July 2005, it became considerably harder. There was no alternative to a fingertip search of the immediate vicinity of the attack, which I defined as the western half of Twickenham Green, from First Cross Road to the bisecting path. I set my two expert exhibits officers, DCs Paul Carruth and Simon Rogers, off with the searchers, ready to collect and preserve anything of potential value.

Of course, at this stage, we didn't know exactly *what* might be of value. The first uncertainty came over the fag-butts. Cigarette ends are often a bone of contention. They are usually an excellent source of DNA from saliva and, as such, can prove the presence of a person at the location where they are found. But there are caveats – they are small, light and easily transported, and so they need not always betray the smoker's presence. Furthermore, in a public place such as this, there will be literally thousands of butts and, since any suspect might have had legitimate, innocent access there on any number of occasions prior to the murder, any evidential value may be significantly diminished.

With the mysterious 'Maradona' it was different. There was a sighting of a suspect in a relatively contained location, and he was seen to be smoking. This made collection of the debris around the sightscreen worthwhile but I was not planning to sweep up every cigarette butt on the Green. Nigel Counsell, it seems, had other ideas and, unbeknown to me, had instructed the POLSA teams to do just that. It was, I know, enthusiasm and a desire to get everything done that prompted Nigel to interfere in this way but it really was taking his acting-superintendent role a little too far, especially without referring to me. The first I knew of it was when an animated Paul Carruth came striding purposefully across the Green towards me. Paul, a tall, dark Glaswegian ex-professional footballer, had recently joined us from another murder team, and was very experienced. Never afraid to speak his mind, he could give the wrong impression quite easily but I knew by reputation he was a very good officer. From about ten yards away, he began the conversation, 'For fuck's sake, Guvnor, do you know how many fag ends there'll be on this Green?'

'A lot fewer now you've given up again, I suppose?'

He smiled and gurgled some mild swear words under his breath; I listened to his proposition that to collect each one was impractical and a waste of time with a great deal of sympathy. I then went and amended the POLSA instructions, made a policy entry and went to tell Nigel. He was never going to force me to do it but we had to agree to disagree. It was, though, for me, an important principle in action – I was the SIO and, while I was,

I had to be allowed to manage the operation, and the risks, as I saw things. To do otherwise would confuse my thinking, confuse my strategies. I was pleased to gain Andy Murphy's agreement on this shortly afterwards.

The afternoon went by quickly: a media briefing by Andy Murphy, interminable POLSA searching on hands and knees, then the post-mortem examination at Kingston Hospital. The media briefing went well – we didn't really have too much to say at that early stage, just the usual appeal for witnesses and expressions of horror at such a terrible crime. The case was arousing quite a bit of interest, with national media as well as London and the locals. While we accepted the possibility of a link with Marsha McDonnell, Andy was rightly quick to deny any thought of a connection to the abduction and murder of Milly Dowler in Walton on Thames in 2002. Quite why the media made such a suggestion was mystifying – sure, it was only a few miles away, but the crime was startlingly different in its nature, in the victim's age and in the way she died. Such a link had never crossed our minds, and we felt that the speculation could only be unhelpful, so it was swiftly put down.

The post-mortem examination was a sombre affair. The pathologist, Rob Chapman, had also examined Marsha's body and so was well-placed to draw any comparisons. I had worked with him many times before, an affable chap with an excellent reputation. But despite him, myself and Richard Ambrose all being of a similar easy-going nature, there was an uncharacteristic absence of even small talk, let alone the usual frequent attempts at gallows humour. It was obvious that we were all aware this was different from the usual one-off murder. Whereas normally we are dealing with the tragedy of untimely death, there is at least some comfort in knowing that it is over; we need to convict whoever did it, sure, but the whole horrible episode is self-contained. Its effects are felt immediately by the family and friends of both victim and suspect, but no wider. What we were dealing with here was much more widespread, more serious, in its implications for a whole community, perhaps even a whole city. As much as we could do no more for poor Amélie, there was a realisation that we had to do so much for everyone else. This apprehension, felt by all, remained unspoken but made for an even more morose atmosphere as we looked on at an examination of a beautiful young girl, perfect and healthy in every way until an animal had left her with a skull like a dropped Easter egg.

The next office meeting was at 7.30pm and we regrouped at Twickenham in the familiar horseshoe with Richard Ambrose and me in the middle. 'What have you found, what does it mean and what do we do next?' – the mantra I always recited to myself as I chaired these meetings. The short answer was that, despite lots of hard work, hundreds of calls and visits from the public, we still didn't really have any clearer picture of what had happened, never mind why. We quickly dispersed again, more people to be seen, more leads to follow. Jo Brunt had seen Vanessa and established that Amélie was in possession of a bag, a Walkman and a mobile phone when she left the wine bar, so we were missing some significant items. The phone might be the easiest to trace; the initial information was that it last contacted the T-Mobile network at 10.23pm on 19 August, just minutes after Amélie was probably attacked. And at the time, it seemed the phone was in Walton on Thames, about six miles away. The implications of that for the investigation were potentially huge but it would be the morning before we got the full details. Quite how the next four hours passed so quickly, I am not sure but, after reading the first few statements and making plans for the morning, it was well into Saturday before I left for home.

CHAPTER FOUR

THE FIRST NIGHT

It was well after 2am when I got home, probably nearer 3am. Despite being awake for twenty hours and active for nineteen of them, there was no way I was getting straight to sleep. Even though I knew I was due back at Twickenham in about five hours, it was always difficult for me to sleep on the first night of a new inquiry. This time, though, it wasn't just thinking about the investigation, what I'd done, what there was to do, nor even thoughts of Amélie and her family. There was a personal dimension, which was impossible to put out of my head, and which led me to sit in the garden with a packet of Marlboro Lights and ponder.

I really fell into being a detective – being a murder investigator – by accident. In joining the police, I had believed my career would be general, in uniform, and my aim was to be promoted, have a career and seize the opportunity to make a difference by controlling and leading things from a senior level. But that all changed, quite suddenly and without warning, in March 1983.

We had left the party at about 3am, even though my colleague and friend PC Andy Taylor and I had only arrived, fresh from a raid on an unlicensed drinking club in Tottenham, about ninety minutes earlier. Truth was that I was tired out and was looking forward to a good long sleep before my 2pm shift the following day. As I drove through a deserted Enfield Town, I noticed the litter bin first – a molten, smoking blob of yellow plastic still doggedly clinging to a lamp post just by the bus stop at Little Park Gardens.

'Bloody yobboes,' I said to Andy, just as we realised the bin fire was only the starters; the main course was obvious to our right. There was a brilliant yellow-orange glow from the street door of a shop, a haberdasher's, where, as I later found out, the primary stock in trade was net curtains.

Two tired partygoers were suddenly awakened and transformed back into coppers. Andy sprinted down to the nearest phone box to raise the alarm while I found my way, through startled kitchen staff at the adjacent Chinese restaurant, into the rear loading yard, where I tore up the fire escape and into the first-floor flat above the now-blazing shop. That's one of the strange things about being a cop: burning buildings, fighting drunks, men with knives – all things any sane individual would flee from, we run towards them. Somehow, the 'escape' bit of fire escape passed me by and it had become my fire access.

But it was completely hopeless. The yards and yards of man-made fabric had, in the space of thirty seconds, turned the burning paper thrust through the letter-box into a raging conflagration. A death trap, quite literally, I realised as I choked on the hot black smoke and felt the heat on my bare arms and face. I had made it perhaps 15 feet into the building, the rear door having succumbed quickly to the adrenalin-fuelled kicks from a size 11, Doc Marten-clad foot. With hindsight, it was probably most fortunate for me that the next door had in it a small wired-glass pane, as through this I could see the fierce blaze on the other side. It was just like looking through one of those little inspection windows on a stove, only much bigger. What would have happened had I opened that door God only knows, but I'm pretty confident still that I would have added to, not reduced, the casualties that morning. I admitted defeat and ran out thankfully into the fresh air.

Jack and Pearl Sedler ran the shop, lived in it and, tragically, died in it. Their bedroom, where they were killed, was on the third floor, at the very top of the building. While I will never know what good I might have done had I continued my rescue mission, and while the overwhelming likelihood is that I would have done nothing except perhaps kill or injure myself, it still hit me hard, wondering perhaps . . .

The following Monday, I found myself not patrolling Tottenham on the beat, but at Ponders End Police Station. It was the first time I had set foot in a murder incident room, and I had to see the Senior Investigating Officer to make a statement. He was a kind, experienced Detective Superintendent, whose reputation as a successful investigator was well-known, even by young uniform PCs like me. His first act was to reassure me that I had done the right thing in trying and then getting out. He left me to write my statement and then asked, almost casually, if I would like to hang around and work on the Murder Squad for a few days. He had 'squared it up' with the bosses at Tottenham, who had agreed that it might do me some good, in that I might feel a bit better about the whole incident if I felt I was at least helping to catch those responsible.

So it was, the next day, that I attended my first 'Office Meeting', as the briefings that take place during an investigation are invariably known. The team sat around in a rough horseshoe, the SIO and his deputy in the middle. And everyone was invited to contribute to the collective knowledge, referring to the red A4 notebooks on their laps and announcing who they had seen, what they had said, emphasising important points and spelling out names and numbers so that the SIO's note was accurate. I had little to contribute but drew in every word, every nuance, from the whole experience.

And what amazed me – excited me – was the SIO. He sat there patiently listening to each team member in turn, noting everything that was said. I swear you could see his mind working, speedily yet in great detail, taking in every fact, comparing it with all the others, and occasionally giving back an aloud thought, which most often was followed by a request for some more action to be taken. The intellectual challenge of it fascinated me, inspired me. As much as it is like the cliché of the boy who wants to drive an engine, it was at that moment in the stuffy, scruffy 1960s surroundings of Ponders End nick that I loved what I saw. I was mesmerised. I knew I had to be an SIO.

Every step I took in the force thereafter was with that aim – to be the man sitting there in the middle of the room, taking it all in, weighing it up, judging the next steps and making sure the team carried them out. That was when the rank, the status, the power and all the other career considerations got put to one side, when that role became the only goal. It had taken thirteen years to get there, another six before it was my full-time job. And just like an actor, or an athlete, I wanted to perform and be victorious on the big stage. That opportunity, which had always been nebulous, theoretical, even fantastic, was now upon me.

What took me two minutes to recall that August morning in my back garden takes much longer to retell here but I needed to make it clear so as to put into context how I came to be in the position, and how taking on Amélie's murder investigation meant to me what it did. Surfers, I think, dream of the great wave; anglers of the record catch; golfers have to believe that, each time they step on to the tee at a par-three hole, today will be the hole-in-one. Police officers are no different. In a job where variety and unpredictability are great attractions, it is often the hope of the capture of the red-handed burglar, the paedophile or the murderer that inspires; similarly, the reality is almost always the equivalent of the wet wipe-out, the tiny minnow or the slice into the trees.

For a Senior Investigating Officer, motivation is never difficult. One is constantly dealing with the most serious of crimes and, therefore, the most serious of consequences. Nobody should need more motivation than that; few, if any of us, do. That it gives the satisfaction of the intellectual challenge, of pitting your wits against the opposition, against the environment and, all too often, against sheer chance is, perhaps, an added bonus only for those like me, who have the sort of mind that enjoys quizzes, crosswords and puzzles.

But for SIOs, the huge wave, the massive trout, the hole-in-one, is the Category A+ murder, the high-profile, stranger attack where there is no connection between killer and victim, save for the misfortune that their paths happened to cross. And if it were part of a series, well, that is thankfully so rare that, despite many being trained for it, each of us knows in our heart that it probably won't happen.

So, as I sat there in a quiet Surrey cul-de-sac and watched the sun come up over the garden shed while puffing my way through far too many cigarettes, it wasn't just the immediate lines of inquiry, the staffing and the existing enquiries that would have to be put on ice that occupied my thoughts. It was the magnitude of what I was embarking upon. It was obvious that this was going to be an extremely difficult case to succeed with. If all the attacks were linked, if one man were responsible for them all, then there had already been a number of investigations, all properly resourced, presumably all competently conducted, but yet he had not been caught. Was he clever, was he lucky – or both? And was I up to the challenge – was I clever, was I lucky – hopefully, both? It was going to be a long job, no doubting that. The comment from my boss, Detective Superintendent Sue Hill, in my recent appraisal rang in my ears: 'Colin is excellent in the on-call role and in completing short investigations. I have my doubts as to his patience and stamina for a long-term investigation, though.'

Like all criticism, it had stung a bit. To be truthful, I didn't know whether she was right or wrong, as I had never really had the chance to find out. Just two months later, the opportunity had arisen, ironically while Sue was on holiday (or else might she have thought I shouldn't take the job).

There was only one conclusion I was ever going to reach. Someone had to lead this. Andy Murphy, my Detective Chief Superintendent, had given it to me. It was the sort of job you dream of succeeding at and that was what I was going to do. There was no element of proving anything else to anyone, just this serial killer's guilt to a jury. It was simply a very difficult job. One that needed doing for the sake of Amélie, the others, their families and, indeed, for those who would, undoubtedly, become victims in the future if we did not catch him. Of course, there was no guarantee of success. There would be highs and lows; eventually, it might just all come to nothing. But it was what I had trained for, what I had craved, what I had worked for. The greatest possible test, the most unpredictable challenge: to take out a madman who was killing young women, at random and for who knew what twisted reason. Wasn't this what I'd joined the good guys for?

I stood up, stubbed out the unfinished last cigarette of a long day and said, audibly, to myself a simple 'Yes!' I went to my four hours' sleep determined and untroubled, actually looking forward to whatever lay ahead.

CHAPTER FIVE

THE FIRST BIG CALL

Saturday morning at Twickenham Police Station. Another office meeting, with a vast number of staff and a huge moment. The Telephone Intelligence Unit at Scotland Yard had all the data on Amélie's phone from T-Mobile. It told them that the last 'handshake' was at 10.23pm on the night she was killed, on a mast in Walton on Thames, and could be pinpointed to an area about 500 yards square, to the north of Walton bridge.

A 'handshake' is the term for the network searching for the location of the phone, and it works like this: the basic premise is that your phone network needs, at all times, to know the location of your phone or else it could not find the correct mast, or cell, to send incoming calls and text messages to. If you make a call from a phone, it transmits to a nearby mast and the network knows exactly where it is, so there is no problem. If, however, someone calls you, the network needs to know which mast to route the call to. It does this in two ways – if you are moving, as you leave one mast's area for another, the handset transmits a signal automatically, effectively saying to the network, 'I'm here,' so the network knows where to place any incoming calls. However, if you are stationary, the phone will not do this and so, to make sure it has the correct location, the network periodically transmits to the phone to ask, 'Are you still there?' These are known as handshakes and can sometimes be heard as a rapid rhythmic noise intruding over, for example, a car stereo if the mobile phone is close to it.

What had happened with Amélie's phone was that a handshake had occurred at Walton at 10.23pm, and the phone had not been 'seen' by the network since. This meant, we were told, that, when the network next transmitted to see if it were still in the same location (which, in this case, T-Mobile told us was about ninety minutes later), the phone could not be found. But there was even more information. If her phone had been switched off conventionally, as it powered down, it would automatically send a signal to the network to inform it – effectively saying, 'Goodbye.' Thereafter, the network would automatically send all calls to voicemail. This had not happened with Amélie's phone; the network had received no powering-down signal – the phone had disappeared from the network in what the network called 'an implicit detachment' – that is, it was assumed to have been off. What did this mean? Well, the phone might have been taken into an area of no signal and left there, or the battery was removed without it being switched off, or it had suddenly been damaged – for example, by being immersed in water.

That information gave me a lot to think about, particularly

when combined with the first, scoping, viewing of closed-circuit-television footage from passing buses. This showed us that Amélie didn't arrive at Twickenham Green until just after 10pm. She had apparently missed her stop at Twickenham Green and got off her 267 bus at its terminus, Fulwell Bus Depot – about a mile away from the Green. However, other bus cameras had captured her on her walk back up to the Green and, while this enabled us to determine her arrival there roughly, further detailed analysis should, in time, give us a much more accurate picture.

So the time between Amélie being attacked and having her phone taken and the phone transmitting to the mast in Walton on Thames was, at most, around twenty minutes. Walton is around six and a half miles from Twickenham Green, so the phone could not have got there by foot or even on a cycle; it must have travelled in a vehicle.

This was to have a major influence on my priority lines of inquiry. Despite London's much-reported mass of CCTV cameras (it seems one's image was captured around three hundred times a day in the city on average), identification of pedestrians was often difficult – particularly at night, when the image quality from even the best equipment was simply rarely good enough. However, identification of a vehicle was rather easier, make, model and colour being regularly discernible, and occasionally even the registration number could be seen.

Since we were almost certainly looking for a vehicle, my reasoning was that, if we were to secure every last piece of CCTV footage on every conceivable route from Twickenham Green to Walton on Thames, the killer's vehicle must be on it. Granted, at that stage, we would not know what vehicle we were looking for but, as the investigation progressed in other directions, we would be able to go to this acquired footage to prove – or, indeed, disprove – the presence of a suspect's vehicle. So it was then that I assigned six officers to CCTV, with the rather optimistic instruction to gather each and every recording across a huge swathe of south-west London. Typically, a murder squad would use one or perhaps two officers on CCTV. My decision to draw the trawl so widely and to employ more than 10 per cent of my team on it drew questioning comment from those both above and below me.

The reasoning, though, was, to me, simple. I knew the killer's car would be on those recordings somewhere and, if we didn't secure the images immediately, they would soon be lost forever. I could not understand why anybody would not want to gather these recordings in and I stuck to my guns. Fortunately, Andy Murphy, for the first but by no means last time in the investigation, went with me – though I knew that the responsibility for the decision was mine alone and I would stand or fall by it.

While the CCTV would be collected and viewed in due course, there was a more pressing action, which could be based on the phone data. Since there was the possibility that the handset could have been thrown into water, and considering that the last handshake was at Walton Bridge, it might be worthwhile searching the river. The data from the phone company suggested the last handshake was in an area to the north of the bridge, and it was here that Mickey Singh made arrangements for the police divers to search. However, I was uncertain about this. Although I was a north-London boy and knew the Walton area hardly at all, I had a very detailed knowledge of the River Thames, having messed about on boats there for the best part of thirty-five years. I knew that where the phone data was sending us there were some footpaths affording public access to the river; at the same time, I knew that just south of the bridge there were car parks, public pleasure grounds and paths that went right to the water's edge and which were much more open and obvious. I therefore insisted that, despite what the data said, we were to start the underwater search there. It was, I thought, the most likely place to find Amélie's phone and, logically, therefore, the best starting point. A little bit of luck mixed with a little bit of knowledge and a fair dash of stubbornness perhaps, but it worked.

The divers, on their second thirty-minute sortie underwater, found Amélie's purse, house keys and CD player. Though her phone and her handbag were never given back by Old Father Thames, these finds were crucial in confirming our developing view of what must have happened. After she was attacked, somebody had, quite quickly, taken Amélie's belongings down to Walton on Thames in a vehicle. Either that somebody was her killer, or it had to have been the outlandishly incredible coincidence of two criminals being on sleepy, safe Twickenham Green that night – one who attacked Amélie, and another who then came and stole her bag as she lay dying. Firmly maintaining my belief that the simplest explanation is usually the correct one, I discounted the latter as being so unlikely as to not matter. If we were to find who drove those possessions to Walton, I was confident we would have found the killer.

That Saturday evening, I went to the Radisson Hotel at Heathrow Airport and, for the first time, met Amélie's parents, Jean-François and Dominique. It was always a difficult moment meeting the loved ones of a victim and this was to be trickier than usual given my lack of French and theirs of English. I was accompanied by DC Gary Fuller, the Family Liaison Officer from my team, and DC Jean-Marc Papworth – lent to me from a murder squad at Hendon – who was to act as interpreter. I hoped that the sincerity of my promise to do all I could to find the man who had killed their daughter (note: never a promise that I *would* find him) survived the translation. As we entered the plush suite we had rented for them, it reminded me of my conviction as to how well we cared for victim families in London. In stark contrast to our efforts to get the Delagranges informed in the first place, when the French police had originally told us we should tell Amélie's parents by phone, then that they would make the call on our behalf. In order to get French police to actually attend the house and speak face to face, it had been necessary to threaten to have British Embassy staff go and do it for us, at which suggestion the *Gendarmerie* grudgingly agreed to visit themselves. As I later found out, they did but in a disgracefully perfunctory manner, the whole meeting lasting less than a minute, with Jean-François being told of his daughter's death on his drive as he arrived home from work with the officers not even entering the house.

Whether or not the implied resort to diplomatic channels had triggered an escalation in the French response I am unsure but I was surprised at the hotel, not only to meet two devastated, humble and dignified bereaved parents but also two smartly dressed French men. One, I soon learned, was Patrick Drul, a senior official from the French Embassy in London and he had brought with him Alain Riboux, a Paris magistrate. They spoke English and explained they were there to make sure the Delagranges were properly looked after. I had no issue with this – victim's families in London almost routinely equipped themselves with lawyers or advisors when meeting the police; it was just symptomatic of how things had come to be done. I did, though, bristle a little when the two men asked me to speak in private with them in the small sitting room off the main bedroom. Drul explained that Riboux had considerable experience of acting as the interrogative magistrate directing sexual and serious crimes in France. Riboux then proceeded to tell me how it was imperative to look at all the known sex offenders who could have been in the area at the time; interestingly, the same classic, almost clichéd advice I was getting from experienced detectives at the Yard. I politely assured him we were pursuing every sensible line of inquiry vigorously. Next, though, I stopped merely bristling and became quite angry.

'We are concerned that you must make every effort to take good care of the Delagranges,' said Drul, looking to Riboux for a nod of support. 'You will, we trust, place an officer at their disposal and meet any needs they have?'

Given that we were sitting in a £200-per-night suite after we had flown them to London, that they had an FLO, an interpreter and a car already and that the SIO was spending as much time as was necessary to speak to them despite the hundreds of other things he had to do that evening, I found this quite insulting. And set against the background of the uncaring efforts of the French police in breaking the news in the first place, it was breathtaking.

'I think you can see that we are taking very good care of them and we will continue to do so. My experience of your police earlier was less than inspiring, so I think we will continue in the English way here.'

MANHUNT

I fully accept that this was, for me, an uncharacteristically blunt response but I was in no mood to take lessons from the French on family liaison – or, for that matter, investigation. We rejoined Jean-François and Dominique in the bedroom and nothing more was said. And I never heard from either Drul or Riboux again.

CHAPTER SIX

CALL IN THE 'OLOGISTS'

Most murders these days are solved, and most convictions for them secured, by the 'Ologists', as the officers of the Murder Squad tend to call the scientists and experts who support their investigations. The reason for this is simple. Murder is largely a spontaneous crime. It results from a spilled pint, a disrespecting comment, a confrontation gone wrong. There is seldom any planning, any thought as to what might lead to arrest or conviction, and, consequently, there is often an abundance of forensic trace evidence – finger-marks, fibres, DNA – as well as CCTV and communications data. When expert resources are pitched in to investigate these crimes on the scale that (thankfully) we are still able to do, it is no surprise that evidence is quickly found and the detection rate for murder is maintained at around 90 per cent. However, the rare and difficult cases are those where there is a degree of preparation and the clever criminal can take precautions to avoid leaving scientific clues. My sense was that Amélie's killer was likely to be in this small minority; he had, after all, probably escaped detection in at least three similar attacks already. Nevertheless, a forensic strategy had to be agreed with the scientists, and the various behavioural and analytical experts consulted, as they still might hold the key to the case.

Hence, by the start of week two of the investigation, I had not only agreed to what samples and items were to be examined by the lab but also arranged a meeting with the experts from the National Policing Improvement Agency (NPIA) at Bramshill, the national Police College situated in a Jacobean mansion in Hampshire. In the tapestry-hung meeting room overlooking the croquet lawn, half-a-dozen police officers, three analysts and two pathologists had a grisly and somewhat surreal discussion about a series of similarly shaped and equally barbaric head wounds sustained by six young women. The conclusion? It was possibly all down to the same man.

During that meeting, I had to step outside to take a phone call. It was Sue Hill, my immediate boss, who was, by now, back from annual leave. She told me that she was worried about the direction the investigation was taking and that she wanted to take a more active role in it herself and so was moving her office to Barnes from the next Monday. As I stood on the terrace, looking on to the lawn where, some eighteen years earlier, I had watched Prince Charles grandly arrive for a race-relations seminar by helicopter, I contemplated how my biggest challenge was about to pass me by. I mumbled some reply but was completely dumbstruck. I knew immediately that, were she to do so, my role as the SIO would be superfluous; Sue would be running the show. I felt completely frustrated – there was nothing I could do to stop her, yet I didn't know why she had taken the view that the investigation needed help. I resolved that I would not continue; that, once she arrived, I would seek to move elsewhere. Bitterly disappointed, I returned to the meeting and somehow managed to keep my emotions from my colleagues on the return journey to London.

The next day was Friday and, while I was considering how best to approach my need to transfer somewhere else, my mobile rang and it was Andy Murphy. He was short and to the point: 'Forget what Sue said to you yesterday. She is not coming to Barnes, you are and will remain the SIO, Sue is not your line manager any more. You will be reporting directly to me.'

This news was surprising and relieving in equal measure. Clearly, Sue had told Andy Murphy of her intentions and he had backed me, not her. As happy as I was with this effective vote of confidence, I actually felt for Sue, who I got on with quite well and who was clearly now in a difficult position within the Command. However, my customary focus on the task in hand soon overtook this emotion. I knew I was going to be in this investigation for the long haul, so best I get on with it.

Next up was another meeting with Ologists, this time the analysts and behavioural advisers from the Met's own rather pompously titled Homicide Prevention Unit. Its analysis had suggested there were possibly six linked offences and proposed a theory that the attacker struck on occasions when he might expect a greater number of potential victims to be out and about. This was based on the coincidence that offences had occurred on the evening of the London Marathon, Bonfire Night and the day of A-level results being announced. I kept my rather negative view of this to myself but I thought, not only was this stretching a point but, in any case, what about the other three offences? While willing to listen to any suggestion, I kept reminding myself that the Marsha McDonnell inquiry had taken the advice of the behavioural people and thereafter concentrated on a suspect who, very probably, had nothing to do with it at all. I was determined to make sure that these hypothetical suggestions remained as such until hard, proper evidence was found to support them.

Following on from this meeting, I had another with DCS Andy Murphy and his boss, Commander Andy Baker. It was here that, for the first time, we came up with the phrase 'Linked Investigative Series'. In the world of investigating major crime, a linked series is a term of art used to describe a series of offences where it is certain that all were committed by the same person. This usually relies upon fingerprints or DNA being common to the linked crimes. There must be no doubt as to the linkage, as the rule is invariably that elimination from one crime will mean elimination from all of them. In the appropriate circumstances, this can lead to reducing the size of lists of possible suspects quite quickly. In this case, although we were fairly confident there was but one man responsible, we couldn't be certain because we had no scientific evidence linking them. Hence the compromise, a linked investigative series, where the same team investigated all the offences but were alive to the possibility of others being involved. There was also a public-reassurance aspect to this; for some reason, a linked series always appears more sinister. As we were trying desperately not to cause widespread fear and panic among the women of south-west London, this enabled us to play down the worries – despite us being privately quite certain that there was a randomly striking killer on the loose.

While I was regularly dealing with these more strategic issues, preparing us to dig in for a long campaign, the team were hard at work exploring possibilities of identifying our man more quickly. Chief among these were the 'MO suspects' – that is, a group of local men whose previous convictions and known habits made them likely to have committed the offences. While such exploration is a regular feature in any investigation where the identity of the perpetrator is not quickly apparent, it is almost always carried out in hope, rather than expectation. Such was to be the case in our investigation: four men were actually arrested to enable us to question them and take samples but each was quickly eliminated.

With both this line of inquiry and all the forensic examinations proving equally fruitless, we eventually settled in for a protracted investigation and, as hard as we were trying, as long as we were working, as we entered the fifth week, we were hoping – indeed praying – for a breakthrough. I tried to make things happen to a degree by returning to the mass of CCTV we had seized – let's start from the scene, work our way outwards and see if something jumps out. Don't forget, I made clear at a meeting with my team on 17 September 2004 that we knew his vehicle was on there somewhere.

CHAPTER SEVEN

'GUVNOR, YOU MIGHT WANT TO SEE THIS...'

Before Amélie was killed, our accommodation at Barnes was probably best described as cosy. Two murder teams, a Child Protection Unit and the Flying Squad were all crammed into a small 1960s police station. With my team being doubled in size, it was hopeless. So much so that my team meetings were held, variously, in a local church hall, a local pub and even once at Twickenham Stadium. This was eventually solved with uncharacteristic speed by the Met with a move to spacious new offices at Putney in February 2005. However, in the meantime, I had commandeered a meeting room in the old cell area for my CCTV team and their equipment – mostly computers begged and borrowed from elsewhere in the Met. The entrance to their room opened directly on to the car park and I had got into the habit of poking my head round the door as I arrived each morning before I entered the main building. It was as I delivered two such courtesy greetings, three days apart, that I heard the next two developments.

On 21 September, I saw that DC Gary Cunningham was in the CCTV office, although he was not actually part of that sub-team. Gary is a very intelligent and practical detective, on whom I knew I could rely and whose views I always took seriously. He had been chatting with DS Malcolm Hudson and DC Paul McGough and, when I arrived, he then explained their thoughts to me. Gary's wife had a friend whose daughter had been seriously assaulted in Isleworth in May 2004. The girl, eighteen-year-old Kate Sheedy, had just got off a bus near her home when she had been deliberately run down and then reversed over. She had been left for dead but, in a display of courage, which I later came to realise she possessed in abundance, she had crawled to her handbag and raised the alarm on her mobile phone.

Despite terrible crush injuries, she had survived and made a remarkable recovery. I was aware of the offence, having happened to see a reconstruction on the BBC's *Crimewatch* a few weeks earlier, but had not really considered it relevant due to the very different method of attack. Gary, though, pointed out that her age, the location and the time, together with her recent bus journey, all fitted with our other offences. I agreed to look into it and, the next day, with Jo Brunt and DS John Pickersgill, I went to Hounslow Police Station to see the officer investigating the incident, DI Steve Leonard, and his deputy, DS Philip Royens.

Their tale was horrific. Kate had been returning from an evening out with her schoolfriends in Twickenham, where they had been celebrating the end of formal lessons before taking their A2 exams. Kate was the Head Girl of Gumley House Convent

School, popular, bright and confident of getting the required good grades to go up and read Politics at Durham. As she had alighted from a bus in Worton Road just two-hundred yards or so from her home, she was aware of a vehicle parked ahead of her, facing the same way. It was a white people carrier, possibly a Ford Galaxy, she thought. It had blacked-out windows and she noticed a defect in the driver's door mirror and that the engine was running although the lights were off. Something – instinct, a sixth-sense or similar – told her the car was dangerous and she crossed the road to avoid walking directly past it. This meant that, as she drew ahead of it on the opposite pavement, she had to cross a side road, which was the entrance to an industrial estate. As she did so, the people-carrier suddenly started forward, at speed, performed a U-turn across the road and ran her down. It halted, its front wheel having driven over her, with Kate lying on the road underneath. It then reversed, the wheel again crushing her slim frame, and drove off. My notes made at the meeting show the salient, almost incredible, features of what happened next:

- *Driver DID NOT get out of the car once it had hit her*
- *Crawls/drags herself to outside #7, then phones Mum*
- *Remains conscious throughout the incident*
- *Blonde, slim build; 5'7"; 8½ stone*
- *Vehicle – Galaxy favoured, blacked-out windows, 2 occupants?, M+/N in number-plate*

The Borough investigation had concentrated on Ford Galaxy vehicles in the area, although there was no certainty that this was the correct identification of it – Kate thought this the most likely, having looked at photographs of similar cars.

Between the three of us, there was no consensus. John Pickersgill thought it was definitely something to do with our investigation; Jo Brunt was equally sure it was not. Perhaps predictably, many cops would say, I hedged my bets in a manner typical of senior officers – I was unsure but agreed to keep an eye on developments in the case and offered some assistance to the beleaguered Borough detectives if they wanted it. We all left there, however, stunned by the senseless and extreme violence. I knew that, if it were our man, he was a lot more dangerous and unpredictable even than I had already imagined.

While Kate's case was filed away in my mind for the moment, a few days later came the second extended visit to the CCTV office. As I said my hellos on the morning of 24 September, DC Paul McGough uttered the words that were to change everything. With his usual efficiency, politeness and understatement, he simply said, 'Guvnor, you might want to see this…'

The team had been looking at the CCTV footage from the many buses which pass along Hampton Road, on the south side of Twickenham Green. What they showed me was stunning in its potential impact, bearing impressive testimony to the thoroughness of their painstaking work. Among all the comings and goings, they had identified a small white van, which had appeared parked by the sightscreen in Hampton Road sometime between 10pm and 10.05pm, but which had departed by 10.08pm. This meant that the van was parked, for a very short while, within seventy yards of where Amélie was attacked, at almost exactly the time she was there. From tracking her movements on CCTV, we knew she arrived at Twickenham Green just before 10.01pm; she had been found by the passer-by at 10.16pm. For the first half of that fifteen-minute period, this white van had been parked right on the spot.

For a moment, the excitement almost took me over. Why should anyone have been there for that length of time? I immediately decided the most likely explanation might well be that it was the killer. Whether or not that were true, the driver might be a witness so he would have to be traced and eliminated. There and then, finding the van and its driver became my top priority – a decision members of the team later suggested was bold, even risky. I never understood their view – I still do not. Was our time and effort better spent chasing MO suspects, doing endless house-to-house inquiries and repeated press appeals, or looking for a person who we knew was right there, at the very spot at the very time Amélie was slain? To me, it was such an obvious decision and I was going to pursue this van with everything I could throw at it.

CHAPTER EIGHT

CHASING CARS

Cars had always been more to me than mere means of transport. From my quaint obsession with classic Minis through to my low-level but immensely enjoyable and reasonably successful forays into motorsport, they were something of a passion. And the opportunity to use my knowledge and interest in my professional life had manifested itself in a series of apprehensions of thieves in 'rung' cars over the years, including Operation Elixir, when I worked on the Met Stolen Vehicle Squad in recovering £750,000-worth of stolen cars in 1989. So I set about trying to identify the crucial van with some gusto, a little expertise and in a hands-on way that, while somewhat out of keeping with my role as SIO, ensured I was completely confident we would succeed. It also got me a reputation as something of a car 'anorak', which survives to this day – and of which I am secretly quite proud!

Obvious at first was that it was a Ford Courier – a small van based on a Fiesta car but with a large cube-shaped rear-load space. I saw it had features such as the shape of its grille and its side rubbing strips, which would probably enable somebody at Ford to narrow it down to a particular manufacturing period. A quick call to Ford, and the ever-helpful Jeremy Burton there, had, by that very afternoon, looked at the emailed images and confirmed it as a Ford Courier van manufactured between 1996 and 2000. He reckoned there might be around 25,000 in existence in the UK – an estimate which was actually pretty accurate, as the Police National Computer records from DVLA at Swansea showed 24,700. That was the haystack; we needed to try to get a bit more information on our needle.

The CCTV team had been busy and, within a day, had found around a dozen other images of what they believed to be the same van. Some of these were in the general area of Twickenham Green more than half an hour before Amélie was attacked. It certainly looked as if the van had been cruising the area for some time. A predator looking for a victim? The suspicions grew and my belief that the van was the key to it all was becoming firmer and firmer. Perhaps more importantly, we had pictures of the van driving away down Hampton Road, all the way to the River Thames near Hampton Court, which was the obvious and natural route to Walton on Thames. Most crucially, all the timings worked.

The van was at Hampton at 10.18pm, just five minutes' drive to Walton and also five minutes before we knew Amélie's phone was there. And that wasn't the end of the good news. From the various images, there were unusual features visible on the van, which not only helped to track it on the various CCTV recordings but also would make positive identification of it much easier when we eventually found it. It had a wheel trim missing on the front left wheel; a black object in the centre of the roof; the left headlight was inoperative; the window areas of the rear doors appeared to have metal, rather than glass, and there were areas to the foot of the back doors that were apparently painted a different colour to the rest of the bodywork.

At the team meeting on 27 September, I'll admit I was probably more animated than usual. Over the weekend, I had compiled a list of actions; all the things I thought we should do to trace the van. My task now was to discuss them with the whole team, agree what was possible and what was not, and allocate jobs to officers. Despite holding the meeting in the rather unusual setting of a pensioners' drop-in centre at an old school on Barnes Green, I was happy to see that the whole team shared my enthusiasm. We had a line of inquiry that was tangible, where the object was clear. Even if some doubted that it would take us to the killer (which more than a few did), there was an appreciation that there was a purpose to what we were trying to do; that it actually related to what had happened on the fateful night. My list was long:

- Cover Thames bridges 24/7
- Ask Ford if they can identify vans with metal rear doors from VIN
- Automatic Number Plate recognition
- Parking/bus lane tickets in the area
- Observations from bridges on major roads
- Intelligence research of Met systems
- Visit all registered keepers in local areas
- Other systems – TfL; census; Congestion Charge

- Internal police appeals
- Public appeals

A postscript to my meeting agenda also shows the first sign of real-world constraints in the operation. We had been working virtually every hour possible for more than five weeks. I had personally had but one day off – during which I moved to a new house – and had averaged over eighty hours per week. Aside from the wear and tear on individuals, the cost was beginning to impact on the overtime budget. From now on, each individual DC and DS would be limited to eleven hours overtime per week. Of course, the DIs and I, being salaried and unable to claim overtime, could work as long as we liked. And we did.

Our search for the van had to be conducted covertly – that is, without alerting the driver to the fact we were looking for it. This was so as not to precipitate its destruction, disposal or even cleaning. Just one speck of Amélie's blood, one hair from her head or fibre from her clothing found in the van might well be conclusive, so we had to try to find it and get hold of it intact – and soon. The most likely way, it was agreed, was to visit all the vans on the list from DVLA that were registered in the local TW and KT postcode areas – around five hundred of them.

While the team set out to find them, I had a pressing problem. Not for the first time, the level of IT support available in the giant organisation that is the Metropolitan Police was not up to the task. All major investigations are recorded on a database known as HOLMES. This is an acronym for Home Office Large Major Enquiry System, which was then in its eleventh upgrade of its second version, but could trace its roots back to the mid-

1980s, when it was introduced to make management of large investigations easier and more comprehensive, in the wake of the mass of information that had mired the Yorkshire Ripper inquiry a decade earlier.

The Met was, by far, the largest single user of the system and had so many accounts on its servers that there was virtually no space for a significant, very large new data set. I was advised that trying to manage the inquiries into nearly twenty-five thousand vans on HOLMES would cause it all to 'fall over'. I therefore prevailed upon my analyst, Gary Hancock, and my wife, Louise (who, as the Principal Analyst for Surrey Police, was frequently a great source of expertise and advice), to construct a separate database in Microsoft Access, which would enable us to log the results of the van inquiries, and search the information as we needed to. This, of course, meant another plea for a non-networked computer on which to run it, which the amazingly patient and helpful Theresa McDonagh in resources at Hendon managed to rustle up for us. This little problem, and its solution, typified the 'can-do' culture that exists in the police service to this day. The bureaucracy, regulations and standard operating procedures are necessary for order but can often be a barrier to swift action. The long history of officers and staff using creative thinking, favours and shortcuts really does make 'The Job' work on many occasions, and this was neither the first nor the last time that I would be a grateful recipient during this case.

While the administration of the van search was, thus, pretty easily resolved, the actual inquiries themselves were not bearing fruit. It became apparent after a week or so that, while it was reasonably simple to produce a list of vans registered in the neighbouring areas, actually viewing them was not so easy. Many of the actions were being returned showing that the van, although registered to a company in south-west London or Surrey, was actually being used miles away. Possibly due to our seeking a commercial vehicle, more than half of the results we were getting showed that, while south-west London was the area of registration for the vans, it was not their area of regular use. We were struggling to look at more than one in three of the vans on our list; a strike rate that inspired no confidence that we would succeed. To come across the van we sought, to identify it from the unusual features observed on the CCTV recordings, we needed to be satisfied that we were looking at every possibility. I thought about the problem and realised that what we had found would be equally applicable in reverse. That is, just as vans registered in 'our' area were being regularly used somewhere that was many miles away, it followed that a similar number of other vans were likely to have been registered elsewhere while being regularly used in south-west London. What we needed to do was to establish the list of Courier vans being used in the KT and TW postcode areas, irrespective of where they happened to be registered.

Automatic Number Plate Recognition, the cameras known inevitably as ANPR, which could automatically read registration numbers and compare them with a database or list of sought vehicles, was in its infancy in 2004. What equipment existed was neither particularly reliable nor portable. Having tried and failed to secure such equipment for the general area in case of a further attack, I knew it would be a slow, expensive and probably ultimately fruitless task to try to obtain it for the van search.

There was, it seemed to me, only one practical answer. So it was that, during an unusually cold and miserable October, pairs of London's top detectives were employed to stand on footbridges, taking registration numbers of passing white vans, from 6am to 2am each day. While I was grateful that they did as I requested, it was not without comment and a certain amount of dissent – and, in truth, I would not have expected it to be any different.

Personally, it represented probably the lowest point of confidence I had encountered since the investigation began. While it was, I knew, the best we could do at the time, I also realised that we were relying on good fortune to a degree with which I felt quite uncomfortable. But what else was there to be done? The only alternative was to systematically visit and identify all 24,700 Courier vans registered in the UK; a task which would be almost impossibly long and expensive. While the cost, ultimately, might not be a barrier, the length of time was worrying. Nobody, with the possible exception of the murderer himself, knew how long we had until the next attack; though I think we all agreed that further attacks were a 'when', rather than an 'if'. This probably motivated us all to try anything we could to find the van. Despite the long working days we were experiencing, I ended almost every night with a couple of hours in the Twickenham area, cruising, parking, waiting and looking – just in the hope that the van would reappear. What was funny, inspiring and even predictable was the number of other officers from the team doing the same thing in their own time, and often in their own cars, that I came across during these unofficial observations. It was quite reassuring to realise that I wasn't the only one obsessed with catching him, and quickly. However, the somewhat strange culture of 'The Job' dictated that we never actually mentioned to each other that this was what we were doing.

While my officers played van-spotters, the October half-term came along. I had a long-standing arrangement to go with Louise and the children to Spain for the week. Although a big part of me wanted to stay at work, Tony McKeown and Jo Brunt persuaded me that a rest was what I needed – my average working week since August was still nearly seventy hours, I had had just the one day off and, yes, objectively, I needed a break. In any case, I could keep in touch on the phone, and a few days lying about by the pool might just be the opportunity for reflection and thinking that I needed.

In possibly a very 'Busman's Holiday' way, my chosen reading for the trip was *Wicked Beyond Belief*, the excellent book about Peter Sutcliffe, the Yorkshire Ripper, by Michael Bilton. Sutcliffe's crimes were of particular interest to me on a number of levels – I had been a student at Leeds University during his reign of terror and, as such, was familiar with many of the locations and features of the cases outlined in the book. News of his arrest the previous evening was what I remember listening to on the radio during the journey to Hendon on 5 January 1981, the day I joined the police force. And I had then, some fifteen years later, served in West Yorkshire for four years and worked with a number of the officers who had been involved in the Ripper investigation. I knew that it had profoundly affected both the individual officers and, indeed, the whole process of major investigations throughout the country.

Quite apart from the historical interest I had, it seemed an obvious choice at the time – a detailed account of that investigation, its pitfalls and its lessons, could only help my thinking as we took Operation Yeaddiss forwards. The most striking feature that was absolutely relevant to us was the Ripper Squad's efforts to identify a vehicle. All they really had to go on was a tyre mark, from which experts were able to ascertain the size of the tyre and, thus, a list of vehicles which might have left the track. It was a relatively common size but, as the number of locally registered cars was much lower back then, the pool of potential vehicles was just over fifty thousand. In hindsight, we were able to know with certainty that Sutcliffe's Ford Corsair was, indeed, within that pool. But I knew, not only from the book but also from first-hand accounts, how desperately difficult it was back in the late 1970s to manage the elimination exercise. All vehicle records were printed on long reels of computer listing paper and the officers using them had to roll them out across the floor of the incident room at Millgarth Police Station in Leeds city centre, ruling out eliminated cars quite literally with a marker pen and ruler while on their hands and knees. This was around the same time that the vast array of filing cabinets containing the indexed cards for the entire inquiry had to be moved to the edges of the incident room, as their combined weight was causing the centre, unsupported section of the floor to bend.

The Ripper Squad struggled impressively with this Herculean task until they were about halfway through, when it started to prove impossible, and they abandoned it to try to find another way. My resolve, then, was that we would not give up. As I explained to a somewhat startled Tony McKeown on the phone from Spain that afternoon, we were going to look at every single van until we found the one we wanted. We had the benefits of a smaller potential pool, computers and databases for information storage and retrieval, and analysts to make sense of it for us. If we failed to learn the lessons from a generation ago, we could have no excuse. We were not going to give up.

I knew how Tony would relay that instruction to the team, in his quiet, laconic way – and also that it would not meet with universal approval. So when my mobile rang while I was awaiting the flight home, I half expected Tony to be wanting to discuss whether it was the correct path to take. But, instead, he had some interesting news. Not only had we found a van that seemed to match the criteria – with a black lump on the roof and missing wheel-trim – but it was registered to the Metropolitan Police. Scarcely able to believe this, and quickly playing out both the investigative and organisational reputation scenarios in my mind (all of which were quite disturbing), I asked Tony not to take any further action until I was back in the office in about four hours.

Louise and the children took care of my bags after we had landed and I rushed out through Customs and on to the Gatwick Express. By about 2.30pm, I was in the office at Barnes, talking to Tony. The Met had quite a few white Ford Courier vans; indeed, we had borrowed one so as to be able to conduct CCTV reconstructions and to assist in witness appeals should we come to them. The vans were mostly used by SOCOs – scenes-of-crimes officers who begin the forensic evidence retrieval at scenes – but some were used for general errands and also some by photographers. The van currently under suspicion was one of the latter, based at the Photographic Branch headquarters in Amelia Street, Southwark. Two officers had visited there to eliminate the van as it was, along with a good few other Met-owned vans, on our list of 24,700. They had found there was the black base stub of a radio aerial on the roof and that the front nearside wheel trim was missing. What added fuel to the fire of suspicion was that it was shown as having been captured by the portable ANPR cameras on Twickenham Green a few days after Amélie's murder. These cameras had been placed there by the local Richmond Borough Police as a visible deterrent to try to placate local fears. Could they have come up with the answer for us?

This was obviously potentially a massive step forward for us, but I proceeded cautiously. I asked who the van was shown out to on the night of Amélie's murder. By this, I meant who had signed the log book, which each Met vehicle has. The procedure is meant to be that each journey or patrol is logged, with the start and finish mileage and the name of the driver. However, particularly where the vehicle is usually driven by only one person, this practice can be lax – one might find a weekly. rather than daily entry, or guesswork, or both. More than once, I have seen police cars running in gear up on a jack so as to enable the mileage total shown on the clock to catch up with that written in the book.

It seemed the van was shown back in at Amelia Street at 6pm that evening, and its (female) driver then took it out again at 8am the following day. The practice there was to store the log books and keys for all vehicles all together, so that they might be readily available in an emergency or for a major incident. The building itself is very secure, with swipe-card access. However, the computer controlling access did not, apparently, record who had entered or at what time; there was, therefore, no way of knowing which employee, if any, might have returned at night and 'borrowed' the van. Frustrated at this, I decided to go down to Amelia Street, both to see the van for myself and to speak with the management there to try to see how I might approach the need to prove that each of the Force's photographic staff was not a serial murderer.

We had always said that, once we set eyes upon the van we had been searching for, we would recognise it immediately. As soon as I swung into the car park at Amelia Street, I knew the reverse was also true. It didn't fit. The aerial stub was too small and too far forward on the roof. Even allowing for the distortion sometimes evident in CCTV stills, it was simply wrong. I called back to the incident room, deflated. We still needed to explain the van's appearance at Twickenham Green, though. I asked for the date and found it to be during the evening of 26 August – exactly one week after the murder. Which was when we conducted the 'anniversary' appeal. It is common practice in murder investigations to stage a reconstruction of the known events one week later, in the hope that those who regularly travel through the area at that time and on that day of the week might see something which jogs their memory. We had borrowed a bus, and a female officer from Twickenham had played the part of Amélie. In what was the first example of the excellent relationship we had with the media during Operation Yeaddiss, ITN had come along and filmed the reconstruction, then passed the footage to the other television stations. However, the Met's in-house video team had also recorded events, and it was pretty obvious which van from Amelia Street they had used. It was just a coincidence, easily explained, and the sad truth was that we were no further on at all. It was time for a rethink about the whole van-elimination exercise.

CHAPTER NINE

'GUVNOR, I THINK WE'VE HIT THE JACKPOT!'

There was no alternative. If we weren't to abandon the van line of inquiry, if we weren't to ignore the lessons from the past, we would have to look at every single one of these 24,700 vans and take the risk that it might turn out to be number 24,699 on the list. The only way to do that would be entirely systematically. While there might be shortcuts – for example, where a company had a fleet of vans all of which (unlike our target) were sign-written, they could all be written off as a block. Equally, we could intelligently prioritise – for example, despite the scare of the previous week, I was happy to put the Met's vans down at the bottom of the list. As we went into November, while the team were still trying to eliminate the locally registered vans, I was making plans for the big sweep.

Essentially, the whole country was broken down into postcode areas, and a list drawn up of every possible van in each area. We would then send pairs of officers to each area, with instructions to book into a hotel and not to come back until they had eliminated them all. Of course, all areas would not be visited simultaneously; that was beyond the scope even of my large team. We would start in London and work our way out spirally.

It was still very necessary to conduct this search without alerting the suspect to the fact that we were on to his van – or else we were likely to spark its destruction and lose any chance of scientific trace evidence. A cover story was therefore devised; we were Metropolitan Police officers (unspecified; the Murder Squad was never to be mentioned) trying to trace a van that had been involved in a robbery. The other suggestion made at a team meeting on 5 November 2004 was that we send letters to the local police, nationally, asking them to make the inquiries for us. I discounted this on two grounds: first, that having been the recipient of similar letters in the past, I had always tried to organise a proper response but, in my heart, I knew that no unconnected, uninterested officer was going to make inquiries with the same diligence as would a member of the team; and second that the chances of keeping our interest in the van secret would diminish considerably as a result. It was our inquiry – my inquiry – and we were going to have to do it ourselves.

Another team meeting on Monday, 8 November saw me outlining the new plan to the team. Despite the impact on their families and personal lives, most of the officers who were to be sent away were happy about it – the overtime and expenses to be earned almost certainly softened the blow of separation. It was another very dark time for me. I knew I was throwing everything in on this van, that the long and expensive exercise upon which

I was embarking had no guarantee of success, and that failure would be catastrophic, possibly to the investigation but certainly to my reputation. Nevertheless, I tried to keep up my usual enthusiastic disposition, briefed the officers and sent them on their way without betraying the fears I had.

The following day was strangely quiet in the incident room at Barnes. The normal hubbub was missing as virtually the whole inquiry team had set out on their mission. As the evening approached, I sat and chatted with the HOLMES staff who were left. DC Mark Leach was one of them, and we were discussing what I referred to as the 'Women Scorned File', more officially referred to as 'Single Suggestions'. In most murder investigations, there will be suspects helpfully suggested by members of the public as possibly being responsible. Such was the impact of Amélie's death that the local community had responded *en masse* and we had received a large number of calls. Many of these had come from women suggesting former or even current partners; they had been collated and, by November, totalled some hundred and thirty men. We were talking about these suggestions because a PC from Twickenham had, just out of interest, asked one of the team if anything had come of a name put forward by a woman when she visited the mobile police station that had been placed on Twickenham Green for a week or so following the murder. That woman was Johanna Collings, and her ex-partner she named was Levi Bellfield.

It occurred to us that, while most of the team were away and we had little chance of pursuing outside actions, we now had the time and could usefully go through the 'women scorned' file and see if there was anything relevant contained in it. By luck, and simply because of the question so casually posed by the PC, we started with Levi Bellfield. Johanna Collings's visit had, like all snippets of information given to us by public and police alike, been recorded as a message in the HOLMES database. Mark Leach began to read the message:

Johanna's ex-boyfriend who she lived with some seven years ago is a male called:

Levi BELLFIELD, date of birth 17/05/68.

White male, 6'01" tall, stocky build, black hair, with tattoos on both arms – 'Lee' on the left and 'TOTTENHAM' on the right.

He is a traveller, works as a bouncer and wheel-clamper and owns a White Van.

According to Johanna, Levi hates women and when he left (7 years ago), she found in the garage a blue biggish coat that had a pocket cut out on the inside. This was where a knife and balaclava were hidden. There was also a *Cosmopolitan* magazine where all the blonde women inside had had their faces stabbed.

Johanna believes there are too many coincidences with regards to Levi and all the attacks that have happened.

He knows the TWICKENHAM area well as he used to drink in the Prince Albert Pub, HAMPTON ROAD. He is known to drink in the WALTON and WEYBRIDGE areas. He associates with a family in WALTON.

He has been harassing Johanna who lives very close by to WALPOLE GARDENS, STRAWBERRY HILL.

His mum apparently lives in SOUTH ROAD,

HANWORTH and he has horses in a field in OAK AVE, which is close to PRIORY ROAD, HAMPTON.

His ex-girlfriend 'Emma' lives in WEST DRAYTON with Levi's 3 children. Again this is not far from HATTON CROSS.

He is currently on bail for GBH and fraud. He attacked a male with a hammer.

Of course, we now know that starting with that particular message was lucky enough; there was more to come. As Mark finished reading the message, he expressed his certainty that one of the inquiries into locally registered Courier vans had mentioned wheel-clamping. A quick check on the standalone database revealed his memory to be correct. P610 XCN, a white Ford Courier van registered to Warren Motors in Isleworth. The garage had been spoken to, and they said they had sold the van to a gypsy who gave the name Levi. He had given an accommodation address, there was no way of tracing him thereafter and, indeed, the garage would be keen to speak to him as they had received a pile of parking and bus-lane tickets for the van since it was sold.

So the name Levi gave us a connection between a Courier van and one of the many suspects suggested to us. Mark looked at me and said, 'My brother knows the bloke that runs that garage. I'll see if I can get a number for him.'

Mark's brother, Dave Leach, was also a DC on my team, at that time working on a different long-running inquiry. Within a few minutes, Mark was speaking to the proprietor of Warren Motors, who could only add one thing to the report on our database – but a crucial fact nevertheless: Levi, when he bought the van, had left a mobile-phone number. Of all the phone numbers we were later to discover Levi Bellfield to have used (and there were more than twenty), the one he left at the garage was, thankfully, one that was associated with him within the Met databases. Levi Bellfield, never one to let sleeping dogs lie, had had an altercation with his neighbour in West Drayton. As a means presumably of making more trouble for him, Levi had phoned the Anti-Terrorist hotline and reported that the completely innocent next-door neighbour was an Al-Qaeda operative. This was almost amusing, since the neighbour was a Scotsman of Italian descent and had no terrorist connections whatsoever. But happily, the conscientious officer who had received Levi's call had taken his mobile number and recorded it on the information log, where it sat in cyberworld, ready to be found by our search.

We had the connections confirmed – Levi Bellfield, who Johanna had told us was violent, hated women (especially blondes) and had connections with Twickenham Green and Walton on Thames, owned a white Ford Courier van.

Not wanting to move too far ahead of myself but feeling the indescribable excitement of actually getting somewhere, I asked Tracy Clarke, the intelligence researcher on our sister team at Barnes, if she would bring me a printout of Bellfield's intelligence record. She returned a few minutes later with an inch-thick pile of A4 paper, which I began to scan. As I went through successive tales of insinuations of violence, drugs, firearms and general lawlessness, I was struck by the charmed life this man seemed to have led – there were very few actual convictions there. But then something big hit me. In April 2004, just a month or so before Kate Sheedy had been run over and left for dead, Levi had been arrested driving a Toyota Previa, which was described as having blacked-out windows. The circumstances of the arrest – that he had apparently kidnapped a pub landlord and had somehow managed to explain it away as a 'prank' – were irrelevant. A Previa was a people-carrier; a large one much like a Ford Galaxy. Kate had described a white people-carrier with blacked-out windows but was uncertain of the make and model. The investigating team at Hounslow had plumped for a Galaxy after she had been shown pictures of similar vehicles and said it looked like a Galaxy. Could it have been a Previa? Could it have been Levi's Previa? The only further confirmation I could get there and then that night was the Previa's colour, which, inexplicably, had not been recorded on the intelligence report. That, however, could easily be solved by a quick check on the Police National Computer (PNC) vehicle file. I asked Tracy to do the check, adding that, if it turned out to be white, we might have hit the jackpot. She brought back a printed record from the check half a minute later and, beaming, gave it to me, saying, 'Guvnor, I think we've hit the jackpot!'

CHAPTER TEN

STICK A TEAM
BEHIND HIM

I always believed that, no matter how decisive a leader one tried
to be, it was essential to keep decisions under review – and that
part of being decisive was being quick to change one's mind as
soon as it was clearly necessary. So, despite knowing the responses
I would get, almost before the elation that we had finally got a
real breakthrough had subsided, I sat by the phone with the team
call-out list and began to call them all back. For me, it was a no-
brainer but, while Jo Brunt understood that, some of the team
were sceptical, if not openly dubious – as she, faithfully as usual,
told me. I had gone, they thought, from having all my eggs in the
van basket to an even narrower approach of staking everything
on this one van, one man. Quite a birthday present for me.

Throughout the investigation thus far, I had a few conversations
with Deputy Assistant Commissioner Bill Griffiths. A revered
investigator who commanded huge respect from all that worked

with him, he had been instrumental in encouraging me to return to the Met in 2002 after I had served for six years in other forces. Accordingly, when I outlined my plan to put Levi Bellfield under surveillance in the hope that he would lead us to the Courier van with its potential for forensic evidence, he was quick to offer up every resource possible from within the force – and one or two from outside of it. He came down to Barnes and we chatted over a cup of coffee, his quiet, polite and encouraging manner making the conversation much easier than one might have imagined when under pressure and speaking to a man of such exalted rank.

I thought that we needed to keep tabs on Bellfield twenty-four-seven for a couple of days and see if we could get the van before we arrested him. I was very mindful that, if he were, indeed, our man, the 'blitz' attacks he carried out would happen very quickly – so quickly that the officers behind him would have to be very much alive to the possibility and ready to intervene. DAC Griffiths asked why I was only wanting to do it for a couple of days.

'Because I don't want us to have another murder witnessed by ten police officers who also video it,' was my reasoning.

'Let me worry about that. We can do everything possible to avoid it but we also need to take every possible chance to get hold of that van. We'll stick a team behind him for a couple of weeks,' was his firm and somewhat audacious reply.

While the logistics of twenty-four-seven surveillance were being organised for me by others, my team spent a couple of days looking for the van itself. It was during this time that I made an unexpected discovery, which was to ratchet up the stakes several notches. DI Richard Ambrose was driving me around as we joined in the search – it really was all hands to the pumps; if we could find the van ourselves quickly, the days of risky and expensive surveillance might be avoided. On the evening of 11 November 2004, we were in the Walton and Sunbury area, scouring the streets near the route of the suspect van. Our car, as well as us, needing fuel, we called in to the BP garage near Kempton Park. While Richard was adding fifty litres of diesel and getting the inevitable tuna sandwiches, I was in the car looking through the thick sheaf of laser-printed pages that were Levi Bellfield's complete intelligence file. Among the litany of suspicious stops, allegations of violence and reports of awful driving, something struck a chord. It was an address, showing that, in 2002, Bellfield was living at 24, Collingwood Place, Walton on Thames. Of course, Walton was where the van had been headed immediately after Amélie's murder and where we had recovered her keys and Discman from the Thames. I didn't know where exactly Collingwood Place was but thought that, if it were close to the bridge, it might be a clue as to where we might look for where Bellfield went on that night. From my backpack, I produced the Met-issue A to Z, a thick, hard-bound blue map book, which usefully included about ten miles around London as well as our actual patch, and so showed Walton on Thames.

And there it was, Collingwood Place, a short, 'F-shaped' collection of cul-de-sacs off Copenhagen Way, virtually opposite Walton railway station. Instantly, I realised the implication of this. In 2002, when I had served briefly in Surrey Police, Amanda 'Milly' Dowler had been abducted from Station Avenue, Walton on Thames and, although I had never worked on the case, I knew that the last sighting of her was at a bus stop near Copenhagen

Way. As hearty as our protestations to the media that our cases were not connected to Milly's had been, I was looking at the very spot on my map where both she vanished and, at the same time our suspect, a violent sexual predator with, according to his intelligence file, strong tendencies towards paedophilia, had lived.

Poor Richard didn't realise why I just grunted as he handed me a packet of sandwiches and a latte. I was transfixed, staring at the map as the enormity of what I had found sunk in. When my power of speech returned, I showed him the intelligence entry, then the map, asking him to check that I had it right. He looked at me agog; for once, he, too, was lost for words. I frantically scrolled through the names on my trusty Nokia 6310. My habit of transferring all contacts from phone to phone and never deleting them paid off – in there, from my Surrey days, was a mobile number for Brian Marjoram, a very experienced Surrey Police DI who I knew was acting up as the SIO for the Milly Dowler inquiry. I looked at the time – 8.45pm. Normally, that would be a bit late to disturb him at home, wouldn't it? Couldn't it wait until morning? Of course it couldn't. I hit 'Call' and Brian's friendly 'Hello, mate, what can I do for you?' began a vital conversation, during which I told him all we knew about Levi Bellfield and which Brian concluded with, 'Christ, the hairs on my neck are standing up now.'

Thus began Surrey's interest in Bellfield, one which was, in many ways, difficult to cultivate but ultimately lasted for seven years until he was convicted of abducting and murdering Milly Dowler.

The following morning, I was back to concentrating on my

investigation, rather than Surrey's. Surveillance teams were crammed into the office at Barnes and I briefed them. Paramount was that they should intervene at the first hint of a new attack brewing. I was able to point out from the CCTV stills how the van had cruised around Twickenham Green, hunting, before Amélie was attacked. The instruction was clear – if he starts doing that, you call for a uniformed car to stop him and, if it gets beyond that, you will intervene, robustly. Yes, I know you are surveillance officers and you usually don't 'show out', but first, you are police officers so you will not watch a murder take place. I was happy that none of them actually *would* have just watched but also wanted to make sure they were clear that there was no room for hesitation. I was petrified by the danger this man posed and determined that we would not let him strike again under our gaze.

While the surveillance team were following Bellfield around west London, without any sign of the Courier van, my team carried on investigating his history. We discovered he had sold his Toyota Previa soon after Kate Sheedy had been run over; that it was now registered to a man in Greenford. The Previa was spotted outside the address but it transpired that the owner was actually a friend of Bellfield's called Noel Moran – who, before Bellfield stood trial, would himself be convicted of an entirely unrelated murder. He had registered it to his home address but in a false name in a half-baked attempt to avoid police attention. The Toyota was seized for forensic examination but it didn't take an expert to notice that the driver's-door mirror was smashed – the exact defect described by Kate Sheedy as featuring on the car that ran her over.

Meanwhile, on the third day of tailing Bellfield, the surveillance team reported a remarkable incident. They were following him and an unidentified friend as they took an apparently aimless drive around west London on a Sunday afternoon in Bellfield's recovery truck. In Uxbridge, they stopped at a bus stop, whereupon Bellfield got out of the cab and spoke with two teenaged girls waiting for a bus. They saw a conversation without hearing it, saw the girls appear to laugh and try to walk away just as a bus came, which the girls boarded. Bellfield returned to the truck and drove off. Using his initiative perfectly, the sergeant in charge of the surveillance team instructed one car to peel off, follow the bus and speak to the girls when they alighted. What they had to say was chilling confirmation that Bellfield was every bit as dangerous as our suspicions told us he was.

The girls were cousins, aged thirteen and fourteen, respectively. They were on their way to meet some friends in the town centre. Bellfield had come up to them and said, 'You two look nice. How old are you then?'

They had told him their ages, to which he responded, 'Ooh, that's good. I bet you're both virgins, then? You look like virgins. I like virgins. I bet you're both nice and tight.'

At which point he had offered them a lift, but the bus arrived, which made it easy for them to escape any further attention from him, save for his parting shout: 'Slags!'

This was, of course, crucial information for me – not only did it show the sort of perverted man we were dealing with but it also added to the belief that he was active on the streets and so the likelihood of further attacks was very real. And the fact that he seemed to view bus stops as a hunting ground gave a potential link to both Amélie's murder and Kate's attack. He was looking ever more a good suspect and I was becoming convinced we were on to something.

After a week of surveillance, we had seen no trace of the Courier van and I started to make plans for Bellfield's arrest. There were two main strands of this plan – the logistics of the physical arrest and associated searches that would be needed, and the legal, evidential side – what we would arrest for, what evidence we had and what we might be able to charge.

The logistics were complicated by the murky worlds Bellfield inhabited. Aside from his current best friend, Brian O'Shaughnessy (who was later to find fame in his new role as a bailiff on TV's *Can't Pay? We'll Take It Away!*), Bellfield was closely associated with a local paedophile, Suraj Gharu – and his brother Sunil, who provided Suraj with a false alibi – as well as an older, more notorious child-abuser called Victor Kelly. The nature of the murders and of these men's past histories gave rise to the distinct possibility that they were somehow involved in criminality, as well as the chance that he had left property or other incriminating evidence with them. The decision was pretty easy to come to – we would need to search their houses and vehicles at the same time. Warrants were duly obtained and my list of targets for simultaneous searches expanded to eight houses or flats and seven vehicles. Which meant, yet again, I was going to have to go begging to borrow staff and vehicles.

The legal aspects were, in truth, much more of a headache. Of course, we would be arresting him for the murder of Amélie and of attempting to murder Kate. But the truth was I knew we had nowhere near enough evidence to charge him and that, if he refused to answer questions and we found no physical evidence, the prospect of releasing him without charge was very real. And it was very frightening – risk-assessment discussions I had held with senior officers came quickly to the conclusion that the danger this man posed to the public was such that, if we were not able to keep him locked up, he would need to be watched, all the time, until we could.

Out of the blue came an opportunity for an easy win to help ensure Bellfield could be charged. Resulting from the publicity surrounding Amélie's murder, a man in Strawberry Hill came forward to say that, in 2002 or 2003, his nanny had been assaulted near to Twickenham Green. She had been hit over the head while walking but had not reported the attack to police and had since returned to her home in Peru. She had, though, told him that she had seen her assailant and was sure she would recognise him again. Despite the obvious problems inherent in relying upon this offence, it did have the potential for enough evidence to charge Bellfield with a serious crime and, thereafter, to keep him in custody. First, we had to corroborate the existence of the crime as described, which was quickly accomplished by examination of triage records at Kingston Hospital. These told us that the nanny, Sonia Salvetierra, had, indeed, attended there with a head injury and gave a history of assault in the street on 3 November 2002, just three months before Marsha McDonnell had been killed. Second, we had to make contact with Sonia, and see if she was willing to come to London and take part in an identification procedure to see if she could pick Bellfield out.

Sonia said yes, travel arrangements were made and her

availability became the milestone around which the arrest date was planned. We would keep the surveillance up until 5am on Tuesday, 23 November 2004 – a further five days – when my team would simultaneously execute search warrants across a swathe of west London at the eight addresses and seven vehicles intelligence told us were associated with Levi Bellfield.

CHAPTER ELEVEN

PLANNING FOR
THE ARREST

The choice of time for an arrest such as this is pretty much a given. Early morning, when the suspect is likely to be in bed asleep, gives police the element of surprise, means that the suspect is somewhat disoriented and also that there are fewer other people up and about to get in the way, assist him to escape or cause a fuss. The chosen day, however, was dictated by more administrative considerations. Most of my team and the thirty or so officers I was to be borrowing for the occasion were rostered to be on a rest day at the weekend. Since the briefing would have to begin at about 3am in order to make the 5am strike time, and the Met Police day is deemed to begin at 6am, they would technically be starting on Sunday and so all be on expensive overtime if we went for it on a Monday. Hence, Tuesday, 23 became the day when three months of hard work would become real and our quarry would be detained.

But there was yet to be a spanner thrown into the works – one beyond my control or, indeed, comprehension. Just after midday on Friday, 19 November, I got a message from DCS Andy Murphy that there was a problem and that I should meet him in his office at Hendon as soon as possible. When I got there about an hour later, I found that the meeting was also being attended by Bob Cox, a wonderfully genial and pragmatic Irishman who was the Met's deputy Director of Communications – the second most senior media officer in the force. He told us that he had been contacted by a journalist from the *News of the World*, who had told him that they knew that we had a good suspect and that we had been tailing him for a week or so. She added that it was her intention to run the story the following Sunday – in two days' time, just forty-eight hours before the arrests and searches were planned. Which, of course, would tip Bellfield off, send him into hiding and probably result in the destruction of any evidence which we might otherwise have been able to find. This was serious; I was furious – yes, that the information had somehow been leaked to the journalist but perhaps more so that she and her editor didn't have the decency and public-spiritedness to hold back and allow us to get on with our job of taking a serial killer off the streets.

Andy Murphy and I knew we could not bring the operation forward to Saturday as, even if we were able to get all the resources in place in time – which would have been extremely difficult – the rest day working would have doubled the cost. Bob Cox was calmly sanguine. What we needed to do, he suggested, was negotiate. What could we give to the *News of the World* that would make them delay their story? My protestations that, if the prospect of letting someone like Bellfield go free wasn't enough motivation, what would be? probably just betrayed my naivety of the world of the media at that time. Bob said he thought there would always be something and, after a few minutes of discussion, we arrived at offering them the opportunity to accompany officers on the raid to Bellfield's house, with a photographer, so that they would have a story from exclusive access when the time came at the end of any trial. This was far from ideal, I thought. First, their presence would be an additional distraction for my officers, who would have an additional couple of untrained and unarmed people to look after during a dangerous operation to arrest a very violent man. Second, their presence was likely to enrage Bellfield, thus making the striking of a rapport with him even more difficult than it was, in any case, likely to be.

There was little choice. As distasteful as I found it, that was probably the best we could offer, so Bob Cox made the phone call and a deal was reached. One that the *News of the World* broke the following weekend, when they ran the story with pixelated photos, despite having agreed to hold off with it until after the trial. To minimise the risk of further leaks creating more problems, Andy Murphy agreed to fund some rest-day working and we brought the arrest day forward by twenty-four hours. Briefing was to be at 3am on Monday, 22 November 2004, in the Simpson Hall at Hendon – which I had not visited since I took the oath of a constable nearly twenty-four years earlier. I went back to Barnes and found all the warrants had been obtained, worked through the details and allocated supervisors from my team to each of the sub-teams, ready for Monday morning.

It was a sharp autumn night, really, rather than morning when around seventy of us turned up at Hendon. Andy Murphy opened the briefing, first explaining the presence of the two journalists and then remarking how 'Breakfast Rules' (the informal punishment whereby any officer late for an early briefing has to buy breakfast for the whole squad) would have been financially catastrophic. Happily, everyone was on time and keenly attentive as I then went through the information everyone needed, their individual objectives and just a few words on keeping safe while they did so. It wasn't difficult to motivate them or to make them appreciate the gravity of what we were about to do. I'm sure I was more John Major-esque than Churchillian – what was needed was patient attention to detail, rather than inspiring rhetoric; they knew exactly how important success was. I then handed over to DI Tony McKeown, who had become a vital part of the machinery as the team quartermaster, earning himself the rather unfair nickname of 'Paperclips'. He handed out vehicle keys, maps and briefing sheets with his customary good humour and efficiency. And, by about 4.15am, we were off.

DCS Andy Murphy had suggested that I keep an overview of the whole operation from his car, driven by his Staff Officer DS Rebecca Hamilton. We drove the eighteen miles or so around the North Circular Road and A4 to West Drayton, to wait for all the teams to get in position before I gave the command for the eleven simultaneous strikes. Everyone was in a position by about 5.10am and, with my heart racing a little, I pressed the transmit button on the Airwave radio and uttered the classic words, 'Go, go, go!'

One by one, the teams reported back that they had secured entry, who was present and that they were proceeding with their evidential searches. Of course, the most important address was Levi Bellfield's home address, a three-bedroom housing-association house in Little Benty, immediately to the side of the M4 motorway in West Drayton. The sub-team there was led by my most experienced Detective Sergeant, Norman Griffiths. Norman was a quiet and practical man, tall and lithe with hands befitting his former trade as a butcher. His normal role was as the office manager, in charge of maintaining the HOLMES database and administration of our investigations, but I had chosen him for this job not only because his overarching knowledge of the investigation so far meant he was unlikely to miss any shred of evidence but also because, quite simply, I trusted him to do a proper job of controlling what might be the most lively encounter.

It was about 5.30am when Norman phoned me to say that Bellfield was not in the house and things looked as if they were about to unravel. The surveillance team had been behind Bellfield on the previous evening and had reported that they had 'bedded him down' – that is, seen him home for the night – at around 11pm. Thereafter, they had been sitting unseen in his road, a cul-de-sac from which there was vehicular access at only one point. There was a footpath at the other end but, they said, if in a car, he had to have driven past them and, if he had walked, they must have seen him. All of which, of course, relied upon their having been awake and watching. Andy Murphy quickly achieved a state of incandescence, suggesting the surveillance team would all be driving panda cars by Friday with such a force and with such venom that I feared I would be joining them. The operation had demanded so many staff that, aside from the civilian staff in the incident room, absolutely everybody I had was already deployed. So it was that the two most senior officers involved went on a whirlwind tour of hotels, guest houses and other possible locations trying to find Bellfield – our efforts hampered by his forty-two different aliases, meaning we weren't actually sure who we should be asking about. It was desperate stuff, indeed, but we knew he needed to be found now that the cat was well and truly out of the bag. I also didn't need to remind Andy that the *News of the World* was on hand to capture this particular spectacular failure.

A couple of hours were spent in fruitless searching until Norman Griffiths rang me again: 'Guvnor, he's here all along. He's in the loft.'

'How do you know, Norman?'

'Gary and Debbie have been talking to Emma, his girlfriend. She said he was in bed and, when he heard us putting the door in, he ran up into the loft.'

'OK, don't do anything until I get back to you. We're going to need some help here.'

The relief I felt that he was there had to be put to one side for a while – there was a more pressing problem. How do you safely enter a loft to arrest a man who you suspect of killing at least two people by hitting them on the head? Think about it. No matter how you do it, entering by opening a loft hatch is likely to expose your head to attack from above. I needed to think of a way to do it with the least risk. Andy Murphy suggested getting the TSG – Territorial Support Group – the officers who are trained for riots and who are not only equipped with shields and helmets but have practised drills by which they can enter hostile premises safely. I agreed but added to this that a police dog might be effective, too – if a suitably protected officer could open the hatch and shout a warning that a dog would be inserted, Bellfield might be persuaded to surrender. We decided that I would call for both and then have a discussion about their tactics when they all arrived. While Rebecca Hamilton drove us back towards Little Benty, I picked up the radio to call the Information Room at Scotland Yard, asking for assistance from our specialist colleagues. Then the phone rang again. It was Norman Griffiths: 'Guvnor, don't worry, we've got him.'

'Got him? How? Did he give himself up?'

'Not quite, Guvnor . . . er . . . I just went up and got him. Thought it would save a load of fucking about.'

'Norman, you do know that was dangerous, reckless and you should have waited? But bloody well done!' I said, unable to disguise either my relief or my admiration for his bravery. It was another great example of coppers doing what they know needs be done without over-thinking the possibilities. The sort of act that no senior officer could ever ask them to do but, equally, that nobody should ever seriously criticise. I later found out the detail of DS Norman Griffiths's courageous act of pragmatism.

After he called me, he sat and thought that it wouldn't do any harm just to look, so he got a stool from the kitchen and took it up to the upstairs landing and stood on it to reach the entrance. He prised the hatch up and gingerly pushed it to one side in the loft. He waited; no movement was apparent. He had a large Maglite torch so he then swung the beam around the loft at arm's length, withdrew and waited. Still no response. Finally, he kept the beam up into the hatch as he stood upright and put his head through. He looked round and the loft was surprisingly free of clutter. He told the other four officers (DCs Gary Cunningham, Dave Leach, Gary Fuller and Debbie Ford) that he was going up, pulled himself up and looked around. Cunningham and Leach went to the stool, ready to assist if needed.

The loft wasn't boarded so he had to tread carefully on the ceiling joists; between them the spaces were filled with sheets of fibreglass insulation blanket, yellowy-orange in colour. He wandered around a bit by torchlight and then, next to the water tank, he realised there was a piece of insulation that was sitting six inches or so higher than the rest, protruding above the level of the joists. He went over, torch in hand and grabbed the end of the piece of insulation, pulling it over on itself slowly like he was opening a freshly-made bed. He had chosen the correct end because this exposed Bellfield's head.

Blinking in the bright beam of the torch, he squeaked, 'All right, all right, I'll come down, sir. I'm just hiding. I didn't know who you were.'

Norman told him to stay there and shouted that he had got him. Cunningham and Leach both entered the loft as well and Bellfield was handcuffed in front of his body so that he could still use his arms sufficiently well to let himself out of the loft. Leach went down again and Cunningham and Griffiths sort of shepherded him down into their arms.

We arrived at Little Benty shortly afterwards and I first set my eyes on Levi Bellfield in the flesh. He had been allowed to dress and was wearing tracksuit bottoms, trainers and a bright-blue polo shirt. He was larger than I had imagined, both taller and fatter, with a huge neck. His hair was shaved at the sides and I instantly noticed his eyes, black as coal and devoid of expression.

The overall impression was of a powerful, frightening man but this was softened instantly when he spoke in his high-pitched, squeaky voice. He seemed to have some sort of tick, blinking and tossing his head nervously every few seconds – but then I suppose he knew what he had done and what was likely to be coming his way. He also was scratching all over his body, or at least as much as a handcuffed man could; lying naked between the ceiling joists having pulled a thickness of about a foot of glass-fibre insulation over himself to hide probably explained his itching. We did though allow him a shower but not until some twenty-three hours later. It is a very small thing in the context of the abject misery this man inflicted but I am so glad that, in those moments, the last few minutes of freedom he would enjoy in his entire life, he was not only very uncomfortable but also utterly devoid of dignity. It is still much better than he deserved.

CHAPTER TWELVE

BELLFIELD IN CUSTODY

Heathrow Police Station, sat on the north perimeter road between a couple of the better airport hotels, was so unremarkable as to be missed by the majority of the travellers passing through the busiest of airports. It was my choice as Bellfield's initial destination for two good reasons – its status as a Category A station, meaning it was suitable for the detention of the most dangerous prisoners was one, but more important to me was that, while it was in close proximity to his home address, there was no information that Bellfield had any history of contact with the officers there. Already it was clear from his intelligence file that he was a man who would try to exploit relationships with police officers and there seemed a very good chance that he had, at some point, been an informant for his local CID. I did not want any familiarity or favours to be a distraction from what we had to do.

I arrived in the Custody Suite around half an hour after Bellfield had been delivered there. He had been searched, booked in and had already called for a solicitor, Mr Smith, who he had used previously. I found Bellfield with DC Gary Cunningham, about to walk through to the caged exercise area to smoke a cigarette. Gary, along with DC Dave Leach, was earmarked to interview Bellfield – they were simply the best interviewers I had. So I had also detailed them to deal with the administration procedures, giving them an opportunity to start to build some sort of rapport with him in a non-confrontational situation before the questioning started. Gary and Dave saw me come in and, as was usual, went to introduce me to the suspect.

'Hey, Levi, this is Mr Sutton. He's the boss.' Gary motioned towards me so as to draw Bellfield's attention.

'Fuck off, prick,' was Bellfield's rather robust and combative reply, which actually set the tone for our 'relationship' over the next four years. I smiled – I was too old and experienced to rise to that sort of bait by then. In years gone by, I'd have retorted with a sarcastic comment about me going home later or looking forward to a pint in the pub that night but I really didn't need to – I had more on my mind than scoring points for banter. There was the identification procedure and interviewing to come and the outcome of those was going to dictate whether this cocky, abusive and horribly dangerous suspect in front of me was leaving in a taxi or a prison van.

While the arrangements were being made, Bellfield was, naturally, placed in a cell. As was usual with high-risk prisoners, he was made to remove his shoes so as to prevent use of them as weapons or of their laces as a noose for a suicide attempt.

This was pretty routine; at this point, we had not had access to Bellfield's medical history and were ignorant of his bouts of depression and talk of suicide. The searching officers and the Custody Sergeant had failed to spot that the elasticated tracksuit bottoms he was wearing also had a tape around the waistband.

It was this that, after just a few minutes detention, he removed and placed around his neck, then tying it somehow on to the fixture on the cell wall that housed the button for flushing the toilet. Since this was less than five feet from the ground, to make the noose effective Bellfield had to lie on the floor; this, in turn, was made difficult because directly below the ligature's anchor point was the toilet bowl itself. Undaunted, Bellfield inserted his large head as far into the toilet as he could, then, deciding presumably that neither strangulation nor drowning in the loo was what he really wanted, he began to shout. The loud gurgling noises echoing around the bare walls of the cell soon caused the jailer officer to enter and, for the second time in a few hours, the fearsome serial killer found himself being extracted from an utterly undignified position by a policeman. How they resisted the temptation to press the flush button before effecting the rescue, I do not know.

A doctor was, by chance, in attendance at the station so I asked him to undertake an examination. With my deadliest-serious face, I said, 'Doctor, obviously, I need you to ascertain his fitness to be detained and interviewed – but also can you ensure he isn't suffering from Harpic poisoning?', which caused a good deal of amusement for everyone present apart from the prisoner himself. The verdict was that, while he hadn't done any real harm with the ham-fisted suicide attempt, his blood pressure was a startling

198/132. The doctor said that any question that caused him the slightest stress might cause something to burst, and recommended that he be removed as soon as possible to hospital for a proper check-up. Prisoners often think they are beating the system by getting a trip to hospital. While it does cause logistical difficulties for the police – specifically in ensuring the transportation and time at hospital are conducted under secure conditions – it also helps them enormously. The time from when he is removed from the station until he is back in his cell is not counted as detention time, so here, it was effectively extra time for us to conduct inquiries, take statements, find witnesses and have scientific work done. Quite frankly, I'd have been glad for Bellfield to be admitted for a week, although the local officers having to guard him might have begged to differ. As it was, he was away for just a couple of hours and the race against time was back on.

Mr Smith, the solicitor, was a pleasant chap in his fifties who told me he had come to the law later than most, spending his first working years as a baker. He remarked, on seeing Bellfield's tattoo of the Tottenham Hotspur cockerel on his leg, that they shared a common interest and was amused when I pointed out all three of us did – but that it wasn't going to help his client. I remarked also that I expected a prepared statement and 'No comment' thereafter; he smiled briefly and replied that he thought, often, where very serious allegations were being made, it was in the client's interests to talk. Gary Cunningham then served him with the written pre-interview disclosure that he had, with my approval, laboriously typed up and we waited for Bellfield and the lawyer to conduct their inevitable long period of consultation. Even in relatively simple murder cases, we were very accustomed to frequent and lengthy periods of inactivity once the suspect was arrested. Because of the high stakes, I suppose, solicitors took great pains to go through every detail and we took similar care in preparing the disclosure. Often, by the time the suspect had been in custody for twenty-four hours, the actual interview time might be just three or four of those, after consultation, rest periods and medical examinations. Almost every time, we were forced to go to a superintendent for an extension to custody time, taking us to thirty-six hours, and, quite frequently, thereafter to a magistrate for a warrant of further detention to take us to the maximum of seventy-two hours. I thought it would be highly likely to be necessary in Bellfield's case – especially if he were to talk to us in interview as that inevitably makes the interviews longer than the more common 'No comment'.

We had prepared one of the small interview rooms at Heathrow, equipping it with cameras and microphones so that every interview could be monitored in a similarly small office nearby. My squad had no prisoner facilities at our base and so we were always dependent upon goodwill from the local officers where we took prisoners; in this case, Heathrow were fantastically accommodating. Everyone knew how important this investigation was and seemed to want to do their bit to help. However, the technology available ended with the CCTV and audio; there was no means of quick communication back to the interviewing officers from the monitoring room. If I wanted to contact the interviewers, it was dependent upon a text or pager message getting through.

The first couple of hours went smoothly enough. To our mild surprise, Bellfield was speaking but he wasn't really answering. Indeed, he was posing nearly as many questions to the interviewers as were they to him. I realised pretty quickly that he was, at this stage, still clearly of the view that he was cleverer than Plod, could outwit them and was using the opportunity of the interview to try to gain an understanding of just how much we knew, presumably to help him come up with the best responses at a later date. I remarked to Jo Brunt that we were better than him, that he couldn't manipulate us and that it actually showed that he had something to hide from us. One thing which also became very apparent was that Bellfield became much more engaged, talkative even, when presented with something to look at – photographs, plans or maps. Again, this was noted and passed on by text to the interviewers as a tactic to use if the conversation was flagging.

While this was going on at Heathrow, my officers were hard at work elsewhere. At Bellfield's home in West Drayton, DCs Gary Fuller and Debbie Ford were patiently talking to his partner, Emma Mills. Emma had been with him for some nine years after they had met when she was a teenager and he was a bouncer at her local nightclub, Rocky's in Cobham. They had moved in together shortly afterwards and she had borne him three children, the last of which had been born just five months previously in July 2004. She was a gentle, shy young woman, well-spoken and bright – very unlike the sort of partner one might expect a man like Bellfield to have. Debbie Ford told me that she was sure that Emma had horrific stories to tell but that she remained utterly petrified by the thought of what he would certainly do to her if she related what he had put her through. I asked her and Fuller to remain patient, to keep explaining how we wanted to help Emma and how that might be made much easier if she told us what had gone before. Elsewhere, I was told that the identification procedure with Sonia Salvetierra was underway. These procedures were now conducted not with live 'stooges' but by playing short video clips to the witness, an excellent improvement as it not only removed the need for many hours of work persuading members of the public to take part but also meant there was no need for the (often very frightened) witness actually to be in physical proximity to the suspect.

The procedures were carried out by officers completely unconnected with the investigation – to ensure there could be no accusation of bias – and so it was simply a matter of us awaiting a telephone call with the result. When it came, it was bad news. Ms Salvetierra had been unable to make a positive identification. This, of course, did not mean she had excluded Bellfield, or that he was not responsible for her attack, but merely that she could not say for sure that it had been him. Nevertheless, it was a blow – I had hoped that her case would be the easy charge to prove, that it would be our 'holding charge', upon which we could have Bellfield safely remanded into custody while we carried on gathering evidence that he was our serial attacker and murderer. Without it and in the absence of admissions or forensic evidence connecting him to the murders, the unthinkable would come to pass. We would have to let him go.

The remaining interviews of the first day came and went with no real change – Bellfield politely denied any involvement at all and continued to press the officers for more of what they knew. At about 6.30pm, I had a meeting with Andy Murphy in a small room off of the Heathrow canteen, which had probably, before the Met became just slightly more modern and egalitarian, been the senior officers' dining room. The main topic of our conversation was proactivity and surveillance – what could we do to make sure Bellfield did not reoffend if we had to release him, and what opportunities for garnering additional evidence might that provide for us? We concluded after an hour or so with a list of potential physical and technical measures we could employ. The message I was getting was that all and any resources of the Metropolitan Police were available to us, so highly dangerous was Bellfield judged to be. Of course, I agreed but, as I then went into a meeting with my team, I decided not to discuss it with them. For now, for our purposes, release was not going to be an option. We had a day or two ahead of us during which we simply needed to turn up enough evidence to keep him in custody: that would be my exhortation.

As it turned out, such inspiration wasn't required. As we settled in to our seats in the briefing room, I was aware that there was a hubbub of chatter between the DCs, with Gary Fuller and Debbie Ford at its centre. They were nodding and smiling. So after starting the meeting with brief details of the interviews and of the failed identification procedure, I turned to that pair first. 'What have you found, what does it mean and what do we do next?'

Gary Fuller began by saying that Emma Mills had realised that this was her opportunity to escape from a terrible relationship, that she had poured out a horrifying catalogue of rapes (one committed under Walton Bridge, in exactly the spot from which Amélie's possessions had been cast into the Thames) assault, abuse, being locked in the house, being locked naked in the garden, being forbidden to call her friends or family – just the most awful tale of domestic abuse imaginable. She had also agreed to make a statement outlining all this and, most significantly, had said that she knew that Bellfield's previous partners had suffered the same treatment. Suddenly, our priorities changed. We had to investigate these allegations immediately so that we might be in a position to charge him with the serious offences disclosed. If we could find the victims willing to help us, we would have our holding charges. Even better, the seriousness of them and the risk of reprisals to the women victims would almost certainly make bail out of the question. This could be the most achievable, pragmatic way of taking Bellfield off the streets. I cut the meeting short after allocating officers to make contact with the ex-partners that evening with a view to arranging meetings in the morning. There was no point in going on with discussions that night; we had all been awake for more than seventeen hours and tomorrow needed an early start to what would be a critical and inevitably very busy day.

CHAPTER THIRTEEN

MILLY GETS RULED IN

All too often we find that those who have a propensity for violence on strangers are also unable to control themselves within their relationships. It was no shock, therefore, to find that Bellfield had been beating and abusing his partners for years. What was shocking, though, was the detail. Emma Mills, Johanna Collings and Rebecca Wilkinson, over the course of half a day, recounted almost exactly similar tales of sexual abuse, psychological control and physical violence. The sequence for each of them was the same: Bellfield is charming, attentive and generous at the start of the relationship. Once co-habitation was established, he forced them essentially to cut off virtually all contact with their former life. They were made to devote all their time and energy to obeying him, forbidden to socialise, spend money, leave the home even, without his express permission. If they went beyond the boundaries he had set, there were consequences – physical assaults, rape or being locked in the house. Individual incidents, which moved even the most world-hardened of us, included being forced to sit on a stool in the kitchen for eight hours without moving, destruction of treasured personal property and being forced to have sex with Bellfield's friends and accomplices.

Of particular interest, too, was a passage in Emma Mills's statement that did not concern his violence towards her. She remembered that, in March 2002, she was house- and dog-sitting in West Drayton for a friend who was on holiday. At that time, she was trying to rekindle her relationship with Bellfield – nearly a year previously, she had left him and sought an injunction due to his repeated violence towards her. Her mother had, through a friend, arranged for her and the two children to move to a rented flat in Collingwood Place, Walton on Thames. It had been her opportunity to forge a new, safe life for herself. Sadly for her – but as is all too common – she relented when Bellfield, during access visits to the children, which she had no choice but to grant him, had made repeated attempts to persuade her to have him back and he had moved into the flat in the autumn of 2001. He was actually redecorating the house at Little Benty in preparation for the planned family move back there in May.

Emma recalled with certainty the events of the evening of 21 March 2002. She was clear about the date because, as a resident of Walton on Thames and a mother, she had that evening worriedly watched the news reports of Milly Dowler going missing from near Walton station. Bellfield had been staying with her at the friend's house and had left early in the morning – as, she thought, to go and continue with the decorating work at their own house. During that day, he failed, as was his controlling custom, to call her every couple of hours to see what she was doing and, indeed, she had tried to call him but found his mobile phone to be switched off. This struck her as particularly unusual in that he was a voracious user of his phone and rarely had it turned off. She had wanted some groceries and was unable to go out as he had taken her car. Interestingly, she recalled that there was only one set of keys to her red Daewoo Nexia car and, on the same ring, was the only set of keys to 24 Collingwood Place. Bellfield had these keys with him all day while he was uncontactable. He came back to the friend's house shortly before 11pm, bringing with him some fried chicken and four cans of lager for them to share. Emma noticed that he had been drinking, which was not particularly unusual, but also that Bellfield had changed his clothes since the morning; he was now wearing a white tracksuit, which she knew had been in the wardrobe at the Collingwood Place flat, so it was obvious to her that he must have been there during the day but she knew better than to ask him for an explanation. They ate the food and then went to bed soon after midnight but Bellfield was restless. By about 3.30am, Bellfield, still awake, told Emma that he couldn't get to sleep and wanted to go back to Collingwood Place. He left, taking their Staffordshire Bull Terrier dog, Shy, with him.

Emma stayed another day then, when her friend returned, gathered her things and Bellfield collected her in the Daewoo to return her to Collingwood Place. He dropped her off outside, having driven past the many police vehicles and officers just yards from the flat on Station Avenue, who were beginning the search for Milly Dowler. He then went off alone. When Emma entered the flat, she found something strange. All the bedding had been removed from their bed. She called Bellfield immediately; his explanation was that Shy the dog had used the bed as a toilet and that the bedding was in such a state he had simply thrown it in the bin. Emma doubted this, at first simply because Shy had always been an absolutely clean dog but then later, when she took some rubbish to the bin, she saw there was no bedding in there. She assumed that Bellfield had somehow soiled the bedding while entertaining another woman and so said nothing – that sort of thing was not only common when you were in a relationship with Bellfield but also something which ought never be mentioned, on pain of violent reprisals. She said, quite pitiably, that it was just what you had to put up with.

That evening, 23 March 2002, there was a further shock. Bellfield told Emma that, despite their plans and there being a further six weeks on her lease at the flat, he wanted them to move back to Little Benty immediately. As usual, Emma complied without asking why and they went together in the Daewoo, with all their things, back to Little Benty. Three days later, on 26 March, Emma realised that the Daewoo was missing from outside the house. She asked Bellfield where it was and he told her that he had been for a drink with friends in Hounslow the previous evening and had left it there and got a taxi home because he had drunk too much to drive. This sudden respect for the law surprised her as being most uncharacteristic of him; nevertheless, the couple called a taxi to go to retrieve her car and found it was not there. Bellfield told her it must have been stolen and made her visit the local police station to report the theft. It was never seen again; Emma eventually received an insurance payout of £800, which, quite typically, Bellfield immediately took from her. She never did get another car from him.

So, aside from her revelations of serious offences committed by Bellfield on her, Emma was outlining a set of circumstances that, for me, aroused a great deal of suspicion. Bellfield was obviously in the area where Milly Dowler went missing during the day, he had changed his clothes and destroyed his bedding, while the car he was using, despite being of little value and a make and model in little demand, had vanished. I knew I had to tell Surrey Police at some point but also that we had more pressing matters to attend to – getting Bellfield charged and remanded into custody – so the exciting and potentially explosive information I had for my former colleagues would have to wait.

While the inquiry team were taking these horrifying statements, the interview team had come up against a snag. When they told Bellfield that he was also arrested for the rapes and assaults on his partners, the solicitor, Mr Smith, told them that he would have to withdraw. Since he had acted for Emma in the domestic-violence proceedings and she was now to be the complainant in a criminal investigation into the same incidents, he was compromised by a conflict of interests and could no longer represent Bellfield. Bellfield himself could not name another lawyer he wanted and so it was that the duty solicitor for the day at Heathrow, the Kingston-upon-Thames firm of Maclaverty Cooper Atkins, was called and the case allocated to its partner, Julie Cooper, who was for the most part represented at the police station by her (then) paralegal sister, Sandra. Both proved over the course of the investigation to be amiable and decent women but their view on

Bellfield's best interests was quite different to that of Mr Smith. From this point forward, Bellfield was to answer 'No comment' to the vast majority of the thousands of questions put to him. Sometimes, though, he found this discipline difficult, especially when presented with photographs and maps. Occasionally, he would also, without ever making anything other than a denial, remark on the contents of a document or question the accuracy of a photograph, protesting his innocence and then, almost comically, glancing at Sandra Cooper and then adding '. . . but no comment,' applying the phrase rather like the '. . . Not!' used in *Wayne's World*, as if it would negative everything he had said before it.

This day's interviews did, though, provide an episode that was, in some ways, comical despite the deadly serious nature of the subject matter. The interview room was small with a desk with two chairs on each side. Bellfield and Sandra Cooper sat one side, DCs Cunningham and Leach the other. Bellfield was in the corner of the room behind the desk and, like almost all our interview rooms then, the furniture was not fixed to the floor. Bellfield, pulling one of his regular stunts to try to show he was in control I suppose, started, during questioning, to rotate his chair while he was sitting in it. Hopping it around with his considerable bulk on it meant my first reaction was one of fear for the structural integrity of the legs but, surprisingly, they held up. He first went through ninety degrees to his right so he was facing his lawyer then, when this provoked no reaction, he continued a further ninety degrees so he was facing the blank wall behind him, with his back to the two bemused officers. To their credit, although they exchanged a few startled glances, they carried on with their line of questions and Bellfield carried on replying 'No comment' as if nothing had changed. Secretly, I am sure he was furious that he had not attracted the additional attention he, as usual, was seeking. So he upped the ante – so close was he to the wall that he was able to rest the soles of his feet on it then, slowly, he walked them up the wall so he was sitting there with his legs out straight, his feet planted against the wall above his head, answering 'No comment' to a series of questions about horrible murders and rapes. Sandra Cooper eventually cracked, telling him he ought to show more respect, and he grudgingly returned to a more sensible orientation. She mentioned in passing that the interview was being recorded but I am sure she knew – as, in all probability, did Bellfield – that it was extremely unlikely that the prosecution would be permitted to play anything quite so starkly callous to a jury. However, after his trial, I made sure that the clip of this staggering show of disregard for what he had done was included in the materials released to the media, who duly obliged by using it on the news. It is immortalised, of course, on You Tube, for all to see.

By the evening of 24 November 2004, I was hanging on the phone with the usual long wait for 'CPS Direct' – the system for getting out-of-hours charging authority from a prosecutor working from home with a dedicated telephone line and fax machine. It is an interesting system, where the central number to be called places your call to the next available prosecutor, who might be physically located anywhere in England or Wales. It has been known, legend has it, for officers who get a rejection of their suggested charges in borderline cases to call again a second or third time in order to find a lawyer who is more sympathetic to their cause. If Dad says, 'No,' try asking Mum . . . I had no need for such chicanery. The lady who received my call and faxed case papers in Nottingham was entirely happy to authorise me to charge Bellfield with offences of rape, of buggery and of assault against each of the three partners or former partners – a total of nine serious offences, for which the Custody Officer was quick to deny him bail on the grounds that he might try to interfere with the witnesses if he were released. He was bedded down in a cell at Heathrow to appear at Uxbridge Magistrates Court the following morning. Our contingency plans for a release were still in place, as they were at every one of the half-a-dozen or so hearings over the next three years when he made an application for bail but, fortunately, no judge ever thought that it was a good idea to inflict Bellfield upon the general public again and all the surveillance and monitoring preparations never had to be tested.

Quite often during a murder investigation, the day of charging is a milestone to be celebrated; indeed, frequently to be toasted. This was nothing of the sort. Although we had achieved the first objective – to prevent this most dangerous of predators from striking again – the hard work was, in many ways, only just starting. Yes, we had uncovered a string of horrible crimes against vulnerable women, a series of offences that, had they been the sum total of Bellfield's offending, would have deservedly earned him many years of imprisonment. But, notwithstanding their severity and the devastating effects they had had on the victims, even these were something of a sideshow when compared to our main aim: to prosecute and convict him for the murders and murderous attacks he had committed against strangers in the street. At this point, there was no cause for celebration because, as certain as I then was that we had the right man – a view shared by every member of my team – we were a long way from proving his guilt. The main chance was still Amélie's murder, especially if we could yet find the Ford Courier van and extract some forensic evidence. However, privately, I now doubted that we would. We would still try, of course – we had to – but the disappearance of the Daewoo after Milly Dowler's abduction worried me. I felt it made it very likely that Bellfield was capable of 'losing' a vehicle in some way if he feared it could incriminate him. His contacts in the motor trade and other nefarious friends might well make this relatively easy for him and, if his appreciation of our ability to retrieve scientific evidence was good enough for him to clean up after that crime, the likelihood was he had done so again. It was one of those things to keep to myself for the time being, though – we had to try to find it and I didn't want to devalue that work by my pessimism. I shared my concerns with Jo Brunt and she agreed, both that it was a real danger but also that we shouldn't make our worries public to the team. She joked with me that I seemed to be learning from her how to judge their mood. I smiled, realising the truth in what she said. The fact was, though, that we had no forensics from Amélie's body or the scene and, if we didn't find the van, it was going to have to be a long, patient assembly of circumstantial evidence. Perhaps, Jo suggested, it was time to look at some of the other crimes we suspected him of to see if there was anything to be found there, now that we had our suspect. I saw the sense in this; nobody had ever considered Bellfield as a suspect for them so it was possible we might turn something up quite quickly. However, despite still having a large, augmented team, to move in that direction would stretch us. Building the case files for the rapes and assaults and continuing to investigate Amélie's murder were each difficult enough tasks on their own. Now I was contemplating looking at Marsha McDonnell's murder and the attempted murder of Kate Sheedy at the same time. Could we manage four live, major investigations at once? Would we need to? While most of the team were busy with inquiries coming out of the material we had seized during the arrest and trying to corroborate the horrendous allegations made by Emma, Johanna and Rebecca, Jo Brunt and I arranged for access to the Marsha McDonnell and Kate Sheedy databases. My plan was to know whether we should assume responsibility for them by Christmas, just one month away.

CHAPTER FOURTEEN

MARSHA MCDONNELL – OPERATION UPWEY

Marsha McDonnell was born on 14 October 1983 and so was just nineteen when she was murdered in February 2003. She lived with her parents, two sisters and a brother in the family home at Priory Road, Hampton. It was a loving and happy family; my subsequent visits to the house, despite the sadness underlying their purpose, were characterised by a hearty welcome and an ever-present atmosphere of love and respect. It was the sort of place you always felt eager to return to.

Marsha had been working in a shop in Kingston town centre. On the fateful night, she went to the cinema with a few friends to see *Catch Me If You Can*, the latest Spielberg film starring Leonardo Di Caprio; the irony of that title not passing us by as the investigation progressed. Marsha got on a route 111 bus at Kingston bus terminus a few minutes after midnight, alone but with her iPod for company during the ten minutes or so it would take her to get home. CCTV from the bus showed her alighting at a stop in Percy Road, less than a hundred and fifty yards from her home. She might have dawdled a bit to smoke a cigarette and ensure that she finished it by the time she was at the front door, but we will never know for sure because she never made it. Instead, she was attacked, hit from behind several times with a heavy blunt implement, causing severe head injuries from which, unfortunately, she would never recover. A neighbour, David Fuller, who lived just a few doors down from the McDonnells, called the police at 12.23am, a mere six minutes after Marsha had got off her bus. A loud thump had first attracted his attention and then a car door slamming but, as he could not see anything outside, he went back to bed. It was then that he heard what he described as 'a long, continuous moan' from outside. He again looked outside and saw what he thought looked like a pool of blood on the pavement, so he went with his wife, Bernadette, to investigate. They found Marsha lying face down with the huge wounds to the back of her head, bleeding profusely and motionless.

Marsha died without regaining consciousness during the afternoon of Wednesday, 5 February, some thirty hours after the attack. Naturally, a murder investigation had been mounted; although my team had been the closest geographically at the time, I had had no capacity for a new investigation, my hands being full with the murders of Bridget Skehan in Paddington on 3 January and David Sheehan in Ealing on 29 January, just a week before. So the new investigation was allocated to the 'in frame' team, Team 2 from Hendon led by DCI Dave Cobb and named Operation Upwey, after an area just outside Weymouth,

Dorset. As I read into that investigation, two things became apparent: first, I understood completely why they thought they had solved it; but second, I realised that, because they had come to that conclusion, there were obviously lines of inquiry that had not been pursued to their logical conclusion. Perhaps, I remarked to Jo Brunt, if we were to reopen the case and follow those leads, we might turn something up which pointed to Bellfield? She nodded slowly and, while she uttered no words, her pursed lips and the look in her eyes spoke volumes.

'It might, or it might be a shitload of work for no result . . .' she eventually said, pausing, then adding, '. . . but I see what you are saying. Got no choice really, have we?'

'Because you know I will insist anyway?'

'Yeah, of course you will – but also, it does need to be done.'

As I knew on the very first day, there had been a young suspect for Marsha's murder who had been sectioned as being severely mentally ill and had been detained in a secure hospital ever since. I now looked more closely at the detail of that suspect, whom I have called Sharpe.

Sharpe was sixteen and lived in Hampton, a few streets away from Marsha. He was well-known by the local teenagers as being a bit withdrawn, not really the friend of any of them but prone to hanging around when they were congregating in the streets and parks. Girls often described him as a bit creepy, but nobody had actually ever seen him do anything other than hang around, unwanted. He had come into the investigation as the result of another incident, which took place earlier on the evening of 3 February 2003 a mile or so away.

In the wake of the terrible news of Marsha's murder, the

community, as it always is in these cases, was desperate to assist. The father of a fifteen-year-old girl I will call Sharon was prompted to tell the police of what happened. Sharon was walking home and became aware of a teenage boy who was following her. She quickened her pace and found that so, too, did he. She had then put her talent as the school 400-metres champion to good use, had run away and lost him. When she felt she was out of danger, Sharon called her father on her mobile phone and he drove to pick her up. As they drove safely home, they again passed the suspect teenager and so Sharon had got a good look at him. Once Cobb's team were in possession of this information, they saw it as a potential lead – after all, what would be the chance of two predatory males following young women in the same small and peaceful corner of London on the same evening? Too much of a coincidence – and detectives really do not like coincidences.

Inquiries with the local neighbourhood officers, using Sharon's description of the suspect's appearance and demeanour, quickly caused Sharpe's name to pop up. He was arrested and, while he had no alibi for the incident involving Sharon, he said that, at the time of Marsha's murder, he was at home in his bedroom watching a recording of the Martin Bashir documentary *Living with Michael Jackson*. His family were in another room but all believed he was in the house at the time. A search of his bedroom revealed library books on macabre subjects and an inquiry of the local library showed he had a history of borrowing books connected with true crime, especially murder. Suspicions were obviously aroused by this; as is often the case, members of the team divided into those who thought he was a good suspect and those who were more dubious. This never influences their actions or diligence in making their inquiries but does make for some lively debate in team briefings – which are often invaluable for the SIO in decision-making.

Sharpe was elevated from being 'of interest' to 'suspect'. Having the comparatively rare luxury of a live witness who felt she could recognise him again, an identification procedure was quickly organised to see if Sharon could, indeed, pick Sharpe out, which she did. Even the doubters were now beginning to be convinced Sharpe was the right man and he became the focus of the investigation. The difficulty for Dave Cobb was that Sharpe's mental condition made meaningful interview impossible; not surprisingly, this also meant that, even if some hard, irrefutable evidence of his guilt had been found, the likelihood of him being ruled as having had the mental capacity to commit the crime was slim – and this meant that it would be pointless to charge him. A report outlining the available circumstantial evidence was prepared and submitted, via DCS Andy Murphy, requesting permission to close the investigation. This had been granted and Operation Upwey was put away as solved.

The difficulty I had in agreeing with this decision was the one that had struck me back in August at the briefing for Amélie's murder: if Sharpe had killed Marsha but was detained and so could not have murdered Amélie, we were looking at two different killers. How likely was that, given the strong similarities in method, victim and location? Taking for the moment a hyper-critical view of the Operation Upwey investigation, I formed the opinion that it was relatively simple to argue against the validity of Sharpe's assumed guilt. He had a reasonably sound alibi; at least there was nothing that actually proved it false.

His reading habits were, at best, capable of adding somewhat to other, more concrete evidence but proved little on their own and, most importantly, the identification procedure proved only that he was the boy who had been following Sharon. There was no provable reason to link that minor incident with the savage murder that took place a few hours later. Sharon had picked out the person who had caused her distress but not the murderer and to confuse the two was a leap of faith, an assumption that, while it might have been understandable as a matter of judgement of coincidences and probabilities – and also one that was rigorously supported by the expert behaviourists and forensic psychologists at the time – did not stand up to simple, logical scrutiny.

Rather than looking backwards at this as an error, I was looking forwards, towards the opportunities this might provide for me. Because the investigation had been suddenly closed, it was very likely that there were outstanding lines of inquiry which might yet yield me important and telling evidence. There might even be some that had never been pursued at all. I carried on reading through the thousands of statements and documents, feeling every bit the twenty-first-century investigator as hour after hour passed at my desk reading my computer screen, consuming endless cups of coffee and Diet Cokes, rather than wearing out shoe leather and sharing halves of bitter with grubby informants. I couldn't even take it home with me as it was just too difficult and lengthy a procedure to get the HOLMES database on my laptop. The dark and wet evenings of December were spent not at any of the scores of Christmas parties to which I had been invited but in my office at Barnes, trying to get my head completely wrapped around Marsha's murder.

Given that our progress so far in Amélie's case had been assisted so much by the CCTV recordings we had recovered from buses and nearby buildings, it is hardly surprising that one action in the Upwey account caught my eye. SIOs tend to be very loyal to techniques that have worked for them in the past so, when I saw that the CCTV from the bus on which Marsha had travelled home had captured a car moving nearby at about the time she alighted, I clicked through every link to see how far it had been taken and to see if it had the potential to tell us more. Despite there being no facility to attach images or video clips to documents in HOLMES at that time, and so having to proceed merely by reading written descriptions, I found this: At 12.17am, Marsha could clearly be seen stepping out of the central exit doors of the double-decker in Percy Road. Her fur-trimmed coat hood down and her handbag slung over her left shoulder, she is alone. Three seconds later, the external camera to the front of the bus shows a car, believed to be silver, travelling south in Percy Road towards the front of the bus. The Upwey team had then 'raised an action' – HOLMES-speak for asking an officer to do something – to identify the car and trace the driver. This had been allocated to a detective constable but had then been returned to the office without completion when the investigation was closed. Obviously, this was not the only action to be so written off but its content and its potential made it, for me, the most notable. What did the CCTV actually show? Could we get a registration number? And where did the car go afterwards – was there any other footage that might help? Just like the first images of the white van on Twickenham Green, I was determined that we should find out. At worst, it might give us an important witness; at best, well, perhaps another jackpot. What if that silver car were Bellfield's? I was sure now that we would have to look all over again at Operation Upwey in the New Year, so I had a week before the Christmas break to see if I would feel the same about the outrageous assault on Kate Sheedy.

CHAPTER FIFTEEN

KATE SHEEDY – OPERATION ZENDA

In May 2004, Kate Sheedy was eighteen and on the brink of a great future. Pretty, slight and great, she was the Head Girl at Gumley House, a convent school for girls in Isleworth; a highly-thought of pupil in a well-respected school. She was approaching her A-levels, predicted to achieve the high grades necessary to take up her offer of a place at Durham University. She lived not far from the school with her mother. Her parents had divorced but she regularly saw her father, who also lived nearby. Thursday, 27 May 2004 was a momentous day for Kate and her classmates. It was the last day of school before they went off on study leave, took their exams and embarked upon their separate life journeys. To mark the occasion, there was a ceremony at the school, where staff and pupils said their farewells and in which, of course, Kate the Head Girl played an important part, delivering a speech of thanks and presenting the head teacher with a bouquet. The formalities having been completed, a substantial group of the girls set off later that afternoon for Twickenham town centre, for one last night out together before the serious revision began. A few bars were visited before the girls finished off in The Sorting Rooms, the former Post Office in the High Street, outside which the bus stop used by Amélie stood. Kate said her emotional goodbyes just before midnight and crossed the road to get on her bus home, towards Isleworth.

What happened to her thereafter was as terrifying as it was incredible. Her single-decker bus came, she got on and almost immediately received a call on her phone from one of her friends she had just left, asking if she had got home yet. Kate said she would be there in a few minutes. The bus followed its route north up Hall Road, passing the County Arms pub to its right and then continuing into Worton Road. This was Kate's stop – like Marsha, she got off a few hundred yards from her home. She walked up on the same side of the road as the bus stop as the bus drove away from her. She saw then that there was a vehicle parked just thirty yards ahead, on her side of the road. Its lights were off but the engine was running. She didn't take that much notice of it, other than to recall later that it was a large, people-carrier type of car, coloured white or silver, and that its rear windows were blacked out. Something – some sixth sense or intuition – told Kate that it was wrong. 'Sinister' was how she later described it. She decided that she would be safer if she put the width of the road between her and this car and so crossed the road, slightly diagonally, to continue her brisk walk. This meant she had to cross the mouth of another road, a cul-de-sac off Worton Road leading to a small industrial estate.

As she approached it, now less than three hundred yards from her front door, she heard the sinister car's engine rev. She looked up to see it pulling across the road at speed, lights still off, performing a sort of wide U-turn in the mouth of the road she was just crossing. It didn't stop; despite her fear, she noticed in that split-second that the car had a broken mirror on the driver's door and that the driver himself was hunched forwards over the steering wheel. Frozen by fear but, in any case, too close to take avoiding action, she was struck by the car, falling in front of it and then feeling the immense crushing pain of its front offside wheel running over her back. It stopped, Kate face down on the road under its side, between the front and rear wheels, in ever-increasing agony. She heard the engine note rise again as the car now reversed, the same wheel running over her body in the same place a second time. Surprised but grateful to be still conscious, she saw the car depart back towards the County Arms as she tried to stand. One step was all she managed before collapsing again on to all fours. Kate told us later that she was determined to crawl all the way home but, having made it on to the pavement, she found her bag, from which she took her phone and raised the alarm. She first called for an ambulance and then her mother, who alerted her father, and both parents arrived at the same time as the paramedics. She was taken to hospital where, as well as it being found that every one of her ribs was broken and that she had sustained some damage to her spine, she had to have an emergency operation to repair her severed liver. That she survived at all is testament to her courage and the skill of the doctors; that she finally took her university place at Durham just eighteen months later and recovered to live a full and happy life is nothing short of a miracle.

Kate's attack was investigated by the local CID in Hounslow Borough. It is a sad inequality for victims in London; if you are killed, you get a team of thirty-eight led by a DCI on your case but, if you survive, you get whatever resources the vastly overworked local office can throw at it. Essentially, Hounslow had a DS, overseen by a DI and assisted by whatever handful of officers had any spare time on the day when they were needed. They also, therefore, recorded their investigation not on the HOLMES system but initially in the ubiquitous red A4 notebooks, with the headline facts later being transferred on to CRIS – the Met-wide Crime Recording and Information System – which was effectively a digital version of what used to be handwritten crime books. This meant looking at the case wasn't as simple as with Marsha's – I couldn't simply log in to the appropriate HOLMES account. I needed to see the hard-copy statements, so I sent DC Paul Carruth over to Hounslow and asked him, while he was there, to collect the physical exhibits too. This was to save him two journeys; officially, I wanted to look at the case before deciding to take it on but, by having him collect everything, it was obvious to him – and, for that matter, to Hounslow – that I had really made up my mind. From what I knew of the case, coupled with us knowing that Bellfield drove a white people-carrier with blacked-out windows at that time, it seemed to me there was a very good chance that it was going to be of interest to us. And anyway, I had reasoned to myself, the crime against Kate was just so awful that she deserved to have a thorough investigation of the type that we could mount and which Hounslow were simply not equipped for – whether or not Bellfield had committed it.

When Carruth arrived at Barnes with the mountain of paperwork and several large plastic bags of exhibits, I got him to leave the papers in my office and take the exhibits to the store in order to note their movement in our logging system. Norman Griffiths had already asked for a HOLMES account to be created and the operation now had a name – Zenda; Z-names were still too difficult for the UK gazetteer so US place names were used in 2005 but whether this was based on the town in Wisconsin or the similarly-named settlement in Kansas, I never found out. Since it was likely to be our most direct route to implicating Bellfield, I turned straight to Kate's statement, looking at her description of the vehicle and its driver, and also to the records of the inquiries the Hounslow officers had made trying to trace it. They had done their best. Kate not being especially car-aware, she had been unable to give them a make and model, just a colour and type. They had taken a number of photographs of people-carriers to her and asked her to do a sort of ad-hoc identification procedure. Of course ,the problem is that these days many car designers follow the same fads and fashions, so models from different manufacturers can appear remarkably similar. This was, perhaps, compounded in this case because the people-carrier genre is pretty prescriptive as to styling – they really do all look very similar, especially in photographs where their different sizes are difficult to discern. So her best guess – that the vehicle was a Ford Galaxy – certainly didn't cause me any concern, since the appearance of that model was clearly similar enough to that of a Previa to keep the possibility of Bellfield's involvement alive. Indeed, when I considered the non-standard blacked-out windows and the damaged driver's-door mirror, I realised these features were much more important than a model identification from somebody who was by no means a car expert. As I was mulling this over, the doubt was about to be expelled in a most dramatic fashion.

Once again, it was the phrase, 'Guvnor, you need to see this ...' from DC Paul Carruth, the exhibits officer this time, and in a phone call. I wandered the short length of the building to the exhibits store, where I found Paul in the small, tiled room which had been converted from the gents' toilet. He had been logging all the physical exhibits we had taken from Hounslow Borough a few days before and had noticed that there was a bag containing a VHS video cassette, which had been sealed, as usual, when it was seized by police, but which had thereafter never been opened. Which meant that whatever the tape had recorded had never been viewed. The label on the evidence bag bore the handwritten description 'County Arms PH 28/5/04'.

The County Arms was a large public house on Hall Road, just before it changes to Worton Road, about a hundred and fifty metres south of the bus stop where Kate had alighted. It had a large number of CCTV cameras, two of which were external pointing north and south, giving a wide view of the road. Of course, seizure of the footage from these cameras was a given – any investigator would have seen the cameras and realised their potential. So why had the footage not been viewed? Carruth and I started to look through the exhibits and found a similar bag containing a cassette – in different handwriting, this one was marked 'County Arms PH 27-05-2004'. Another crucial difference was that it also bore a record of being unsealed and resealed for viewing. The conundrum facing us was why the officers on the original investigation would have looked at one recording but ignored the other.

It took us half an hour or so of speaking to detectives at Hounslow to work out what had happened. Although Kate had been attacked just after midnight – and so on 28 May – the officers who went to the County Arms to check the CCTV had originally thought of the offence as having taken place 'last night' and so had taken the tapes for 27 May. The CCTV system there automatically switched to a fresh tape each night at midnight and so the recording on the 27 May tape was of little use. Even before it had been viewed, the officer leading the investigation had realised this and so had sent officers to recover the tape for 28 May. Hence the two bags, which were logged in the exhibits record book several pages apart because there had been quite a few seizures of other exhibits in the meantime. The lead officer had then gone on annual leave for a few days and asked another officer to view the tapes while he was away. This officer went to the exhibits book, found the entry for the 27 May tape and duly viewed it, correctly reporting that it contained nothing of interest. However, he was unaware of the 28 May tape logged three pages further on in the book and, not being so familiar with case, failed to spot that what he had watched did not cover the time of the attack. The action to analyse the CCTV was then considered to be complete, so that, when the officer in charge came back, he was told there was nothing of any use recorded on it. Hence, the 28 May tape had remained sealed and not viewed, and nobody was aware of it sitting with its secrets sealed in polythene.

Having established all this, Carruth and I strode expectantly to the video machine, opened the bag and started to watch. At

00:32, we saw from the camera pointing south down Hall Road a bus heading north; the bus on which Kate had travelled from Twickenham. Forty seconds later, the next vehicle driving in the same direction behind the bus was a white people-carrier, which I immediately recognised as a Toyota Previa. We then switched to the view from the north-facing camera, which showed that, as the bus pulled in to the stop just opposite the entrance to Worton Hall, the Previa overtook it and then went out of shot. Although it was not visible on the recording, we knew that Kate had got off the bus and walked north, on the same side of the road as the bus stop. We then saw the Previa drive south on Worton Road and on to Hall road, past the cameras, back in the direction it had come from when following the bus. It was 00:34 – the murderous attack that left Kate with devastating injuries had taken less than two minutes. Paul Carruth and I were both uncharacteristically speechless, looking at each other for a good thirty seconds with our mouths open. This was dynamite.

When our faculties had returned, we looked closely at the frames containing the Previa. As was so often the case, footage from cameras situated to protect premises was not focused on events in which we were interested on the public road and so there was no chance whatsoever of identifying the Previa's registration plate, less still the identity of any occupant. However, as it made its escape down Hall Road it presented its passenger side to us and we were able to make out a large mark about 20cm by 6cm on the paintwork at the rear corner. We quickly looked at the photographs of the Previa taken after it was seized from Noel Moran and there it was – a stain where petrol had been leaking from the filler cap and had eaten into the paint, the same size, in exactly the same place and at the same angle as the mark visible in the grainy CCTV still. That was enough to convince us; would it convince the scientists and, ultimately, a jury? We had to be hopeful.

Once the excitement of such genuine progress had subsided, I had inevitably to consider the wider implications. While, from my perspective, this was an important breakthrough, from an organisational point of view, it was a disaster. While the failure of the borough investigators to view the CCTV was explainable, this didn't make it acceptable. Sure, mistakes happen, especially in overworked and understaffed borough CID offices but this was one which, especially in such a serious case, ought not have been made. And sometimes, unfortunately, the consequences of a mistake magnify its gravity. This was such a case. White Toyota Previas were by no means common and so, once the vehicle in the CCTV had been identified — which, with its very distinctive styling, would have happened very quickly — a search of the DVLA database would have thrown up those locally registered and given a starting point for investigations. But even if the trail from the previous registered keeper to Bellfield was tortuous (he, of course, had not registered it to himself), there was 'CRIMINT', the Met's intelligence database. A search of Previas in the area would quickly have returned details of Bellfield being arrested in such a vehicle just days before the attack on Kate. There was no doubt that the CCTV would have led quickly to Bellfield and, while there might not have been enough evidence to charge him with Kate's offence, at worst, he would have been on the police radar. At best, he would have been charged, remanded and simply unable to kill Amélie.

Everything could have been different if only that tape had been viewed back in May 2004.

That day was one of very mixed emotions; elation at having concrete proof of the link between Bellfield and Kate Sheedy, uneasiness at the criticism the Met would undoubtedly (and rightly) be in for, anger that my colleagues had let Amélie down so spectacularly and sorrow for Jean-François and Dominique Delagrange, who would have to deal with the new tragedy that their daughter's murder ought to have been prevented. It was the last feeling that I dealt with first – I would go to France to tell them, as soon as possible. I travelled with DC Gary Fuller, their Family Liaison Officer and DC Jean-Marc Papworth, the French-speaking murder detective from Hendon. We tried to enjoy the benefits of an unexpected upgrade for the short hop to Paris Charles De Gaulle but even the BA lounge and spacious seats failed to raise our spirits. This was going to be very difficult. I told the others that I had worked out a plan that, if the news were met with anger, we should withdraw for an hour or two, returning only for me to set out how their complaint would be recorded and what would happen in that process. I had already made tentative plans for family liaison to be taken over by officers unconnected with my team if that were necessary. It wasn't our fault at all but I was prepared for an extreme reaction. Expecting it even.

We arrived at the Delagerange's detached house in the idyllic Picardian village of Hanvoile the next morning, exactly on time at 5pm. Jean-François, an architect, had designed the house himself some twenty-five years previously. It stood on a wide plot of well-kept but very natural gardens and inside his skill as a carpenter, though just a hobby, was evident in some beautifully crafted furniture. Both parents had noticeably lost weight since I had first met them, Jean-Francois especially looking gaunt and aged. The strain of their loss was apparent, even before I gave them more terrible news. As ever, they were impeccably polite and hospitable to us; more than ever, I regretted taking Russian, rather than French, as my second modern language at school, then at least I would have a few words. It was so cumbersome conversing through the brilliant Jean-Marc and, in such a delicate situation, nuance and intonation would say so much – but with the inevitable delay through translation, they were lost.

After a few minutes of catching up and explaining the progress on their daughter's case, I started. Slowly and deliberately, I went through the whole story of Kate, our taking it on, why we thought Bellfield was responsible and then the mess of the CCTV viewing. I stressed that my team had done everything properly; even in such a pressurised and delicate situation, I was determined to defend them. I let the facts sink in and there was silence for a minute or two. Jean-François and Dominique looked at each other but said nothing. Dominique could not help but let a tear escape but she wiped it away quickly with the tissue she seemed to have permanently in her hand. During the pause, I remembered the sound advice given to me by David Stobbs, my wonderful first inspector in my probationary days at Tottenham in the early 1980s, when he said, 'Never advise anyone to make a complaint against the police; there are enough made without us encouraging them,' and immediately decided to ignore it. Sorry, Dave – it is a good rule of thumb, which I had often recalled and obeyed, but it wasn't for this situation. What would be the point in leaving them distraught and confused? I needed to resolve it there and then. Whatever they wanted me to do, I had to take it away and get on with it. There was no way I could leave things unsaid and go back to London.

'You do realise what this means, that he might have been caught before?' I said, breaking the silence and then suffering an extended wait for the response as Jean-Marc translated. Jean-François Delagrange replied, looking me straight in the eye as he did, despite knowing I would have to wait for the translation. His manner, though, spoke to me. Volumes. His sad eyes and the drawn, bearded face shouted sorrow yet, at the same time, were friendly, sympathetic almost. There was no trace of hostility in the man, which given the nature of what I had just told him – that my police force had messed up so badly it resulted in a man being free to kill his beautiful daughter – shocked me. As I was taking this in, Jean-Marc began to translate even as Jean-François was still speaking: 'Of course we understand what it means. It is a shame, a great shame, but we are where we are, it has happened and we cannot change what has happened, as much as we would like to. Mistakes get made, we are humans. Thank you for telling us, for your honesty. We know the French police would never have been so open with us and we respect you for that. What is important to us is that you carry on and bring this evil man to justice. Now, are you three going to stay here for dinner tonight?'

And that was it. What I expected to be the most difficult conversation of my career by a long way was nothing of the sort. It was my turn to shed a quickly disguised tear, so moved was I by the patient and reasonable dignity of the Delagranges, which they displayed consistently from start to finish. I muttered that, equally, the British public were unlikely to be so understanding and that I was so, so sorry we had failed Amélie. And, yes, we would love to stay for dinner.

What a dinner! It was simply perfect: a typical home-cooked French five-course feast, with three different wines and finished off with some remarkably lethal locally brewed liqueurs, from the special trunk Jean-François had made and that only got opened 'for ze special guests'. Poor Gary Fuller got thrown the keys to the hire car; rank sometimes does have its privileges. As we sat sipping the cloudy fire-water, Dominique suddenly put her glass down, took a deep breath and exclaimed in a strong French accent, 'You know, Col-een, I learn a leetle English in ze school.'

I stopped and looked at her. This quiet yet cheerful woman who had been through so much gave a beaming smile and put on her best posh, received-pronunciation English, albeit still unmistakably spoken by a French woman: 'I can speak English just like ze Queen.'

Jean-François resignedly responded, in French and through the interpreter, 'My God, she must be really pissed to do that.'

The whole table erupted in laughter; as it subsided, I reflected on how the day had unfolded in a way I simply couldn't have begun to suspect it might. We left for our hotel still wondering at the spectacular generosity and steadfastness of Amélie's remarkable parents. Yes, it was still a very memorable day but in a completely different way to that I had expected. Not that I needed any greater motivation but I was now completely determined that I would do absolutely everything I possibly could for this thoroughly decent and kind family.

CHAPTER SIXTEEN

NEW YEAR, NEW OFFICE, NEW DIRECTION

As my old boss, Eddie O'Connell, used to say, good detectives don't need desks, they need coat hooks. And it was true – most of the team spent most of their time out on inquiries. Yet, even so, there had barely been room for my team at Barnes Green before all this began; the space available would have suited a team of twenty but nearly forty of us made it difficult. Once my team grew to around seventy, it was almost impossible. It was the briefings that were so very difficult; those crucial hours when we were all together sharing what we knew. We had started using the old custody office but this was now occupied by the various viewing machines and hundreds of tapes and disks being worked on by the CCTV team. And in any case, the room couldn't take nearly eighty people at once. This was brutally brought home when DC Mick Laverick sidled up to me at the end of a briefing during which he and others had huddled in the yard near the door straining to hear, saying that the 747s overhead on the flight path to Heathrow had been so frequent that he really hadn't caught much of what had been said. While we had tried using a local pub, a pensioners' drop-in centre and a church hall, all of which were gladly loaned to us free of charge by the ever-supportive local organisations, I had been lobbying for a new home virtually since the investigation began.

By February 2005, just five months later, we were able to move in. Our new space took up most of the fourth floor at Jubilee House, a tower block wholly occupied by the Metropolitan Police on the south side of the Thames at Putney Bridge. It was open-plan, a complete blank canvas and had two 'arms' around the emergency stairwell at its northern end with wide views over the river. I allocated one of these to myself and the DIs, and the other became our briefing area. The rest of the room had plenty of space for intelligence, DCs and DSs and the HOLMES team. Only our exhibits store was to stay at Barnes. The whole set-up was a much nicer place to work in, the area was better served by public transport and the high street, with its many bars and restaurants, was just a short stroll away. The uplift the move gave to our spirits and to our efficiency was immediately noticeable.

This was just as well as there was an incredibly huge amount of work in store. In order to move the investigation forward, we needed either to find some forensic evidence – our best hope of which was probably to locate the Courier van – or we were facing a lengthy and slow slog to accumulate hundreds, if not thousands, of pieces of circumstantial evidence to build our case. While I never gave up hope of working out what had happened to the van, my instinct told me that it had gone and that we were in for a very long haul. It was time for a team meeting where I outlined this – that the investigation had entered a new phase. We had come so far, done so well, to identify and arrest our suspect from a starting point of having nothing to go on. We were united in our belief that we had the right man. Now we had to prove it. And this was complicated by having to do so working on three fronts – Amélie, Marsha and Kate – and within the context of keeping our existing investigations into other murders going, as well as 'losing' every ninth week as we had been reinserted into the on-call rota, having to be available to offer the first investigative response to murder and potential murder throughout a third of London. As pleasant as our new surroundings were, Team 7 was, at that time, no place for passengers or shirkers and I made this very clear to the team, reminding them that they were free to move elsewhere if they felt it was all going to be too difficult.

'Why would anyone want to move from the best investigation any of us will ever be a part of?' was the gladdening and honest response I got from one officer as the meeting broke up – and, of course, she was correct: nobody was leaving unless they had to.

Others in the murder command were not privy to what we were doing and, inevitably, there was a degree of resentment at the huge resources we were being given, the overtime my officers were earning and especially the fact that other teams had been required to cover our on-call weeks for five months. My fellow SIOs had coined a new nickname for me – I became Colin 'One-job' Sutton. Which was, in a sense, true but what a 'one-job' it was! Andy Murphy, helpful and supportive to the last, came up with a potential solution; at an SIOs' meeting in the rather grand surroundings of the Honourable Artillery Company on the edge of the City of London, I was given, at his suggestion, a half-an-hour slot to present an update to my peers on what we were trying to achieve. My PowerPoint show took them through the whole story, emphasising at every opportunity the vast scale of what we had already done and what we had left to do. I concluded with an unashamed appropriation of their sarcastic tag for me – I signed the last slide 'Colin Juan-Job Sutton' and advised them not to deride my (entirely fictitious) Spanish heritage. It is fair to say I made quite an impression. To a man and woman, they spoke to me afterwards expressing their admiration and, in a few cases, outright jealousy at what my one job was. The serial killer, the Holy Grail of the SIO, and there I was, not only living and breathing it but actually getting somewhere. It was almost a coming-of-age for me within the group, realisation and acceptance that not only was this a 'proper job' but also that I really was a proper SIO.

The evidence-gathering operation was expanding. Slowly but surely, we were getting snippets of information and then finding ways to prove them and thereby secure new tiny but crucial parts of the jigsaw. The one area where no progress was made was with the scientists; despite throwing everything they had at the items we had recovered from Bellfield's house, and a few moments of false hope, no hair, no speck of blood, no fibre and no mark linking Bellfield to any of the victims was to be found. As much as I would have welcomed some sort of breakthrough, I had virtually resigned myself to there being none. Part of me – a masochistic part possibly – was quite pleased with this: although forensic evidence would have made it much easier, what an achievement it would be to do it with none. Doesn't everybody rely on DNA these days? How fantastic would it be to get there without it? The only downside to that would be the somewhat bizarre fact that, with the preponderance of CSI-type programmes flooding the television channels, members of the public – and so our potential jurors – had come to expect police always to be able to find some DNA or trace evidence. If we had none, it would be an issue on which we must be robustly clear to them that, in the real world, it was entirely possible to commit horrific crimes and leave no trace. I resolved to make sure that I stressed this to our lawyers when the time came.

Our search for evidence from witnesses was progressing much better, though. While we had always enjoyed great support from a frightened community only too pleased to try to help, we now found, post-arrest, that those who knew Bellfield were coming forward to speak to us. While his family remained aloof and staunchly supported him, friends and acquaintances were far less entrenched. Their view was, in many cases, that they always knew he was a bad and evil man – indeed, they had been surprised that it had taken the law so long to catch up with him. Many were, though, quite understandably, reluctant to commit their knowledge to a statement lest he were released and had the opportunity to exact inevitable and bloody retribution. This presented a problem for us: we were tantalisingly close to having a wealth of proof of his nature, propensity to violence and strange behaviour coinciding exactly with the aftermath of his attacks but, unless we could convince those speaking to us that they would thereafter be safe, we would be unable to convert intelligence into hard evidence.

I wrestled with this, imagining some creative solutions.

I thought, if we could convince the friends that he really was guilty and was likely to remain incarcerated, they would be happier to commit to a statement. If we were to 'leak' to the witnesses just how much we knew, that might convince them. The risk was, though, that such underhand tactics would prove not only embarrassing but fatal to any court proceedings were they to be discovered. I had never been prepared to compromise propriety to advance an investigation and so certainly wasn't going to start during the biggest case of my life. I then floated the idea of formally, openly briefing them as to the state of the evidence, as we would often do for families of victims. All the advice I received was that this would infringe Bellfield's right to privacy and so this, too, had to be discounted. However, sitting watching BBC's *Crimewatch UK* one evening it came to me. If we were to get a slot on the show, it would enable us to show our hand to a degree for everyone to see – and while it might or might not bring new witnesses and information, that would not really matter, but it would definitely help to show the dithering witnesses just how certain we were that Bellfield was the man. Getting on to *Crimewatch* was sometimes tricky – they, just like the police, had performance targets and so preferred to take on crimes where there was a large degree of public support and interest – it made for more calls and more chance of being able to show the programme's effectiveness. This meant that murders where the victim's lifestyle had contributed in some way to the crime – for example, gangland killings or the murder of a drug dealer – were almost never chosen. I didn't face that problem. I was sure that the Bellfield investigation was just the sort of shocking and high-profile crime they would want to help with.

But we had publicly made an arrest for Amélie's murder so that was a non-starter. The programme had, though, covered Kate's attack soon after it had happened so that was a possibility. Would they help us by making a further appeal? Of course, previously, there was a vague appeal for a white or silver people-carrier but now we knew the exact make and model. And everybody who knew Bellfield knew he had owned and driven the white Toyota Previa. The idea was crystallising in my mind. If I went on to *Crimewatch* appealing for help in identifying the Previa, Bellfield's friends and acquaintances would see it and recognise it as his car. They would know then of his wider involvement and feel much more secure that we were going to get him convicted. There was just one slight issue that we would have to gloss over: I would be appealing for information about a car that we had already seized and examined minutely, knowing virtually everything about its history and ownership. So long as *Crimewatch* never knew that, I was sure they would have us on their show.

Vish Patel, the Homicide West Media Officer, quickly obliged and set me up a meeting with the BBC. I went over to Television Centre at White City and over a cup of coffee chatted with the editor of *Crimewatch UK*, Doug Carnegie. I had never met Doug before but immediately warmed to his no-nonsense attitude, every observation delivered laconically in a soft Scottish accent. He was not only keen to help, agreeing almost before I had asked to give me a slot, but also genuinely interested, concerned even, with the whole Bellfield investigation. As we chatted for a bit, two things struck me: that I was confident he would do absolutely everything he could to help; and also that I liked him. He was trying to be so helpful and I therefore could not, in good conscience, carry on the deception as to the status of the Previa. So I took a chance, hoping that his desire to assist was genuine and that he would understand. I took a deep breath and told him the truth. We knew all about the Previa. I just wanted to use his programme as a means to publicise just how much we had on Bellfield, speaking implicitly but directly only to those who knew him. Doug smiled, immediately agreeing and adding that he understood exactly what I wanted to achieve and that he felt it was his duty as well as honour to help. One week later, I was there on *Crimewatch*, the CCTV stills of the Previa before and after Kate's attack beamed in to millions of households across the UK but, most importantly, showing twenty or so people in west London that our arresting Bellfield was no mere fishing expedition. They saw his car was the one that had so nearly killed Kate and realised that their worst fears about this man they thought they knew were actually true.

CHAPTER SEVENTEEN

PIECING IT TOGETHER

The effect of the Crimewatch broadcast was almost immediate and, as intended, it worked to help us more on the Amélie case than the one about which I had appealed. The next morning, I sent out every officer available to revisit anyone who had been reluctant to nail their colours to the mast and who we thought could take us further. Within hours, the statements, all properly signed up and evidential, started to come in. As winter turned to spring and the trees outside my office window showed signs of growth, so, too, the case against Bellfield began to sprout.

Richard Hughes, more a friend of Emma than Bellfield, told us of being given a bloodstained top to burn by Bellfield in 2002, of how Bellfield had painted the rear windows of the Courier van white in May 2004 and at the same time rivetted alloy plates to the bottom of the rear doors to cover rust, both of which helped explain exactly the appearance of the van in the CCTV pictures we had. He also told us that he knew Bellfield had used the van to go to Kent to visit a friend, Michelle Wickham, for a week or so immediately after Amélie's murder, and that Bellfield was trying to sell it just afterwards, in early September 2004. Most crucially, also, Hughes described seeing Bellfield at Little Benty in August 2004. He was 'crying his eyes out' over a period of three or four hours, at one point saying to Hughes, 'I think I need some help.'

Hughes took him to Hillingdon Hospital, where he was detained overnight in their mental-health unit. This happened on 27 August 2004, about a week after Amélie was murdered, and was the first example we found of the regular pattern of Bellfield sinking into the depths of depression soon after he had committed an atrocity.

Michelle Wickham then told us that Bellfield, Emma Mills and the children arrived at her house in Kent in a green Vauxhall in late August 2004. They stayed for two weeks, having originally planned to stay just for the weekend. About a week into their stay, a white van appeared on her drive, rather than the Vauxhall. She believed it was a Ford, smaller than a Transit. She also recalled that the front light on the passenger side of this van was not working, reinforcing again what could be seen on the CCTV on the night Amélie was killed. The green Vauxhall, Hughes told us, was his and he had asked Bellfield to return it when it became obvious the stay in Kent was being extended. The obvious inference from this was that Bellfield had driven back to West Drayton, returned Hughes's Vauxhall and returned to Kent in the Courier van, clearly putting the van in his hands in the first week of September 2004.

Belfield's friend and clamping associate Joe Ryan said that, in July or August 2004, he went fishing with Bellfield in the Thames, close to Walton Bridge. They used Bellfield's 'clapped-out' Fiesta Courier van. Ryan remembered that, on that evening, it had no nearside headlight and they tried to use a bulb from his own Ford Escort. This didn't work so they stopped at the Esso Garage near to Walton Bridge and bought a new bulb. He found Bellfield had broken the light fitting in his ham-fisted earlier attempts to effect a repair, and so had to use tape to secure the bulb; Ryan described this as only a 'temporary measure', which, of course, allowed for the possibility of future malfunction. I was also reminded that a Ford Escort left-headlamp unit, minus bulb, had been found in the front garden of the house at Little Benty when Bellfield was arrested on 22 November 2004. Ryan also told us that, on 28 July 2004, he helped Bellfield by fitting a new front, nearside wheel, which was black and lacking a silver trim, to the Courier van, this being necessary because Bellfield had had a minor collision with a kerb, damaging the front, nearside wheel and tyre of the van. All this information from Ryan helped enormously in proving the van on the CCTV was, indeed, Bellfield's, the headlight and wheel being entirely consistent with all the CCTV recordings from the night of the Amelie's murder, explaining some of the distinctive features which were clearly visible in the pictures.

This was all pointing pretty conclusively to confirmation that the van in the recordings was P610 XCN, Bellfield's Ford Courier. An independent witness also emerged to help in this regard – Simon Redston came forward to describe two incidents involving a white van. He regularly cycled home from work along Hampton Road and said that, on 17 August at about 8.45pm, he was passed very closely by a van being driven in excess of the speed limit in Fourth Cross Road, Twickenham. More important, though, was what he told us about 19 August 2004. He said that, sometime just after 10pm, he saw the same van driving along Hampton Road towards Fulwell bus garage. He described it as being driven at 'crazy speed'. Redston remembered the van as a small, box-style white van, distinctive due to having two metal plates on the bottom of the rear doors. He memorised the registration number and later wrote it in his diary as P240 PXN. A check of the Police National Computer showed that the registration number P240 PXN had never been issued. I checked with the CCTV team and we found Redston had been captured in the same CCTV footage that showed what we believed to be Bellfield leaving the scene. It was clear Redston's account was accurate and obvious that he had merely recorded the registration number of the van inaccurately. But was P240 PXN really so far from P610 XCN? I was absolutely happy that what he had seen was Bellfield fleeing, leaving Amélie for dead on the Green – and that Redston was going to be vital to our case.

While I knew that I would have to get an expert, scientific view to support our assertion that the van we saw on sixteen different occasions around Twickenham Green during the hour leading up to Amélie being attacked was the same one each time, what these witness statements added was a powerful case that the van was, indeed, Bellfield's. That was definitely progress but what was needed next was to show that the van had been on the same road at the same time as Amélie, thus giving the driver the opportunity to spot her, and then to prove that it was, indeed, Bellfield driving it. This last fact was always going to be the most difficult but, before we looked at how to do that, I asked Gary Hancock, my intelligence analyst, to see what he could make of all the timings. Within a day, he was sitting in front of my desk with some papers in his hand as I arrived for work. Gary was a quiet, unassuming man who had worked on the team for many years. His work was always first class but he was quite shy about it. I had tried to get him to take a bigger part in our discussions and briefings – he always had something useful to add but I think he was a bit cowed by the big personalities around him, which was a great shame. On this occasion, though, he was buzzing, so keen to show me what he had that he was there waiting and started to speak even before I had hung up my coat.

'Have a look at this, Guvnor. I reckon he spoke to her.'

What Gary had done was to painstakingly look at the timestamp on every one of the sixteen separate pieces of CCTV we had of the van during its hunting patrol around Twickenham Green, and then to do the same with the nine clips that showed Amélie walking up towards the Green. By reference to the times shown on the recordings from buses – which were known to be accurate because the hardware took time updates and then adjusted itself from the so-called Rugby Time Signal – he had managed to ascertain exact timings for every clip. From this, he was able to make two important conclusions. First, a static camera in Hampton Road showed the van passing towards Twickenham Green and then Amélie walking past it sixty-two seconds later. Since further back down the road minutes before, Amélie had been in front of the van, it was obvious that it had passed her and, therefore, the driver must have had the opportunity to see her. Not content with that vital discovery, Gary had carried out some time, distance and pace calculations and proved that, while Amélie had walked from the bus garage at a strikingly constant (if slow) pace while she was in front of the van, her speed between the last two sightings – so before the van was seen to have overtaken her – had decreased markedly. The only rational explanation for the minutes she had taken to get between the two points was that she was, for some time, stationary. As she, of course, would have been if the driver of the van had stopped to speak to her. This made so much sense to me. Bellfield had been cruising looking for a girl for nearly an hour. He then saw Amélie, so he stopped and propositioned her. She told him to get lost and walked off. He was so incensed by the rebuff that he drove on past her, waited for her to arrive up at the Green and then assaulted her as she walked across in the darkness. Her only crime? To dare to have insulted the great Levi Bellfield by turning down his advances. A hypothesis which, I knew almost instantly, would be almost impossible to prove in its entirety without his confession, but which fitted so neatly in to all we were beginning to understand about how this wicked man operated. Putting him in the van was the next hurdle we needed to clear.

CHAPTER EIGHTEEN

PROVING BELLFIELD DROVE THE VAN

I knew we could prove Bellfield's van was the killer's vehicle. Analysis of the CCTV from buses and static cameras in the area of Twickenham Green showed us that the white Ford Courier van was in the area from 9.32pm to 10.09pm on 19 August. It had spent around forty-five minutes just cruising around an area of less than a square mile, during which we were able to pinpoint it no fewer than sixteen times. It was then parked by the Green, about fifty yards from where Amélie was killed, for about three minutes at exactly the time she was attacked, before driving swiftly away to the south, along Hampton Road. What was needed was to name the driver, so I pondered how to prove it was Bellfield behind the wheel. We had no forensics, no van, no live witnesses and the CCTV was nowhere near clear enough to see any detail of the driver. So I strolled past the room dividing screen and in to the intelligence unit to chat things through with DS Clive Grace, recently promoted to be my Intelligence Manager. What about his mobile phone: could that give us what we needed? For that to work, I would need two things: first, to prove that one of Bellfield's phones was active in the Twickenham Green area at the relevant time; and second, that it was really him who had possession of it. Hadn't Jo Collings told us that, Bellfield being very aware of what could be done with mobile-phone records, always switched his off if he knew he would be out committing crime? I was confident Clive would know, almost certainly without checking, if we had any data from the service providers which would help.

Clive did not disappoint me – he genuinely never did. He told me that telephone data showed that the landline at Little Benty had called Bellfield's main mobile number at 9.37pm on 19 August 2004. This was potentially a great help to us as, when we brought up the huge unwieldy spreadsheet of cell-site data on his oversized screen, it told us that, when his phone was called, it was transmitting to a mast in Fourth Cross Road, Twickenham, which had a coverage area including Twickenham Green and the surrounding roads. This was exactly when and where the CCTV analysis had shown the van to be, cruising on its hunt for a victim. We needed, though, to shut down any possibility of Bellfield being able to explain this away. It was still open to him to say that he had lost his phone, or lent the van to somebody else, or even both. To make this the clinching piece of evidence it had the potential to be, we needed to develop it; to put the phone in his hands, in the van. The interesting thing was that the call had hit the mobile and then been sent immediately to voicemail. It was easy to imagine that Bellfield – if he were in the habit of switching his mobile off when he was thinking of committing crimes – had made a mistake. The phone would have rung, perhaps just once, and I could just imagine him panicking and hurriedly turning it off. But that was too late; the call had been placed through the mast and left its digital trail for us to pick up months later. How could we prove that, when that call was made, the phone was with him in the white Courier van? That could be the most valuable piece of evidence we could find, since the proximity of the van to Amélie's murder and its odd behaviour in the hour leading up to it were striking. Putting Bellfield in the van at that time might be the final piece of convincing evidence.

The first step was to return to Emma – it was logical that she was probably the person who made the 9.37pm call; if she could once again remember the circumstances around it, there might be an opportunity for us. Gary Fuller and Debbie Ford went again to see her and, once more, she came up trumps. Her ability to recall detail and relate it to events and dates was to help us enormously. She told us that she remembered 19 August – she had seen the reports of Amélie's death on the TV news the next day and, knowing Bellfield's attachment to the area around Twickenham Green (where she had rented a flat with him for a short while early in their relationship), she had paid special attention.

Emma recalled that the night before she saw those news reports was the first time she had left the house since the birth of their third child some three weeks previously. She had agreed with Bellfield that, in the evening when he returned from his day of wheel-clamping, he would take her to Hayes to do her shopping at the large Tesco store there. By 7.30pm, he was still not home so, needing nappies for the baby and other essentials, she had no choice but to call for a mini-cab to take her there. At about 8pm, she had received a call from Bellfield, asking her why she was no longer at home. She explained where she was and he said he would come to Hayes and meet her in the supermarket – which he did. Bellfield then took the two older children across to the Toys Я Us store while she continued with her shopping. After a short while, he had phoned her again, excitedly telling her about some toys he had bought and to say he would wait for her outside. So she would find him easily, he stressed that he was in the white Courier van.

Emma finished her shopping, paid for the groceries and left the store. In the car park, she located Bellfield and the whole family returned to Little Benty in the Courier van. Bellfield had backed it up the drive and opened the rear doors so that Emma could unload the bags into the house. While she was struggling unaided with the many bags, Bellfield sat in the driver's seat and was making a call on his mobile. Once she had finished, she closed the doors and Bellfield drove off, not having entered the house or even leaving the van. She believed this was around 9.10pm. She had then, about half an hour later, gone to make herself a drink and realised that she had forgotten to buy milk. She had, therefore, called Bellfield from the landline to ask him to bring some in but, after ringing, the call had gone to voicemail – this was clearly the call we had the log for at 9.37pm.

Debbie Ford called a break in the interview at this point and called back to the office. She spoke to Clive Grace, who looked at the other calls on the record and was able to confirm to her two calls by Bellfield on his main mobile on 19 August –

one at 8.22pm hitting a mast at Hayes and another at 9.08pm logged on to the mast nearest to Little Benty. So these coincided exactly with Emma's story, obviously being his call to her from Toys Я Us and then his call on the drive while she was unloading the shopping. Clive came and told me this and naturally I was excited – but still I wanted more. I wanted to make sure this potentially case-clinching piece of evidence was watertight. I asked for Ford and Fuller to carry on the interview to see if Emma had a bank record of her payment at Tesco, as this would be the final link to prove her story exactly correct and also give us yet more irrefutable proof of the date and time. Emma told them she had used cash but, using the sort of initiative my officers had in abundance, they did not give up. Patiently and in detail, they asked Emma what she had bought. What sort of nappies, what brand of coffee, cereal, washing-up liquid – all her usual weekly purchases. Emma was able to go through virtually her entire shopping list; she also recalled that she had spent slightly over £70 in total.

While I was back in the incident room wondering why they were taking so long, Ford and Fuller were in a dusty loft at the Tesco superstore at Hayes. They had asked the manager if any records were kept and he had told them that the till rolls were all retained for a couple of years, adding that he wasn't really sure why but they were. He jokingly suggested that it was probably because his deputy was suffering from mild OCD. This was a stroke of great good fortune for us because, in the loft, they not only found the pile of cardboard boxes containing the till rolls but also that each box had been carefully and accurately labelled with the date range of the rolls it contained, making their search immeasurably easier and quicker than it might otherwise have been. Despite this, it still took them an hour or so to go through the records for the twenty-odd tills at the store until, quite incredibly, they found it. Pampers, Nescafé, Fairy Liquid – all the things Emma had recalled, no milk – and a total of £71.08. Printed at 8.46pm on 19 August 2004, paid with cash. A quick return was made to Little Benty, where Emma gave a further statement, identifying the receipt as hers, and we had some independent, documentary confirmation that what Emma had told us was true. She gave us Bellfield in the Courier with the phone, the call data and the CCTV gave us the phone and the van at Twickenham Green. Suddenly, our case was looking firm.

CHAPTER NINETEEN

THE STRANGE TALE OF SPANISH PETE

As the investigation into Bellfield widened – as we searched for every snippet that would indicate his lawless and violent nature – we uncovered tale after unbelievable tale. None of those was any stranger than the case of Peter Rodrigues, a most complex and incredible set of circumstances in which Bellfield was involved in the summer of 2004. Despite my intimate knowledge of the whole case and those involved, it was the one aspect that kept me puzzled for weeks and that I had to read, analyse and reread many times before I could finally work out exactly what had taken place. While it had little, if any, bearing on the murders and attacks we were looking at, it served to show the ruthless nature of our suspect and gave a frightening glimpse into the murky world in which he dwelled. Peter Rodrigues, known to his friends as 'Spanish Pete', was in many ways typical of the type of acquaintance Bellfield exploited and abused. Cheerful in nature, slightly built and lacking in confidence, he was perfect for Bellfield to employ, deride and bully. However, their relationship was to end not just in exploitation, sarcasm and hurt feelings; at Bellfield's hand, Rodrigues was to suffer conviction for a serious offence and injuries so severe that his life hung in the balance for several weeks.

The complicated tale began in May 2004. Bellfield had acquired 250 ecstasy tablets, which he hoped to sell on for a good profit. His natural instinct to protect himself from the law meant that he was unwilling to have them lying around at home any longer than absolutely necessary. While wheel-clamping with Peter Rodrigues one day, Bellfield learned that Pete's aged and infirm mother had been admitted to hospital for what was likely to be a lengthy period. Bellfield, therefore, knew her flat in Battersea would be left empty and realised it would be a perfect place for storing his stash of drugs. Reluctantly, not wanting to anger his employer and fearful for both his personal safety and his job, Rodrigues agreed. Bellfield gave him the bag of drugs, instructing him to keep them cool so as to preserve them. Rodrigues followed the instructions to the letter and the bag of tablets was duly placed in the salad box at the bottom of his mother's fridge.

A week or so later and Rodrigues was getting increasingly nervous about this arrangement. He was hoping that his mother would shortly be released from hospital and wanted the drugs gone. He was, though, as always, frightened of asking Bellfield to remove them and, thus, decided to keep quiet and try to choose an opportune moment to broach the subject. He had discussed this on the phone with Bellfield's ex-partner, Jo Collings, with whom Rodrigues maintained a friendly relationship, and she had advised that he proceed carefully lest he angered the unpredictable Bellfield.

On a Saturday evening in early June 2004, while Rodrigues was mulling his dilemma over, Bellfield was at the flat in Crosby Close, on the Oriel Estate in Feltham, which he illegally sub-rented as his 'love nest', the place where he spent time with his sixteen-year-old lover whom I shall call Amy. With them that morning was Amy's younger sister, Emily, aged just fourteen. Emily received a phone call from her schoolfriend, Megan, also aged fourteen. Megan had been having a difficult time, being on bail to Uxbridge police after her arrest for supplying an ecstasy tablet to a friend at school. This crime was not related to Bellfield's venture into the drugs market but had brought Megan into conflict with her mother. Megan told Emily that, after a serious argument, her mother had thrown her out of their home. She had gone to her father, but he had not allowed her to stay at his flat as he was going out. He had, instead, given her five pounds and told her to 'sort herself out.' She was now desperate for help and asked Emily if she had any idea as to what she could do and where she could go.

Emily turned to Bellfield and asked if Megan could come to the flat. He quite predictably saw this as a wonderful opportunity to have a young girl deliver herself to him for sexual abuse, removing the need even for him to go out and find one. As usual, his mind worked quickly and he formed a plan. He rang Rodrigues and asked him to go and collect Megan and take her to his mother's flat. Once there, Rodrigues was to give her a couple of the ecstasy tablets from the fridge and await Bellfield's arrival.

Rodrigues, compliant through fear as usual, obeyed. Megan went to the flat and later remembered taking the tablets – but not much else afterwards. She awoke on the Sunday morning, still at Mrs Rodrigues's flat, finding herself dressed in clothes that she didn't recognise. She realised that she had soreness, which told her she must have been raped the previous evening. Uncomfortable but not understanding really what had gone on, Megan again phoned Emily, who asked Bellfield to go and collect her – which he did, bringing her back to Crosby Close, where she joined Amy and Emily with Bellfield. She told the other girls that she must have been drunk or drugged or both and that she simply did not remember what had happened to her but that she must have slept with somebody there.

Rodrigues was now even more uncomfortable. Not only was his mother's flat being used to store drugs but now Bellfield was also using it as a safe house for the sexual abuse of children. He knew that Bellfield and two or three of his friends had been there with Megan the previous evening and, knowing their propensity for drug-assisted gang rape, he guessed what had gone on. He again called Jo Collings and the upshot of their discussions was that he resolved to go and confront Bellfield, to make him remove the drugs. This was something he really did not want to do – he knew the likelihood was that it would enrage Bellfield – but he felt he had no choice. He spent a good two or three hours plucking up the courage to make the journey across to Crosby Close so it was Sunday afternoon before he arrived there.

The girls went into a different room and let Bellfield and Rodrigues have their discussion alone. They did, however, hear raised and angry voices coming from the living room – mostly,

Bellfield shouting and swearing at Rodrigues. They heard a mobile phone ring, not knowing that it was Jo Collings calling Rodrigues to check that he was safe and that the confrontation with Bellfield had passed off peacefully. As they both knew that Bellfield must not get to know of their friendship, they had a pre-arranged code, so Rodrigues told Jo that he couldn't hear her properly because the line was bad, and she knew this meant that Bellfield was within earshot so she ended the call. The last thing the girls heard was the front door of the flat slamming twice, more shouting and heavy footsteps running down the external stairs.

Shortly afterwards, the flat door opened and shut again. Bellfield burst into the room where the girls were, bellowing that he needed to use one of their phones to call an ambulance because 'the Pakis have done Pete'. The clear implication from this was that his friends, the Gharu brothers (who he always referred as 'the Pakis'), had assaulted Rodrigues. This was an assertion he was later to repeat in a call to Emma Mills, in a stage whisper obviously intended to be heard by the police officers who had, by that time, attended Crosby Close. Rodrigues had staggered out into the parking area by the block of flats and then collapsed, unconscious. He was bleeding profusely from a large blunt-instrument wound to his head. He was taken to hospital, where he was treated for a fractured skull and brain damage, spending six weeks in a coma on a life-support machine. He was close to death several times and that he survived at all is a testimony to the skill and patience of those treating him.

Of course, the ambulance crew who attended had informed the police that they were dealing with what was obviously a very serious – indeed, murderous – assault. A cordon was set up and Bellfield was there, chatting to the officers and trying to give the impression of an innocent man whose friend had just been attacked. His story was that Rodrigues had been in the flat, had left and that he then saw him on the floor in the car park from his window. And that he thought he had seen two Asian men running away. Rodrigues himself being in no position to give the true account, the police had, initially, to take Bellfield's story as their starting point. The local CID from Hounslow was called and the investigation taken over by Detective Sergeant Craig MacKinlay. Despite Bellfield's assertions of innocence, it was decided that his story did not ring quite true. The girls had all given a similar, vague account, which itself appeared as if it had been scripted – as it almost certainly had, by Bellfield. He was arrested on suspicion of assault and his vehicle – the white Ford Courier van for which we were to be searching so frantically a few months later – was seized for forensic examination. Bellfield was interviewed, stuck to his story implicating the two mysterious Asians and was, therefore, released without charge. He had, though, during his time in custody, the opportunity to use his charm and persuasion on the investigating officers. As he had done for most of his adult life, he gave a good impression of a man who was a friend to the police, who knew lots of people and lots of things, and who could be a very useful contact for the future. It seems he succeeded, once more, in manipulating a difficult situation to his own advantage. Even he though probably didn't realise how useful that was to become in the coming days.

On the day after the assault on Rodrigues, while Bellfield was being interviewed by police at Hounslow, the other strand

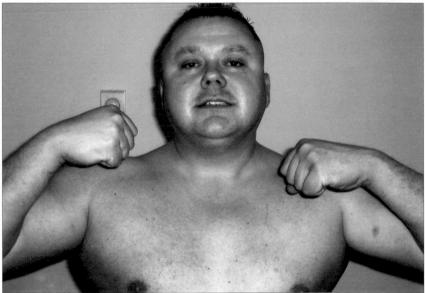

Above: The face of evil: triple murderer Levi Bellfield.   © *Rex Features*

Below: Showing off the intimidating bulk which made his distressingly brutal attacks possible.   © *Rex Features*

Bellfield, in a display of utterly childish behaviour, turns his chair one hundred and eighty degrees, and refuses to engage with his police interviewers. His behaviour could not be held in more sharp contrast than by that of his attempted murder victim, Kate Sheedy, who bravely gave evidence in court after he ran her over in his van.

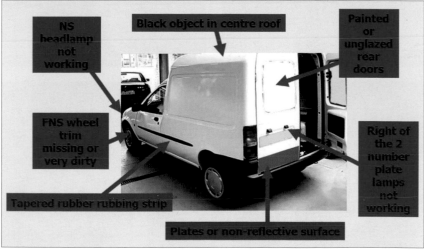

Labels on diagram:

- NS headlamp not working
- Black object in centre roof
- Painted or unglazed rear doors
- FNS wheel trim missing or very dirty
- Right of the 2 number plate lamps not working
- Tapered rubber rubbing strip
- Plates or non-reflective surface

Above: Above: Detective Chief Superintendent Andy Murphy briefs the press at the scene of the Amelie Delagrange's murder. Bringing down Bellfield was a team effort through and through. When the race to stop a killer is on, having supportive bosses like Andy makes all the difference.   © Rex Features

Below: The exact diagram I supplied to my team identifying the vehicle we were looking for in connection to the murder. It's not glamorous – you'd certainly never see this in a TV crime drama – but it's the attention to detail which builds or breaks a case.

Above: The deeply moving sight of Milly Dowler's mother and father laying a flower on the site where their daughter was discovered, in Yateley Heath Woods.

© *Rex Features*

Below: Amelie Delagrange, Milly Dowler and Marsha McDonnell (*l-r*). As a murder detective, their faces are all the motivation you need to keep the pressure on and hunt down monsters like Bellfield to make them face justice. © *Rex Features*

It is easy to forget that Bellfield's crimes extended beyond murder scenes and sensational headlines. Bellfield's partner, Emma, pictured here, suffered rape, assault and degradation at his hands. Her courage in giving evidence against him, in the face of intimidation, was vital.

1A

2008030004508

**JUDICIARY OF
ENGLAND AND WALES**

THE HON MRS JUSTICE RAFFERTY DBE

13th March 2008

Sir Ian Blair
Commissioner of Police for the Metropolis
New Scotland Yard
10 Broadway
LONDON SW1H 0BJ

Dear Commissioner,

**Re: R v Bellfield, Central Criminal Court,
2nd October 2007 – 27th February 2008**

I tried Bellfield for five events, each alleging violence to a lone female in hours of darkness, in West London, at or near 'bus stops. Save for two, the evidence was circumstantial, and the case for the Crown required close attention to detail across a number of topics. The length of the trial indicates its complexity, and the depth and breadth of challenge.

The Senior Investigating Officer was DCI Colin Sutton, who gave evidence, during which he was criticised on several fronts. One answer in cross-examination encapsulates his calm, firm, dignified demeanour. He was castigated for ordering, post-hazardous scientific tests, the destruction of a relevant vehicle without consulting Bellfield or his solicitors. He told leading counsel "it is absurd to suggest I should canvass the views of a suspect or those who represent him. In any event, Mr Boyce, we are not here to discuss the philosophy of investigation." I reminded the jury of it in the summing-up.

I addressed him, once I had sentence Bellfield, as he stood in the witness-box to receive what he must have known was a commendation. He fought his emotions, lost the battle and wept, and I am certain the driving emotion was relief that he had given three families at least something out of a long chronicle of uncertainty and misery.

He emerged as a leader of men. It was plain that from his arrival the team made marvellous effort, undiminished by the passage of time, setback, and complication. His was the firm, determined, motivating hand on the tiller, and I should not be surprised to find that he led his officers to heroic instances of redoubled labour.

A commendation from Justice Rafferty, the judge in Bellfield's trial. It is a letter that I am, and always will be, truly proud of.

He was quick to agree that grand pronouncements do not lead to convictions. Dogged, well-directed, painstaking, unglamorous police work does, and, in this case, did.

I list below those whom he feels played a noteworthy part in the exercise he headed, and I am confident he is correct. If nothing else, DCI Sutton merits these comments finding an audience in you.

> DI Joanna Brunt
> DS Malcolm Hudson
> DC Neil Jones
> DS Paul McGough
> DC Clive Grace
> DC Paul Carruth
> DC Jayne Farnworth.

Yours sincerely,

Anne Rafferty.

Bringing down Bellfield was a long road – from the day he appeared at Bow Street Magistrates to be charged with the murder of Amelie Delagrange (*above*) to the day, at the Old Bailey, when he was finally put behind bars forever (*below*). Can you tell I am pleased?

of this story was developing in another police station at nearby Uxbridge. Megan returned there to answer her bail for the supplying-ecstasy offence and, while talking to the officers before receiving her caution, she almost casually mentioned that she had been raped on the previous Saturday night. The officers took this very seriously as, indeed, they would do when a fourteen-year-old girl makes such a shocking allegation. They asked her to divulge the detail and arranged for her to be medically examined – this more in hope than expectation, given the passage of time since the incident. She could give a rough location of the flat and so the officers liaised with their counterparts at Battersea, that being the police area in which the offence had taken place. She also told them about the assault on Rodrigues and so the Battersea officers spoke to those at Hounslow investigating that crime, with the intention of establishing the exact address of the flat. Since it was not possible to ask Rodrigues himself where his mother lived, MacKinlay asked Bellfield, who had by now been released, where the flat was. Bellfield told him that he did not know but would find out for him the next day. Bellfield, of course, was now deep into self-protection mode. He had to tell the police where the flat was but knew there was a mass of incriminating evidence there – not only the bag of ecstasy tablets but also trace evidence that might show Megan was there, which would support her allegations. He needed to get access to the flat and clean it up before the police got in. He needed the key.

Turning up at the intensive-care unit at Ealing Hospital, Bellfield knew he was unlikely to be granted a visit to Rodrigues as an interested friend so he presented himself as Lee Rodrigues, the tearful and concerned brother of the patient, and was allowed a short visit. One can imagine him rifling through the bedside cabinet while left alone with his comatose victim, but he was unable to find the key. He was stuck, breaking in not an option because that would serve only to elevate suspicions, as MacKinlay would know he knew that the police visit was imminent. The best he could hope for was that there would be no DNA or fingerprint evidence found. The drugs were history now; he had to accept they would be discovered. Once again, he thought quickly to extract himself from suspicion. He rang MacKinlay and told him the address, adding that Rodrigues was a dealer in ecstasy tablets and that his supply was kept in the salad drawer of the fridge. MacKinlay responded by telling the rape investigators at Battersea the address but stipulating that he would lead the search as he had information relating to other crimes. So it was that the raid took place with a joint team of Hounslow and Battersea officers. MacKinlay held the briefing and stated that the objectives for the Battersea contingent was evidence relating to rape but that the Hounslow officers would look for everything else. So the drugs were found, but the Battersea officers found nothing relating to sexual crimes – not even Megan's missing clothing – and a thorough scientific search also proved fruitless. The rape investigation looked as if it would be going nowhere.

MacKinlay spoke to Bellfield the next day, thanking him for the information and explaining that, if Rodrigues recovered, he would be facing an investigation for possession with intent to supply. Bellfield asked how the rape was panning out and MacKinlay told him that they had found nothing. Bellfield then, curiously, said that he had the clothes Megan had been wearing that night and that he would drop them in to MacKinlay when he had time. MacKinlay, even more curiously, agreed to this without questioning why and how Bellfield came into possession of them. Bellfield did, indeed, take a few freshly-laundered items of clothing in to Hounslow a few days later, yet nothing ever came of it. And Bellfield, for reasons I cannot explain or discern, was never investigated as a potential suspect for Megan's rape and that investigation was closed.

Rodrigues eventually recovered and was released from hospital some ten weeks later. His memory of the attack was flimsy. He told Hounslow Police that he had argued with Bellfield about the drugs, wanting them removed from his mother's flat. He remembered Bellfield becoming agitated, shouting and swearing, threatening him with violence if he persisted. At that point, he had left the flat and his last vivid memory was of Bellfield following him down the stairs carrying what looked like a mallet. Which, it occurred to me, was probably not an image anybody would want to see. After that, he had no recollection at all. He told the police about the drugs, how Bellfield had leaned on him to store them and how he had been told to give Megan two tablets. Despite this, he accepted that he had himself technically been in possession of them and so was charged and pleaded guilty, receiving a suspended prison sentence. The Crown Prosecution Service, acknowledging that Bellfield might also be guilty of the same offence, took the view that, as he was by this time charged with murder, attempted murder and several offences of rape, it would be better to await the outcome of those trials before deciding to proceed against him. As he was convicted of the murders and received three whole life tariffs, ultimately, the decision was that it would serve no purpose to charge him with the drugs offence and so it was never proceeded with. Similarly, although Rodrigues's recollection was *prima facie* evidence of Bellfield having attempted to murder him, pursuing that too was considered to be an unnecessary use of public funds and so nobody was ever charged with the attack on Rodrigues.

Despite these decisions, I felt there was unfinished business in this episode, which it would have been in the public interest to investigate. In my view, although he had probably acted naively and there was absolutely no question of personal gain, the way in which MacKinlay had dealt with Bellfield was unprofessional. Bellfield was not registered by him as an informant, but he had used him as such. (Indeed, Bellfield had once been a registered informant for another officer but was de-registered, as the controller of informants felt that he was dangerous, and that there was evidence to suggest that he would abuse the system by setting up criminals and then informing on them so as to 'bank' goodwill from the police for his own future criminal enterprises.) I had no doubt that Bellfield's behaviour throughout this episode had been criminal and yet he had never been properly investigated. The concept of him being allowed to drop off a rape victim's clothing without further inquiries being made as to his role in the offence was staggering. The information we had gained from the victim and the other young girls placed him squarely at the centre of events, yet he had been ignored. I took my concerns to the Met's Department of Professional Standards (DPS), with a full written report detailing what my inquiries had uncovered. They took the report and said it would be looked in to, but nothing ensued.

There was little I could do about the inactivity of the DPS.

That department had come into the investigation in another way and that, too, had never been resolved to my satisfaction. Early in the Amélie Delagrange case, when we first identified Bellfield as our prime suspect, we had obtained all available call records for his mobile phones. One of these, his 'main' phone, which he used every day, showed twenty or so calls being made during early 2004 to a landline number used by the Metropolitan Police at their offices in Jubilee House, Putney. Ironically, the very building to which my team moved in February 2005 when the squad had grown too large for its cramped accommodation at Barnes Green. In 2004, the building housed three main teams: the Stevens Inquiry into the death of the Princess of Wales; Operation Trident, which was then dealing solely with offences of murder committed within the black community; and the DPS. Unfortunately, the call records we had obtained showed that Bellfield was calling the switchboard for the building but thereafter we could not tell to which individual extension the call had been routed. I had asked the question of all three teams. Both Trident and the Stevens Inquiry assured me they had never heard of Bellfield and they had not spoken to him. The DPS said they would get back to me but, despite my repeating the question on several occasions over many months, they never did.

Why would Bellfield be calling the DPS, and why were they reluctant to tell me he had been? I know for sure that he was never officially registered as an informant to that department. Were they, with the deepest irony, using him as an unofficial informant, contrary to both internal rules and the Regulation of Investigatory Powers Act? If so, did that affect their decision whether to investigate the misconduct I had alleged against

MacKinlay? Did Bellfield have the ability to embarrass the DPS to the point where the whole tale was a stone they preferred to leave unturned?

CHAPTER TWENTY

PERSUADING SURREY

The silence from Operation Ruby – the Surrey Police investigation into the murder of Milly Dowler – was puzzling me. I had given them, I thought, a good suspect to look at by highlighting Bellfield's character, his known activities and where he lived on the day Milly was abducted. Yet it had been six months and I had heard virtually nothing back. I asked Louise if she knew anything: she told me that she had effectively been cut out of the communication loop on Milly – presumably because Surrey feared she would leak information to me over the dinner table. Well, breakfast table, actually – I was still pulling twelve-hour shifts most days and it was accordingly rare that we sat down together in the evenings. The lack of trust Surrey had in her was hurtful to us both and completely misjudged. There actually might have been advantages in two people in our positions discussing the cases – they would have been effectively getting free consultation time. I was troubled further but never mentioned it to Louise. It seemed obvious to me that Surrey felt they had something which needed keeping from us; I was determined to find out, in case it was something which might harm my investigation.

I decided to try to arrange a meeting with the Surrey team. I explained that I had some exciting new information for them – I had yet to disclose what Emma had told us and thought that such a promise would at least get me through the front door. On reflection, it is astounding that there should have been any question of my having to persuade them to meet me but that was exactly how it felt to me. After having set a date and time to go down to Mount Browne, the Surrey Police headquarters in an old country house just outside Guildford, set in rolling hills now littered with modern, ugly office buildings and parked cars, I received a call back from Brian Marjoram telling me that Steve Scott, his Superintendent, was to attend the meeting and that he was to be replaced as SIO by the newly promoted DCI Maria Woodall. Steve had joined Surrey on promotion from Sussex Police just as I was leaving Surrey to return to the Met. We had met a couple of times socially through Louise and he seemed a pleasant and reasonable chap. I had no issue with his presence; indeed, I thought it might make things easier – Steve might be more able and prepared to make decisions needing resources than Brian or Maria would have been.

I decided that I would take Jo Brunt with me. She had a dental appointment that morning in Hounslow so we left the office early and, after she had had her scale and polish, we had a spare hour or so. As we had to drive virtually past my front door on the way to Guildford, I suggested we stop off for a cup of tea. As we sat drinking it, with Jo fussing around my springer spaniel, Sally, we were chatting, naturally, about the dog, my house, the furniture, the weather – anything really except our investigations. It was then that I realised how Jo had become more than just another capable colleague; she was a real friend too. One which I was glad to have and upon whom I knew I could utterly rely. This made our combination at the head of the investigation team even more effective – it had developed to a level where I had no inhibitions about discussing absolutely anything affecting the case with her. I was able to share so much that I had been internalising and agonising over in my head with no real support from those above me. My fears, hopes, hare-brained ideas – all of it had a sounding board that I could be confident in using. To realise that lifted a huge weight from my mind.

Given how I felt that day, it is very ironic that I then, unwittingly, put Jo in a terrible position. We went to our meeting in one of the modern offices at Mount Browne, where, coincidentally, I had been the occupier for a few months some four years earlier. I was pleased to see Maria Woodall there. She had been a detective sergeant on the only murder investigation I had led in my short spell working in Surrey and, as well as knowing she was a pretty good detective, we had got on well together. I feigned surprise when she told me she had just been promoted to DCI and was taking over as SIO for Operation Ruby, but I told her I welcomed it. I did – if we were to be working more closely with Ruby, it would make things run much more smoothly if my opposite number was someone like her, I thought. Of course, this meant that Brian Marjoram was out of the picture, so I accepted that I was probably going to have to 'sell' Bellfield as the suspect all over again.

The introductions having been made, I proceeded to tell them what we knew about Bellfield. The first part, of course, they knew and Steve Scott nodded and muttered that Marjoram had told him that. When I started to speak about Emma – and the rapes on her, Rebecca and Johanna – I sensed by the glances he was exchanging with Maria that they were wondering what the hell that had to do with Milly. I needed to get their attention so I posed that exact question: 'You might be wondering what all this has to do with your investigation. Well, I'll tell you . . .'

Of course, that made them sit up and listen silently as I led them through every detail of Emma's suspicions and what Bellfield had been doing on the very day that Milly went missing. It took me six or seven minutes and, when I finished, there was a pregnant pause. Maria looked at me with an unusually serious expression, then her eyes darted across to Steve Scott. It was as if she didn't quite know what to say, or at least never had the confidence to say it. It is natural for somebody new to a position to defer to senior officers and I think this was what inhibited her. I followed her gaze to Steve, who was looking down at his papers. He started to speak a couple of times but then looked down again. To keep the momentum going, I took the initiative once more.

'So what I was thinking, you know, do you have any CCTV pictures of Emma's Daewoo that day? That might be a good starting point for corroborating what Emma says.'

Scott once again looked over to Maria but this time they exchanged very serious expressions and then Scott broke his silence.

'Er, yeah, we do. There is a red car coming out about twenty minutes later. We never identified who was in it.'

The Surrey intelligence analyst who was at the meeting – sitting where, of course, Louise might have been had she not been 'banned' – rifled through a sheaf of printouts and papers and passed Scott an A4 sheet with a grainy print of a red car on it. He passed it to me silently, just like my officers had passed countless things across the table to Bellfield during his interviews. Not that I needed any encouragement to become engaged; I immediately saw it was a red Daewoo Nexia. The registration plate couldn't be read but I knew already that Emma's car was the only one of that colour, model and type registered in the KT12 postcode area. Thus, it was very likely to be her car and the only person with the keys that day was Levi Bellfield. My heart rate quickened and I felt that pang in my stomach that comes only with great fear or excitement. This was huge.

Trying to be restrained and professional, I calmly said, 'Well, I think that is him. All we need to do is look at the rest of the CCTV from that camera and the others in the town and we can trace his movements for most of the day – job's a good 'un.'

Steve Scott looked down at his papers, then to his colleagues, then to me again and said, 'Er, we're not going to be able to do that. We haven't got it. We've just got about ten minutes either side of the last sighting of Milly, from that camera.'

I tried not to let my emotions show in my face (although Jo later told me I failed miserably). I could not believe what I had just heard. Forget the car, what about looking for Milly on foot? Had they not done the absolute basics and tried to find her on the many other nearby cameras? Did they really only seize twenty minutes of footage from one camera at the start of what was to become the biggest, longest and most public investigation in the force's history? For once, I was lost for words. I had plenty to say but realised immediately that none of it would have been of the slightest help. I turned to Jo and she looked horrified – not so much at what she had heard but because she could read me and was worried about what I might say next. In the event, I muttered something about it being a shame, realising that my tone was partly patronising and partly in that sort of detached, matter-of-fact way in which you express disapproval to a child at whom you would like to yell but who isn't actually yours to chastise. The atmosphere was heavy and horribly uncomfortable, quite unlike I had ever experienced in a police meeting. I knew they had messed up, they knew they had messed up, and now they knew I knew they had. Yet it was all unspoken, people shuffling papers and looking at the floor. It was as if a teacher would walk in any moment and sentence us all to a detention because the person responsible wouldn't own up.

Steve Scott was the first to speak: 'Well, we do have a very good suspect of our own that we are working on. We are hopeful that analysis of mud from his car will show similarities with pollen found in Minley Heath Woods where Milly's remains were found . . . er . . . perhaps when we resolve that one way or the other, we could find some time to have a look at your man . . . er . . . perhaps, in the meantime, you can bear us in mind and let us know if anything else comes up?'

If she could have done, I know Jo would have put her hand over my mouth. But she knew she couldn't really do that in front of our Surrey colleagues so she had to be content with giving me her best death-stare. She knew what I was thinking – she was thinking the same – but she also knew I was likely to say it while she never would. I rarely got angry at work; it is, I suppose, not really my nature to be anything but calm and reflective. I was once told by one of my team that this was more effective than being full of bluster because, when I only exploded once or twice a year, they knew I really meant it. And this was going to be one of those occasions.

'We are giving you a suspect who is not only a paedophile but a killer and a rapist too, and who not only lived right on the plot but is provably there at the exact time she goes missing. And you want to let us get on with it while you are waiting for some pollen analysis? What the fuck is wrong with you? I'm struggling here, completely struggling to fathom why anybody would do that. Why? Don't you want to solve this?'

Of all I said, of course, it was the last sentence which stung. For me to suggest that they didn't want to solve the case would be a red rag to any detective. I wish I could say that I said it for effect, to elicit a reaction, but it was far simpler than that. It was me vocalising my pure anger and utter disbelief, with no real thought of the consequences. Steve Scott was understandably cross.

'How dare you say that we . . .'

He boomed across the desk at me but the rest of his sentence was drowned out by my mobile phone going off. I saw it was the Forensics manager calling so I didn't want to miss the call. The timing was, of course, perfect.

'Sorry, I really need to take this,' I apologised to the others as I stepped out into the corridor. I was aware that the bellowing was continuing from inside the office for a bit and then, while I was still on the call, I heard the door open and the meeting broke up. Jo came up to me and motioned towards the car park so I followed her, not completing my phone conversation until we were both sitting in the car. I apologised again, this time just to Jo. I had abandoned her to take the full force of an angry Surrey superintendent when I was the one that had enraged him and then rushed out of the room.

'He just sat there shouting and swearing a jabbing his finger across the desk at me. I thought he was going to have a heart attack. I was actually a bit scared. And you'd buggered off to let me take it all!'

Then we started laughing as it dawned on us what a ridiculous set of circumstances it had been. When that subsided, I asked Jo what else had happened after I left and where we could go from there? She said she had given Maria Woodall some papers outlining what we had and that Maria had promised to take it forward as best she could. Which was a typically pragmatic thing for her to do to try to rescue things. Ultimately, I said, it mattered not to us and our investigation whether they took Bellfield seriously as a suspect or not – but it did matter that they investigated their job properly.

I was still incredibly angry about the Surrey attitude after I had dropped Jo off at her house and made my way home for a rare early finish. I was also surprised when Louise came home and knew nothing of the outcome of the meeting. Despite the embargo on her knowing about Operation Ruby, I would have expected something like that to have made its way back to her. It was about 7.30pm and I was in the kitchen cooking dinner when

Louise came and told me Steve Scott had texted her asking for my phone number, which she had sent him. Just a few minutes later, before I could even explain to Louise why he would want it, my phone rang and it was him calling. I braced myself for a difficult call, resolving to stand my ground on the principles but thinking it would probably be right to apologise for the way in which I had expressed them. But there was no need.

'Colin, I wanted to call to apologise for the way I went off today. I was a little bit thrown by the embarrassment of what those before me had failed to do, I think, and I have thought about it and you are absolutely right. We need to make Bellfield our number-one priority. There's just too much in what you have got for us to ignore. Can you pop over again later in the week and we can go through what you have got together?'

'Of course I can, Steve. I'll be only too pleased to. And I'm sorry for going off on one a bit, too.'

'Don't worry about that, Colin – we only do this if we are passionate. I understand. Let's just make sure we get it all done, shall we?'

And that was it – Surrey were on board.

CHAPTER TWENTY-ONE

RETURNING TO KATE AND MARSHA

By the autumn of 2005, the team had settled down into a comfortable working structure. Like everything in the Metropolitan Police, it was something that I had had to document and submit to my senior officers for approval but, in practice, they had just rubber-stamped it. In practice, too, it was probably one of the all-too-rare occasions when bureaucracy actually helped, as the structure I was forced to think about and implement really did make managing a sprawling investigation much easier. Each of the main cases we were investigating – Amélie, Marsha and Kate – had a sub-team with a Detective Inspector responsible for it. The other cases were allocated to their sub-teams too and the HOLMES Unit, Intelligence and Exhibits teams supported them all. I had the overview of everything and had meetings almost daily with the DIs, with a full team meeting at least once a week. The Intelligence Unit had responsibility for day-to-day liaison with Operation Ruby in Surrey, too. There was a considerable overlap in terms of investigating Bellfield himself – the evidence we were finding of his habits, his repeated bouts of depression, his tendency to go away on holiday just after he had done something terrible and his general background was, of course, relevant to every case. Once more, the responsibility for collating that fell to the indomitable DS Clive Grace, whom I knew I could trust to keep on top of a difficult task without fuss or error.

A notable development in Operation Zenda, the Kate Sheedy investigation, came about like this: When Bellfield was arrested, three mobile phones were seized from his house at Little Benty. One of these was a Samsung with a camera, capable of shooting video clips as well as stills. This feature was still relatively new in 2004 and, when all the phones were interrogated at the Met digital lab at Newlands Park, it was clear that Bellfield and his teenaged girlfriend, Amy, had enjoyed experimenting with it. The fifty-seven low-resolution clips, most of less than a minute in length, were pored over for hours to see if they contained any evidential material. Aside from showing the disdain Bellfield held for others during his wheel-clamping, his penchant for driving quickly through puddles to soak pedestrians and the narcissistic and utterly revolting clip entitled 'Levi pissing', there was very little. The one which was relevant to us provided a very welcome additional piece of circumstantial evidence relating to the attempted murder of Kate Sheedy; however, it was not easy to prove and was another example of our lateral thinking and painstaking work.

During the evening of 27 May 2004, while Kate Sheedy and her classmates from Gumley House Convent School were enjoying drinks and dancing in Twickenham, Bellfield had left the Samsung phone at the flat he illegally sub-rented in Crosby Close, Hanworth. There, that night, his sixteen-year-old girlfriend Amy and her younger sister were drinking too. Cider, vodka, and a lot of it. Throughout their binge, they were intermittently shooting video clips – just fun clips showing a pair of teenagers getting drunk and eventually throwing up. They kept going through to the early hours of 28 May when, just after 2am, Bellfield returned to the flat. This was less than two hours after Kate had been run over and left for dead a few miles away in Isleworth. Amy videoed him and we could see that he was wearing a blue coat of some sort, obviously showing that he had recently come in to the flat from outdoors. The ten-second clip is blurred and chaotic but clearly shows Bellfield testing a torch by switching it on and looking into the beam, which lights up towards his face and bleaches out the video. With a cheery 'Fuck off' to the young girls, he then apparently walks off and the clip ends.

I thought this clip had the potential to be of great importance. If, as we believed, he had just been responsible for running Kate down, this proved that he had been out of the flat, that he was wearing outdoor clothes and that he had, for some reason, come indoors, grabbed a torch, checked it was working and then gone back outside again. Which, I hypothesised, was exactly the behaviour you might expect from somebody who had just been involved in a hit-and-run and wanted to check his car for damage or tell-tale signs. For this to have the evidential impact I hoped for, we needed to be able to prove that it was taken on the date and time it purported to have been. The phone software, helpfully, automatically assigned a file name to its clips in the format 'date_time.mp4'. While it was possible for the user then to rename it (such as with 'Levi pissing') it had not been done in this case – so we had a starting point, as the file name was '28-05-05_0215.mp4', indicating 2.15am of 28 May 2004. But it wasn't quite as simple as taking that to be the date and time; it was possible for the user to set the date on the phone manually and so this could have been wildly inaccurate. If we were not able to prove that it was correct, it would be open to Bellfield to say that the settings were hours, or even days out – a claim that we would have great difficulty in disproving.

I checked the lab report for the phone. As was usual, the first thing the scientist had done was dial the speaking clock from a landline and compare the actual time to that shown on the phone (contributing to an annual bill to the Met of over £35,000 for calls to the speaking clock, which was more recently the subject of some public criticism from those who did not appreciate why it was necessary). He had found that the date was correct and the time was eight minutes fast. This, though, did not really help us too much, since this was proof only of the state of the handset when it was examined. We could not be sure this error was present several months previously when it really mattered to us. In order to use the clip as the powerful evidence it might represent, we needed to work out how could we prove that the file name given by the phone was accurate and, thus, the actual date and time of the video.

The clip was played and replayed hundreds of times; every member of the team had seen it and all knew the importance of proving its relevance. As well as the video, there was, of course, the sound track; apart from Bellfield's cursing, there was some music. It was a long shot, but was there any way in which that might help? I asked everybody to play the clip again but, instead of watching, to listen and see if they could recognise the tune. An amateur episode of *Name That Tune* for the highest of stakes. Of course, if the music emanated from a CD or tape, it would be of no use at all – but what if it came from the radio? Could we trace back playlists from all the probable stations to see if we could pinpoint the time? What sounded to some like yet another hare-brained idea from the SIO actually worked better than I could have imagined. Gill Patterson, one of the team's civilian HOLMES indexers, was convinced the music was a theme from a TV show, not a record. But she wasn't sure which show. Once again, I asked everyone to listen and the consensus was that the music was the theme tune to the game show *Wheel of Fortune*. Thank heavens for shift workers watching daytime television, I thought. I got the audio lab to separate out the music from the sound track and, after comparing it with a YouTube video of the show, it seemed that we had, indeed, identified it. From a huge leap forwards, it was then a relatively easy job to consult the TV schedules for that night and then to get a statement from the TV channel, which not only told us the transmission times of the programme but also the exact time the clip of music we had was broadcast. We had the time down to the second – and, most pleasingly, it showed that, even back then, the phone time setting was eight minutes fast. Which was really the most likely outcome, one which we had expected, but precisely the sort of detail which could make the difference between a comprehensive, watertight case and jurors entertaining the slightest doubt. We were somehow making real progress despite having so little material to work with.

Operation Upwey, Marsha McDonnell's murder, was always going to be the weakest of the three. Not that there was any doubt in my mind that Bellfield was responsible, just that the passage of time and the absence of CCTV or mobile-phone data from that day meant we were struggling to prove it. The one thing we had was the Vauxhall Corsa, visible on the bus CCTV. By viewing not only the external bus cameras but also by looking through the windows on the internal, footage we had been able to plot the Corsa's movements quite accurately. One second before Marsha alights from the stationary bus, the Corsa is driving towards it. It has passed the bus two second later, by which time Marsha is level with it, on the pavement to the driver's side. The Corsa then arrives at the crossroads where Percy Road and Priory Road intersect. The Corsa pulls over in the mouth of Priory Road to its left, the brake lights coming on as if it is stopping, then the bus pulls away and we lose pictures of it. Marsha would have approached the crossroads and turned right into Priory Road, where she lived, and so was walking away from the Corsa but clearly visible, in the street-lit residential street, to its driver. We knew the Corsa line of inquiry had not been progressed by the original Upwey team because they thought they had arrested their suspect and so there seemed to be potential in it – especially in light of the fact that we knew Bellfield, at that time, owned a silver five-door Vauxhall Corsa, registration number Y57 RJU. The best (black-and-white-only) image of the Corsa on the CCTV showed it was probably silver and, despite the registration number being an illegible smudge, looked very much as if it contained only six characters, the second of which could be a '5'. If we could prove that the Corsa was Bellfield's despite the other limitations in what we could find, it might be enough when on the same cross-admissible indictment as the stronger cases of Amélie and Kate, and when put together with his knowledge of the Hampton area from his family ties there, to get him charged.

DI Joe Farrell drew my attention to an article he had read in an American journal suggesting that blurred or low-resolution photographs could be read more easily if they were displayed on extra-large screens. Not just 21-inch monitors or 50-inch televisions but really big, supersize, cinema screens. The unlikely proposition seemed to have some complex science supporting it, so what, I thought, was there for us to lose? Where was the biggest screen we could find nearby? The Odeon, Leicester Square, somebody suggested. So a call was made and, early one weekday morning, a group of us met in a nearby coffee shop and took the best stills from the Corsa CCTV to the incredibly helpful projectionist, Eric, who told us he was honoured to help, it making an unusual change from his normal hot-and-thirsty job. It was, for me, too, one of the strangest things I did in my career, five detectives desperately moving about an empty cinema, craning their necks and straining their eyes trying to look at a fuzzy black-and-white car at about four times its normal size. All to no avail; it was no easier to read on the big screen than it was on a phone. Back to more conventional methods it was.

I sent DI Richard Ambrose to meet an expert in video interpretation to see what he could make of the footage. Richard returned buoyant the afternoon of his meeting, presenting a statement saying that, in the opinion of the expert, there was 'strong support' for the proposition that the number plate of the Corsa in the recording was Y57 RJU. Job done, he thought. Except it wasn't. From my days working on the Met's Stolen Vehicle Squad fifteen years earlier, I was aware of a concept known as confirmation bias: that the human mind finds it impossible to forget about something and disregard it after it has been suggested. Practically, and in this sort of context, it means that the person attempting to identify the number should have no idea of what you think it is, less still what you would like it to be. What we were used to doing when heating and applying chemicals to retrieve ground-out engine numbers, Richard and the expert should have done here. Richard knew no different; the expert should have known better. The statement proved nothing; it was useless for court. However, all was not lost. Richard was duly sent to see another expert, who made a proper, blind assessment of the possible numbers shown on the CCTV. The plan was then to combine the two experts' findings and arrive at a list of possibles, which we could seek to eliminate. For once, luck was not with us. Expert number two concluded that, since the vast majority of registration numbers have seven characters, the flare caused by the bus headlights being reflected by the number plate was possibly completely obscuring the first character of seven. Therefore, while he opined as to the possibilities for characters (as he saw it) from position one to position seven, he thought there might be a position-one character that was completely unknown. As only 'I' and 'Z' are never used in that place on UK registrations, this multiplied the possibilities by a factor of twenty-four. When we combined all the possibilities suggested by both experts, we came up with a staggering total of more than 610,000 possible registration numbers. As if 25,000 vans weren't bad enough, no team could ever hope to see such a huge number of cars.

Talking it over at a supervisors' meeting the next day, Clive Grace, as ever, was positive: 'All might not be lost, Guvnor. We can probably get that down.'

'How do you suggest?' I asked, more in hope than expectation.

'Well, as well as "I" and "Z" at the start, "I" and "Q" aren't used in positions five, six or seven. So that takes out a few more. Then we can take out loads by ignoring all the cars that aren't Corsas. Then, if we work on the features visible, colour is obvious but also like the number of doors, whether it has a sun roof – we can probably tell that from some code in the VIN number, which Vauxhall can tell us about. It still might not be doable, but we need to try.'

I said that, of course, we must try, thinking that it would still probably be impossible but that, if anybody could pull it off, Clive Grace was the man. It took a few weeks, during which time Clive presented me with an expense claim for a book costing £49.99, entitled *Registration Marks of the World* – a weighty hardback tome, which I looked at once and which I instantly put down as it appeared to be something that would send even the most fervent car nut to sleep. I also had to authorise a reconstruction, whereby we got the actual bus on which Marsha had travelled and parked it in Percy Road, recording CCTV at night while a succession of light-coloured Vauxhall Corsas (including R57 YJU, which we had, by that time, seized from its innocent new owner) were driven past so that the experts could be certain of the colour of the suspect car. This enabled another large tranche of Corsas to be eliminated.

Finally, one morning, Clive came to my desk with a pile of paperwork and a cup of tea, sat down and said in his deep Hampshire burr, 'Well, it's nowhere near as bad as we feared. You know we started with six hundred and ten and you said get it down to a thousand? Well, it's better than that. Quite a bit better, actually. One hundred and seventy-eight.'

And with that understatement, he showed me the results of one of the most detailed and fantastic pieces of police work I ever encountered. The final list of 178 was arrived at by eliminating, in order: all that were not Corsa C-model cars made before February 2003; then all with only three doors; then all with a sunroof; then all other than silver; then all exported, scrapped or written off before February 2003; then 'sister' models badged as Opels or Chevrolet and imported (as their grille badges were markedly different); and, then, finally, he had ensured that there was no record of any Nigerian or Romanian Corsa being imported – as the definitive book showed these countries to have, at the time, number plates most closely resembling those in the UK. It was a masterpiece of logic, patience and tenacity. And it put us just 177 statements away from proving Bellfield's car was there when Marsha was murdered, which would take us very close to being able to charge him with her murder. It was time to take what we had to the lawyers.

CHAPTER TWENTY-TWO

CHARGING MURDER

I called for a full meeting of the legal team to discuss the evidence we had, knowing that an immediate charging decision would not be forthcoming. It would need a comprehensive written report before they would support us but, as always, it was prudent to clear the ground first by talking things over. I went with Jo Brunt and DI Joe Farrell to meet the lawyers.

Andrew Hadik, the Special Casework Crown Prosecutor assigned to the case, was one of those men who might as well have had 'Character' tattooed across his forehead. Tall, well-built and in his early fifties, he had the manner and bearing of a man directly descended from revered Hungarian nobility. Some described him as Dickensian. He wore square, wire-rimmed glasses, was rarely seen without a waistcoat and had a mop of greying hair, which had once been sandy. He spoke in the expected RP accent but with the odd habit of ending almost everything he said with a sort of grunted 'huh?', almost as if he were asking you to agree. Which you often found yourself doing just to be polite, even if you really did not. He had a penchant for small cigars and, in his small talk, often referred to his Parson Jack Russells.

Andrew first struck me as too detailed in his thinking; in our early conferences (barristers always have conferences, or 'cons', never meetings), I feared he was getting us bogged down in minutiae that really weren't relevant at that point. As the case progressed, though, this feature of his work became all the more important and, by the start of the trial, I was very grateful for his thoroughness in interpreting the law and trial procedure.

Lead counsel Brian Altman had prosecuted a few murder cases for me in the past. We knew each other well and, crucially, had a good working relationship based on respect. He had earned a justifiably fine reputation for his mastery of facts, his being demanding of thorough investigations and his low-key but devastating style when on his feet in court. One of his oft-repeated phrases was 'No surprises' – meaning that he needed to know absolutely everything before the trial had started. It was a degree of preparedness I wholly appreciated and concurred with. He was, at the time, holding a position known as 'Number One' in the Treasury Counsel's room at the Old Bailey, which meant that he effectively had first option on all the high-profile cases coming through there. Naturally, he fancied Bellfield's case and I was absolutely delighted that he did – I really would not have wanted any other of the many talented lawyers available to work with; for me, he was the very best of them.

Altman was supported by his 'Junior', Mark Heywood, junior describing their relationship but being wholly inappropriate for an experienced and brilliant lawyer who would himself soon be appointed as Queen's Counsel and become the 'Number One' Treasury Counsel. Together, they made a formidable team.

I had usually met Hadik in his large but cluttered office ('Terribly sorry, Colin – I have had somebody squatting in my room with me and there is rather too much paper and rather too little furniture') in a modern yet now demolished block on Ludgate Hill, just 200 yards from the Old Bailey; however, the conference which really counted in early March 2006 was in a very ordinary meeting room in the Old Bailey building itself. None of the corporate niceties like coffee or biscuits, simply half-a-dozen people at the top of their game trying their very best to ensure a serial killer could be held behind bars forever. Nervous but pumped and ready to argue my corner, I exchanged the usual handshakes and we went through the evidence that we had, the realistic prospects (or otherwise) of adding to each strand and the difficulties and pitfalls we might face. I came out of the conference hopeful that we had not been discouraged – at all. Indeed, Brian Altman's attitude had been extremely positive, talking always of when, rather than if. Andrew Hadik was more cautious, using the phrase, 'Well, let's see what you have in your report, huh?' on more than one occasion. It was time for me to sit down with Joe Farrell and write it, a task I took on with even greater hope when Altman whispered to me that he was sure it was going to be charged as we exchanged our goodbyes.

Faxes from the CPS were to become a frequent source of consternation and, indeed, work for us over the coming months, often arriving on a Friday afternoon and sending the team into furious action. However, the one which came a week or so after we had submitted the full report was the most important and the most welcome. It addressed the vital question of whether we were able to charge the murders. A negative response would not have been fatal to our chances, but it would mean further months of slogging, painstaking assembly of snippets of information, turning them into evidence to fill the gaps Hadik still saw in our case. Left to me, I'd have charged him months ago.

Andrew Hadik's 'Advice' was long, deliberately written in very precise language, almost as if he were making a reasoned submission to the Court of Appeal. There was nothing at all sadistic about this – while he was thoroughly, and perhaps understandably, immersed in the drama of it all, he wanted, I think, to show that he had considered it all carefully and properly. There was no doubt that he had. He went through the cases as an overview, remarking that Amélie's was the strongest, Marsha's the weakest and Kate's not much better. The whole thing would hinge upon getting all on the same indictment and arguing cross-admissibility – that the jury would be entitled to take the stronger case into account when deciding if he had also committed the weaker cases.

That was, he thought, extremely likely to be allowed by the judge. So he went through the evidence we had for Amélie, the van, the phone, the CCTV, and concluded that made out a compelling case, one with a realistic prospect of conviction and, therefore, one which he would authorise us to charge. My mood lightened; at least we were on for one. Hadik then continued that, in the light of that, the CCTV and identification of the Previa in Kate's case, together with witness evidence that Bellfield was using it on that evening and, of course, the torch clip, made a reasonably convincing case for charging the attempted murder of Kate, so he would authorise that charge too.

His carefully crafted prose then turned to Marsha. At the outset, he said he did not think we were quite there, even if the jury were happy that he was guilty of the other two. However, what would tip the balance would be for us to complete the Vauxhall Corsa elimination exercise Clive Grace was battling with. With extreme clarity, which made my immediate focus so simple, Hadik said that, if we could eliminate every Corsa except Bellfield's, he would authorise charging Marsha. I was relieved and elated. Two out of three wasn't bad and I knew exactly what we had to do to make it a full house – and knew that we would achieve it soon.

Once the elation had subsided, my mind turned to the practicalities. We could not charge the Marsha McDonnell murder until we had finally eliminated all of the potential 178 Vauxhall Corsas that could have been on the bus CCTV as she alighted. We had done very well but, despite months of hard work, there were five cars we could not trace. I realised that was going to take a few further weeks at least and so we could not sensibly delay the other charges to give that investigation time to catch up. It meant there would have to be two charging days and I asked Clive Grace to prepare the written request to produce Bellfield from his remand cell at Wood Hill prison to the local police station in Milton Keynes for the first of them, so that our suspect could at last be charged with murder.

In the Custody Suite at the modern Thames Valley Police facility, we were strangers yet known. Bellfield had been interviewed there several times already and his notoriety as a putative serial murderer meant that the locals were extremely friendly and helpful. A mysteriously large number of the local officers seemed to find spurious reasons to pop into custody that morning in early March 2006; I knew they were just trying to get a glimpse of this man they had heard so much about and I didn't even consider trying to prevent it. Charging people like him makes coppers happy, even if they have had nothing to do with the investigation, and I wasn't going to begrudge our colleagues from TVP a share of our feel-good factor. There was plenty of it to go around.

As is usual when anybody is charged with an offence, fingerprints, photographs and DNA were to be taken, so Gary Cunningham and DC Andy Murray took Bellfield into a side room to go through the various procedures. The door was open and I kept an eye on them as they did it; I was thinking ahead to investigating other offences in the future and so had asked them to make sure that we had good and comprehensive photographs of Bellfield's many and varied tattoos – they could be very useful aids to identification, especially since we were dealing with a man who had used no fewer than forty-three aliases. This, of course, meant they had to ask him to strip naked and, suddenly, there was a commotion, Bellfield yelling abuse at the officers. A few of us went to the door and, for the first time since I had set eyes upon him, I saw the angry Bellfield, the dangerous Bellfield. He was snarling, his upper lip curled like a wild dog about to strike, his jet-black eyes fixed, staring, even more menacing than usual. Cunningham and Murray had each taken one of his arms and were holding them (and him) up against the wall. He was cursing into the room, his huge belly hanging down, almost providing modesty to those parts of his body the exposure of which he had apparently taken so much exception to. Murray, ever helpful, said, 'Come on, Levi, we've all seen dicks before!' which, surprisingly, did seem to calm Bellfield.

Although, if he had heard Cunningham's whispered but entirely accurate observation of, 'Yes . . . but never quite *that* small,' I am quite sure the altercation may have gone on longer.

We returned to our seats and I decided to broach something with the youthful Custody Sergeant, something about which I felt a little embarrassed. From my earliest days in the police, there was a tradition for the Senior Investigating Officer to sign the charge sheet for murders. I had never bothered to make a fuss about this; it seemed an unnecessary expression of self-importance to me, as if it were all my own work when the truth was I was successful because I had the privilege of leading such a brilliant team. On occasion, usually when the Custody Officer was especially aged and remembered the tradition, they would seek me out for the signature and I would, of course, oblige but it was never important for me to perform this wholly symbolic task.

This time it was different for me; this was going to be the defining moment of my career, I thought, almost certainly the only serial killer I would be involved in snaring. I was going to make sure my name went down on the record.

'Sarge, would you mind if I signed the charge sheet for this one?' I asked.

The smart, young, well-spoken man with the stripes looked up at me and smiled.

'What, do you still handwrite them in the Met then? We're all modern here. It is all on the computer.'

I was crestfallen, embarrassed both that I had asked for something and been refused and also that the Met – the glorious Met of which I was so proud – was shown to be falling behind the times. I muttered an 'OK' and then heard him say, 'But because we have so many from the prison here from all over the country, we are instructed not to do the charging ourselves at all – we end up spending hours on trains going to court in far-flung places, otherwise. So I will need somebody from your team to physically read them out to him.'

I didn't need asking twice. In fact, I virtually barged the poor chap out of the way as I leaped behind his desk. He handed me the mouse, I scrolled to the start of the charges and cleared my throat as Bellfield, my quarry for the last eighteen months, was walked in front of me by Murray and Cunningham, still buttoning his clothing as he came. He stood in front of me. I looked him straight in the eye, and saw only hate. Not violence, cunning, nor greed – not even contempt. Just burning hatred directed towards me, for the simple reason that he knew I had beaten him. Trying to appear casually disinterested but with pride and elation welling up in my chest, I went through the words I had to formally read to him. In truth, I could have done it without the prompt. I knew the charges off by heart. I had practised hearing them in my head so many times, never thinking it really would be me doing it if we ever got there. Having my name on a piece of paper would have been one thing but this was the memory of a lifetime. I stood there and it was me. I was to be the one – on behalf of my team, of all the victims, of all London – who stood there two feet away from this sickening apology for a human being and told him what he was going to have to answer for. I was the one all his malice bent itself upon and never before, nor since, have I so loved being hated.

The following day at Putney, there was an office lunch. Lunch is a euphemistic term for the practice carried out three or four times a year by Met squads and CID offices. It usually involves everyone hitting a pub at about 11.30am, finding somewhere to eat around 2pm and then rushing to catch the last train home – the celebrated 'vomit comet', as it is often known. They always take place on a Thursday, not a Friday, despite most detectives usually not working on Saturdays and Sundays. The reasoning, since the earliest days of the Met, has always been that there is no point having a hangover on your day off; better to suffer on the firm's time.

I had to miss the early part of the festivities, being required to attend another meeting with the lawyers at the Old Bailey. It was, therefore, about 4pm by the time I arrived at The Boathouse, a busy and modern Youngs pub on the River Thames at Putney. As I walked from the towpath towards the pub, I heard some mild cheering from the first-floor terrace. I looked up and realised that almost all the team, even the non-smokers, were outside, enjoying the unusually mild spring sunshine.

I had taken just a few steps into the building when somebody pressed a pint of beer into my hand, reminding me that I was at least five behind everyone else. As if the noise they were making didn't make that abundantly clear to me. I made my way up to the terrace and a table of six or seven shuffled along the benches at Jo Brunt's behest to make room for me to sit down. I was opposite Gary Cunningham, who was finishing some story or other, which was greeted with the real hilarity that his tales usually inspired.

He then turned towards me and, using the perfect comic timing that came so naturally to him, said, 'Guvnor, we've been having a bit of a discussion, and want to know: when they make the film of this investigation, who do you want to play you . . . given that John Candy is dead?'

Roars of laughter spread out around the terrace, and rightly so. I joined in – it was a genuinely funny moment. I looked around at the smiles, the tipsy crowd of thirty or forty people, happy and carefree in the sun. Every one of them I knew could tell a story of remarkable sacrifice and redoubled effort. Each had contributed to making us successful and each would remember this case for the rest of their life. It had been a couple of years of hard work, highs and lows, sadness and fear. But at that very moment, I was so proud of them, of us, of what we had achieved together. If ever a group of people deserved a day to let their hair down and celebrate, it was this lot. And I was so proud of every single one of them.

CHAPTER TWENTY-THREE

BUILDING THE CASE

Two other cases we had uncovered, where Bellfield had attacked but not killed women in the street, were also authorised for us to charge, forming an indictment of two murders, two attempted murders and an attempted abduction. The 'extra' attacks were those on Anna-Maria Rennie and Irma Dragoshi.

We were told by Clint Stevens, one of Bellfield's acquaintances who was undoubtedly frightened of him but who was emboldened by his incarceration, that he was a passenger in Bellfield's white BMW car as they passed a young woman near Twickenham Green and that Bellfield had said to him, 'I want to talk to that slut,' and stopped, leaving Stevens in the car as he got out and approached her. Stevens saw a conversation begin, which then became heated, and Bellfield started to manhandle the girl towards the car. Stevens had got out to try to stop Bellfield but was told in no uncertain terms that he should mind his own business, and so began to walk home. Several minutes later, Bellfield had driven alongside him, alone in the car, and shouted at him again to 'Mind your own fucking business.'

We had researched Stevens's statement and could not find an incident like the one he had referred to as having been reported to the police. However, we did find that Anna-Maria had reported a very similar incident as a crime at about the same time. Although her description of Bellfield's passenger could not have been Stevens and she was sure Bellfield was driving a dark Ford Mondeo, her description of the actual assailant was very close to Bellfield's. It perhaps just goes to prove just how often he committed acts of this nature.

Anna-Maria Rennie was just seventeen in October 2001. She had had an argument with her boyfriend and had left their flat to go for a walk and clear her head. It was about 11.30pm and she was sitting at a bus stop in Hospital Bridge Road, Twickenham, about a mile from Twickenham Green. A dark Mondeo pulled up in the lay-by with two white men in it. The driver had got out and offered her a lift. When she declined and walked off, the driver followed her and, once he had caught up, grabbed her and lifted her off her feet, then marching her back towards his car. Anna-Maria was naturally terrified; she screamed and he put his hand over her mouth. Despite her small frame, Anna-Maria screamed and struggled, frantically flailing her arms and legs in an attempt to get free from the large, heavy man's grip. Perhaps surprisingly, she succeeded, wriggling free and running away towards her home.

When reporting this attack to the police, she said she believed the Mondeo had a registration number beginning with 'L651'.

Bellfield, at the time, had possession of a dark-blue Ford Mondeo, L620 FLJ. Her description of her assailant as being tall, thick-set or fat and with close-cropped hair was obviously consistent with Bellfield; any doubt that it was him was removed in March 2005 when she positively identified him as the man who had tried to abduct her at a formal identification procedure. Indeed, as Andrew Hadik rightly pointed out, it was not a mere attempt; Bellfield had actually succeeded in abducting her, the offence being complete once her feet had left the ground. A lovely example of his technical thoroughness, which was reflected in the actual charge preferred.

Irma Dragoshi was a hairdresser who worked in Slough but lived in Hillingdon. Her employer used to help her get to and from work by collecting her from a bus stop on the Old Bath Road in Longford, a village at the end of the Heathrow runway, dropping her off there again on the return journey. On 16 December 2003, Irma was at the bus stop at around 7.15pm. It was cold and dark, she was speaking to her husband Astri on her mobile phone and told him that, as usual, the bus was late. That was the last thing she remembered when she later woke up in hospital. Astri recalled that, during the conversation, he had the incredibly distressing experience of hearing his wife scream and the phone going dead. She had been attacked in the middle of their call. She had suffered injuries to her head consistent with having been struck with a heavy, blunt instrument, perhaps owing her life to the heavy fur-lined hood of her coat, which cushioned the blow.

We were alerted to Bellfield's involvement in this attack by another of his friends, Sunil Gharu. He told us that he had been the passenger in Bellfield's black Volkswagen Golf that evening. As they drove along the Old Bath Road, Bellfield had suddenly pulled over to the kerb, switched off the car's lights and got out, saying, 'Here you are, watch this!' as he exited. He jogged over to Irma at the bus stop and grabbed or hit at her, pulling at her as she fell to the floor. He then ran off, crossed the road and returned to the Golf, driving off at speed, laughing. Gharu said he had not mentioned the shocking assault at all because it served only to make him more scared of the man he thought was a friend.

Armed as we were with a positive identification from the victim in one and an eye-witness account in the other, it was hardly surprising that the CPS brought the charges in these cases. Of course, the common factor in both was that the victim was at a bus stop; given that buses played such a prominent part in the attacks on Amélie, Marsha and Kate, there was little doubt that having them all on the same indictment would add considerable weight to the proposition we were trying to establish for the jury – that Bellfield preyed on women using buses and bus stops as his hunting ground.

We turned then to another series of offences, which had come to light while we had been researching Bellfield's habits. From early 2005, some of his friends had told us about a sex tape, which, while many were certain as to its existence, none had actually ever seen. It was rumoured to have been taken while a young teenage girl, under the influence of some drugs, had been repeatedly raped by Bellfield and a few of his friends. This information, albeit uncorroborated, chimed with other information we had found – that Bellfield had a peculiar interest in girls between thirteen and fifteen and liked to pick them up in the street, drug them and share them with his friends, as had been evident in the events surrounding the attack on 'Spanish Pete' Rodrigues. While I had no doubt he was capable of such outrageous offending, I had been cautious about pursuing the line of inquiry. My view, quite simply, was that, while such a string of offences would ordinarily be worthy of detailed investigation, I had a responsibility to ensure that my team's time and energies were focused on our main priorities – the murders and blitz attacks. Despicable and distressing as they might have been, these drug rapes didn't really advance our knowledge of those offences, nor would they add evidential weight to our prosecution. It was the tough sort of resourcing decision SIOs had, on occasion, to make. However, the handful of officers on the team who nevertheless wanted to investigate everything got their chance, all because of a lolly-stick.

In October 2005, I had spent a week away near Nerja in Spain. One day on the beach, I was ambling across to get some drinks when I felt a sharp and severe pain in the sole of my right foot. I found I had a piece of wood protruding from it and, when I pulled it out, I realised a sharpened lolly-stick had penetrated about an inch into my bare foot as I had stood on it. I hobbled around for the rest of the holiday and then for a couple of weeks when back at work, as the wound was not healing and was still very painful. Eventually, I sought medical help and, to my astonishment, was admitted to hospital. Part of the stick was still in my foot, it had all gone horribly septic and I needed an operation to remove the wood and surrounding infected tissue. Which was just what I really did not need – while the hospital stay was just three days, I was then unable to walk or drive for some time and the upshot was that I was off work for five weeks.

During this time, the reins of the team were handed over to DI John McFarlane, a burly, bluff and quite menacing Scotsman who had been drafted in to assist a few months earlier. John was one of the three supervisors I called my Praetorian Guard – two Sergeants and an Inspector, the shortest of whom was still 6' 5" tall. John had succumbed to pressure from some of the team and, I suspect, his own preference too and ordered some work around the drug rapes. This had turned up an allegation of rape made by a sixteen-year old girl called Charmaine Hook. She had identified Bellfield as having picked her up in the street in West Drayton, taken her to a night club in north London, where he plied her with drink, and then back to West Drayton, where he gave her some Malibu from a small bottle. He had then taken her back to her home, a narrow-boat on the Grand Union Canal at Cowley, which she shared with her mother. However, Mum was away for the weekend, Bellfield entered the boat with Charmaine and the next thing she remembered was waking up the following morning, realising that she had been raped. She felt as if she had a hangover and was sick into a bowl. With remarkable forethought, she covered the bowl and called for police, realising that she had probably been drugged and that the vomit might contain useful evidence.

The investigation had failed, at the time, to identify Bellfield as the rapist; Charmaine had contacted the incident room because she had seen the publicity surrounding the white Courier van and realised it was the van she had been taken in. In her detailed description of her attacker, it was clear she was talking about

Bellfield. At this time, there was a court prohibition on publishing his photograph (which, indeed, existed until he was convicted of the murders) so her description was evidentially valid. Scientific examination of her bowl of sick confirmed the presence of large quantities of chemicals, which resulted from the metabolism of the so-called date-rape drug GHB. It was developing into a pretty good case.

A further four similar cases, involving victims aged between thirteen and sixteen, were identified that fitted this method, within a relatively small geographical area, suggesting Bellfield might be responsible. When I returned to the office and found that the work had been done, I was a little annoyed that my instructions had not been followed but, practically, realised that, having made contact with the victims and perhaps given them an expectation of investigation, we had little choice but to pursue it further. A plan was devised to produce Bellfield from prison and to arrest four of his friends who we suspected of involvement. They would all be taken to Wimbledon Police Station and each would have his home address searched in an effort to find a copy of the almost-mythical sex tape. Despite our best efforts, the tape was never found and all denied any involvement. It left us with the quite disappointing situation where we were certain we knew what had been going on but where there was nothing like enough evidence to bring charges in any case other than Charmaine's – and that was pretty thin. I wrote a report for the CPS and submitted it to Andrew Hadik, seeking advice as to how to proceed.

The advice, when it came through on the customary Friday-afternoon fax, was short and absolutely clear – there was, at present, insufficient evidence to proceed. What the fax did not contain, though, was what Hadik had said to me in a phone call shortly before it arrived. Paraphrasing, he asked what the hell we were playing at. Did we not realise that the case against Bellfield was complicated enough as it was? That the indictment was already about as much as we could reasonably expect a jury to cope with in one go? And went on to say that, in his view, we ought to concentrate on the murders. Every word of which I wholeheartedly agreed with. What did come out of this, though, was my acceptance of the need to care for the many victims of Bellfield who, for whatever reason, would never see their cases before a court. This developed into my setting up a support network for these women, assisted by multiple Family Liaison Officer deployments, engendering a mutual feeling that 'her justice is my justice'; that what was important was that Bellfield was imprisoned forever and unable to create more victims, whatever the route to that incarceration might be. This novel approach was a total success, measured perhaps by the 'unsatisfied' victims never pressing for further investigations and, indeed, by the presence of several of them on the day he was sentenced, sharing with us all the moment of satisfaction.

CHAPTER TWENTY-FOUR

MORE ON MILLY

Operation Ruby, the investigation into Milly Dowler's murder, was of great interest to me, because I was convinced Bellfield was responsible. However, it was a Surrey Police investigation and, while we were trying to assist them as much as we could and some members of my team were in virtually daily contact with their opposite numbers at Guildford, my personal involvement was minimal. I did, though, keep abreast of developments and a couple of things puzzled me. One was that, in an attempt to share information and prevent the duplication of effort, I had allowed them access to our HOLMES databases. This meant that officers from Surrey could read any statement, action or other document which we had recorded during our investigation.

This openness was, however, not reciprocated. There was no technical reason for doing so – HOLMES is a system operated to national common standards and conventions and so it was simply a matter of allowing access and we could have read what they had too. But despite my frequent requests for real-time access, the best we ever achieved was being sent DVDs of selected data from their account. I knew that there had been some sensitivities over the Surrey treatment of Milly's father as a potential suspect early in their investigation and so assumed this might be the reason for their selective sharing. Like anyone outside their team, I was completely ignorant of the mess they had made of dealing with the hacking of Milly's phone by the *News of the World*; when that became public knowledge in 2011, their coyness became, to me, a lot more understandable. I am not sure proper access to their data would have helped our investigation much, if at all, but I still suspect that, had we been able to read it, we might have been able to assist them achieve a satisfactory conclusion more easily and more speedily. I guess we will never know for certain.

I was, though, invited by Brian Altman to attend a conference at the Old Bailey, where he and Andrew Hadik were going to discuss their decision on charging Milly's murder so that it could be added to our indictment. I don't think for a moment I was a welcome attendee as far as Surrey were concerned but the lawyers told them I was coming as it was felt that, given my intimate knowledge of our investigation into Bellfield, I might be able to add to the discussions. I took DI Joe Farrell with me; Superintendent Steve Scott led a Surrey party of three or four detectives. Arriving early, Joe sat in the meeting room and I went to seek out Brian Altman in the Treasury Counsel's room. In what was probably a breach of official protocol but equally a measure of the close relationship we were forming, Altman took me in, shut the door and said in deliberate and hushed tones, 'Colin,

I must tell you that I don't want that case within a thousand fucking miles of our indictment.'

Sensing the shock on my face (which was more as to the strength of his view, rather than the outcome), he continued, 'Yours is a good case, a good chance with lots of hard-earned evidence, which comes together in a coherent package. Theirs is piecemeal, it is bitty, there are so many holes and avenues of escape. I don't want to be putting that to a jury and jeopardising what we have already got. I really think there is a danger of it dragging us down. Just so you know.'

I muttered a quick acknowledgement and we went into the meeting. Steve Scott opened with a summary of the evidence he thought he had and which had been submitted in his written request. Altman replied for the lawyers, asking Scott about the evidence that Milly had not made it past the Bird's Eye building in Station Avenue after the last confirmed sighting of her. This was crucial because, if the hypothesis that Bellfield had abducted her close to the Collingwood Place flat were correct, she could not have walked past the building's two CCTV cameras. That she had not was a fact, I thought – from the very start, Surrey were saying that she was not on the CCTV recordings and that meant they could be certain she had not walked past. Altman, though, with his usual thoroughness, would not take this on face value. He wanted to be told not just that they knew but exactly how they knew.

The cameras on the Bird's Eye building were mounted at each corner of the roof on the side facing Station Avenue. They pointed down, their field of view encompassing the whole roadway and pavement of both sides. However, the width of their view was quite narrow; they rotated from side to side in order to make a wider and more useful sweep of the area. The cameras rotated at different speeds, meaning that, while their view sometimes overlapped, they were, at other times, pointing in different directions so that a section of the street was frequently, if briefly, not covered. This was the gap Altman wanted to explore. Scott appeared slightly flustered. Not having been involved in the investigation at the start when this 'fact' was determined, I imagined he didn't actually know. He looked at Tim Barrett, a detective constable who had been on the team from the start for guidance. Barrett obliged, saying, 'Well, we got a PC to walk and run past the cameras – on both sides of the road – and looked at the recordings. It got her every time.'

I immediately felt embarrassed for my colleagues; I knew what was coming. As useful as that reconstruction might have been as a guide to whether it would be impossible to pass the cameras and not be recorded, it clearly would not be conclusive. There was no way, I thought, that Brian Altman would be happy with such an unscientific method of proving what would, one day, be the foundation of a prosecution he was leading. I knew what he would want – and I knew it was something that would be relatively easy to arrange. I found it incredible that Surrey had not done it already. What was needed was a study of the time and motion of the cameras to enable a reconstruction to be made of the area they were viewing, extended over one full cycle of their movement. From this, it would be possible to see where the windows of non-coverage were – and for how long. Finally, from that, it could be calculated if, indeed, it would be possible for a person to move from Milly's last known location past the building without being captured on the recording – and, if so, how quickly she would have to have been moving. It required patient and validated calculation by an expert, not the finger-in-the-wind method of having somebody walk past a few times.

Steve Scott looked aghast. Andrew Hadik passed him a written report, saying it was the official decision not to charge and that there were other issues outlined within it. Scott, understandably not wanting to prolong the embarrassment, spluttered that they would take it away with them and consider it. He hurriedly stuffed the report into his bag; I got the real impression that he had done so almost in panic, desperate that Joe and I shouldn't see what other horrors it contained. And that was it; the meeting was over within just a few minutes. I hadn't even had the need, let alone the opportunity, to speak.

On the tube back to Putney, I reflected on the decision. I had hoped the decision would have been to charge. I knew that, had Milly been added to the indictment, it would have pushed 'my' victims to the side of the stage; it would have become the Milly Dowler trial, such was the huge profile her tragic case had maintained. I was completely at ease with this. As terrible and notorious as the Met cases had become, it didn't matter to me that they would be overshadowed by Milly. All that was important was that Bellfield was convicted, the victims and their families saw justice and that he would not be able to kill or rape or maim again. He had killed Milly, I was sure, so I wanted him to be tried for it. I knew it was by no means the end of the road for Surrey either – they now had a template for what they needed to do; what the lawyers wanted them to prove. And if they were able to achieve that, the charges would be forthcoming; what I needed to do was to ensure we gave them as much encouragement and assistance as possible. I resolved never to discuss the failure to prove the cameras properly with them. What would be the point? But I also remembered the lack of CCTV seizure, which I had found out about during that first explosive meeting at Guildford, and I couldn't help but wonder how different things might have been if they had been better at doing the basic initial investigation back in March 2002. It would not have saved Milly, sadly, but what about Marsha, Amélie and Kate?

Another staggering fact had come to light. On the day before Milly was abducted, Rachel Cowles, an eleven-year old schoolgirl, was walking home from her school in Shepperton, just across the River Thames from Walton. She was dressed in her school uniform. She was approached by a man in a red hatchback car who spoke to her from the window. He said he had just moved in down the road from her, he recognised her as living near to him and he had forgotten the way. Would she get in and help him find the road? Being suspicious, she said she had been told not to get in cars with strangers and, as the conversation continued, completely by chance, a marked police car came around the corner. At this, the man gave up and drove off. Rachel continued home and told her father what had happened, explaining to him that the car was about the same size as his Rover 214, that it had four doors and that in the back were two baby seats. She remembered thinking the man must have a son and a daughter because one was pink and the other blue. She said the man was fat with short, dark hair and a squeaky voice. Mr Cowles naturally phoned the police, who quite correctly said that, since the incident and the danger were over, they would not deploy to it but would record the facts as intelligence, which they did.

Somehow, inexplicably, when Milly was reported missing the next day, just a mile distant as the crow flies, Surrey Police did not find this information in their intelligence trawl. Worse, perhaps, the staff who had taken the call and recorded the information on to the intelligence database did not make the connection and alert the Operation Ruby team to it. Of course, Bellfield was, at the time, using Emma Mills's red four-door Daewoo hatchback, with its blue and pink baby seats in the rear, and the Ruby team had the Bird's Eye CCTV showing it exiting into Station Avenue about twenty minutes after Milly disappeared. But the information stayed hidden on a server somewhere, not accessed by the detectives so nobody was prompted to ask the question that might have, back then, led to Bellfield: 'What were the chances of two different men with red cars being at the scene of two separate abductions of young girls in school uniform within one mile of each other in suburban Surrey on successive days?' Indeed, the information remained unread for years; it was only in 2005 when Mr Cowles saw Surrey's new media appeals about the red Daewoo that he posed the question in a letter to the Chief Constable, which drew attention to yet another opportunity missed due to very basic investigative work not having been done.

CHAPTER TWENTY-FIVE

PREPARING FOR COURT

In early May 2006, Bellfield was further charged with murdering Marsha McDonnell. This came after Clive Grace had completed his Herculean task of eliminating all the other possible Vauxhall Corsas to the satisfaction of the CPS. The team settled down to completing outstanding statements, fine-tuning and honing the rest of the evidence as best they could, but there was little in the way of new breakthroughs. I embarked upon my third read-through of all the documents – no small job since there were more than 60,000 of them. Once we had served our case on the defence, we would have to complete the formal disclosure of all this mountain of paperwork, the statutory process of assessing each document that we did not plan to use, as to whether its contents could undermine the prosecution case or assist the defence. Not that we knew what the defence was likely to be.

The trial had been set for March 2007. Notwithstanding this

apparently distant date, the sheer amount of work meant we would have to work fast. I calculated, roughly, that we would have to process 300 documents every working day for 3 months to complete it, given that our other investigations and on-call weeks would eat in to the time available. While, normally, disclosure would be completed by one or two officers, I needed more. I made a successful case for every officer below Inspector rank to be trained to carry out this dull but crucial task and, exceptionally, received an extra overtime grant of £20,000 to be spent on it. Which we used, although it was impossible to ask the team to spend more than nine or ten hours per day doing disclosure – there is a limit to how long you can ask somebody to sit at a computer and maintain the level of concentration needed. We completed disclosure in time and it was yet another example of the wholehearted dedication my officers showed in their determination to do a proper job.

One decision made with the lawyers did remove a large piece of work from the team. A serving prisoner, whom I shall call Kevin, had written to us, claiming that Bellfield had, while on remand at Woodhill Prison, admitted to him that he had killed Amélie and Marsha, and insinuated that he had also killed Milly. At first blush, this was, of course, exciting – it was the first (and, indeed, would be the only) occasion where Bellfield had given even the slightest inkling of admitting what he had done. However, these cell confessions always come with huge and serious caveats. Essentially, my rule of thumb had always been to use them evidentially only in cases where you really had to. While it is, of course, possible for a convicted criminal to tell the truth – and it is relatively common for career thieves and robbers who have every reason to hate the police nevertheless to be willing to give evidence against sex offenders – they will always be challenged as to their veracity by the defence in a trial. It can be extremely challenging to present a man as a witness of truth when the jury are read a long list of his previous convictions for dishonesty.

Kevin presented such a dilemma. In his late forties, his life had consisted of a succession of spells of imprisonment for theft, burglary and drugs offences, punctuated by odd weeks – or, quite rarely, months – of freedom before being caught again. He was an engaging, animated man who had led a wholly dishonest but ultimately very interesting life. When I went to meet him after his release, it was on a beautiful spring day in the garden of an idyllic country cottage he was renting with his girlfriend, who just happened to be the prison drugs counsellor he had been supported by while serving his most recent sentence. Not that his idyll lasted; almost inevitably, he was caught burgling a neighbour shortly afterwards and found himself back behind bars.

What he told us was convincing, not only in its substance but also in that the words and underlying attitude of the conversations he reported sounded exactly like Bellfield. We had been (openly and quite lawfully) monitoring all Bellfield's phone calls out from prison from the day he was first remanded and, by now, we had a very good feel for his phraseology and tone. Most telling was that Bellfield had told Kevin of his fears that we would discover the Corsa he used during Marsha's murder, but this was before we had gone public with it and before we had put it to Bellfield in interview. So neither Kevin nor Bellfield could have learned about it elsewhere and added it to the story. However, when we started to look more closely at Kevin's background, not only did we find an atrocious history of crime but also that he had been confessed to in prison by murderers on no fewer than four previous occasions. While there was no suggestion that any of these were anything other than true, it presented yet another line for the defence to attack – was this a man who deliberately sought confessions from fellow inmates in order to gain favours during his sentence?

Once the defence knew that we had Kevin's statement, they asked for full disclosure of all of Kevin's contacts with the authorities since the age of twelve. Which consisted of thousands of social-worker, probation-officer, medical, police and prison reports. We drew his prison file to assess the magnitude of responding to the request. Flicking through it, there was an ironically hilarious moment when I found a certificate, presented to him while an inmate at HMP Bedford, for taking a course in 'Listening Skills'. I would imagine he had passed with distinction. Before we embarked upon the gargantuan task, I needed to be absolutely sure that we wanted to use his evidence. I had an informal conference with Brian Altman. We had both been uncertain as to whether Kevin would help or hinder the case; I was most relieved when we agreed that the risk outweighed the possible benefits. Altman thought that we had enough without him, that the sniff of desperation arising from his use would taint our case and that the lengthy challenges to him from the defence would only confuse the jury and weaken our overall case in their eyes. And besides, we didn't actually need to use him. I was very grateful this was the outcome, even more so because of the reduction in demand on my hard-pressed team it resulted in.

Mine was not the only team which was hard-pressed. The defence had suddenly realised that there was an awful lot of material to get their head around too. So much so that they found from somewhere a small army of trainee solicitors who were to descend upon us in Putney to go through the unused material. They were not allowed access to the HOLMES system but instead had to read through hard-printed copies and so it was more practical, given the mass of lever-arch files they consisted of, for them to come to us. I arranged for the conference area in our office to be available to them and deputed a completely reliable, unflappable and sharp officer, DC Jayne Farnworth, to be their liaison. On the appointed day, eight or so bright young men and women, each with a shiny new MacBook, turned up, were given visitors passes, shown the toilets, the fire exits and the canteen and then set loose on our paperwork. They asked Jayne for a document and she went and got it for them, then another, then another. This went on for a couple of days then, one evening, Jayne came to ask my advice after the lawyers had all gone home.

'Sir, I'm not sure what I should do. Different ones of them keep asking for the same document. Four of them have separately asked for the same thing today. I didn't say anything but do you think I ought to?'

I thought about it for a moment and said, with a smile, 'No, I think it would be very wrong for us to interfere in how they are doing their job. All we do is facilitate what they want. If they keep asking for the same document, just say "OK" and get it for them.'

I went on to draw an analogy for Jayne. It was like when a team of police officers are searching a house – if there is no structure, no plan and, crucially, no control, it is very likely the search will be incomplete; the bookcase gets searched three times by different officers but nobody looks in the cupboard under the stairs. What was happening here was very similar. It seemed the defence team had panicked at the scale of what they had to do and put together a team with no plan, no structure and no leader. Ultimately, it would make no difference; we really did not uncover any piece of evidence that remotely exonerated Bellfield or which undermined our case so there was nothing for them to find. And while I could have offered advice to the defence as to how they could have completed their task much more efficiently, it certainly wasn't my place to do so. I had worked out the best way for my team to work but I was under no duty and had no reason to try to do the same for them.

Knowing that the trial was likely to last at least five months, I realised my summer was going to be completely filled up, so I took a break in the Canary Islands in February, a last battery recharge before the impending battle. I was lounging by the pool enjoying remarkably warm February sunshine when the phone rang, Jo Brunt being the caller name on the display.

'You're not gonna believe this . . .'

Which were precisely the words I didn't want to hear interrupting my relaxation.

'. . . the defence have listed the case for tomorrow to go back to the judge and apply to have the trial put back for six months. Apparently, there is more for them to read than they had imagined and they are not ready.'

Immediately, I knew that it would be pointless to oppose their application. No judge in the country would force a defendant to go ahead with a trial if his legal team was, due to the volume of material, not ready to proceed. Despite that, we had moved heaven and earth to make sure we kept our side of the case on schedule. They would be given the time. Summer was reinstated; the trial would begin on Monday, 1 October.

Before that, though, we had a handful of court appearances to settle pre-trial matters. It was during these that we first appeared before the judge who would preside over the trial, Mrs Justice Rafferty. In these preliminary hearings, she made two notable decisions: one which was undeniably crucial to our case and one which we hoped would not diminish it too much. In our favour, she agreed that the cases on the indictment were capable of cross-admissibility – that is that the jury would be permitted to consider evidence in any of the other cases when deciding upon another. So the evidence in the strongest case (Amélie's) could be considered as making Bellfield more or less likely to have murdered Marsha or attempted to murder Kate. And, of course, the evidence of assaults at bus stops in Anna-Maria and Irma's cases could legitimately influence their thinking on the more serious counts. This was vital to the prosecution; indeed, the decision to charge Marsha and Kate's offences was made on the basis that this cross-admissibility would be allowed. It was, of course, rigorously opposed by William Boyce, QC, for Bellfield, but the decision in our favour, which the lawyers had assured me was the correct outcome, was most welcome.

Where the learned judge found against us was the question of admissibility of the evidence from the two young girls accosted by Bellfield at a bus stop in Uxbridge while he was under surveillance. To me, this was a powerful piece of evidence, showing not only Bellfield's preparedness to make sexual advances against strangers in the street but also reinforcing his use of bus stops as his hunting ground. It was likely to have a strong impact on the jury and, of course, the defence knew this, which is why they argued it should be excluded – on the grounds that what Bellfield was doing on that occasion was very different to the blitz attacks and, therefore, the prejudice to him outweighed the probative value of the girls' statements. They had a point; if we had been able to prove that the blitz attacks followed from a rebuff from a sexual approach, perhaps the connection would have been firmer and the evidence allowed. As it was, while we suspected that to be so and it could be inferred from the timing and pace of Amélie's walk, we could not be conclusive. The judge erred on the side of caution, sensibly, I suppose, trying to make sure any subsequent conviction was 'appeal proof' but, at the time, I was bitterly disappointed and fearful that it might diminish our chances of success.

My mood was lightened almost immediately, however, by an amusing encounter outside the Old Bailey. As I exited the building, I saw a barrister who had previously been involved in prosecuting one of my cases, leaning against the wall casually smoking a cigarette. I went to join him and, his knowing about the Bellfield case and who was trying it, he asked me, 'How are you finding Mrs Justice Rafferty?'

'She seems very switched-on and fair-minded,' was my deliberately uncontroversial reply.

He then went on: 'You do realise there are members of the

Criminal Bar who like to call her the JILF, don't you? Standing for 'Judge I'd Like to F—'

I cut him short just before he uttered the final word. 'Yes, yes, I can guess what it means. I don't suppose there are many on the bench you can say that about.'

He replied in a heavily exaggerated, camp tone, 'That, my friend, depends entirely on your point of view!', smiling through a cloud of cigarette smoke as I suddenly remembered that he was gay, and we both roared with laughter.

CHAPTER TWENTY-SIX

THE CASE FOR THE CROWN BEGINS

The letter 'P', or more accurately, a number of letter 'P's, have a special place in Metropolitan Police wisdom and lore. As recruits, we were enjoined to beware of the 'three Ps' – Prisoners, Property and Prostitutes – as these were the dangerous things likely to bring trouble for a young officer. Later, and for those in positions of leadership, it became essential to remember the 'six Ps' – 'Prior Preparation Prevents Piss Poor Performance'. As 1 October 1 2007 dawned, I was running over our preparation, hoping I had thought of everything but expecting that the coming months would throw up a curve ball or three. We had a van full of exhibits and a room at the Old Bailey in which to store them. With very rickety shelving, as we were to find out later when what was first thought to be a peal of thunder turned out to be the whole lot collapsing under the strain of 65,000 documents and hundreds of DVDs of CCTV recordings. We had a dedicated phone line back to the incident room and a rota for staffing it, so that any emergencies could be quickly dealt with. We had two laptops, the second begged from somewhere, with the entire HOLMES account loaded on to each, enabling us to follow statements and find documents quickly in the court room. Monitors and players for CCTV viewing were being set up in Court number six, not the famed number one with its historic decorations but one of the larger, modern rooms with sufficient space for us, the defence, all the victims and families and the hordes of press who were to follow the case every day. All the practical things had been sorted. All we needed was a full set of judge and lawyers, for which we were going to have to wait until the next day.

The trial proper opened on 2 October 2007 at 10.35am. Brian Altman was the first to speak. The first task was to select a jury but William Boyce, QC, rose to make the first of his many submissions for the defence. It concerned reporting restrictions, ostensibly to prevent the facts around the rape and assault charges on former partners being leaked to the jury but its real purpose was something we were all frightened of – that the speculation about Bellfield's involvement in Milly Dowler's murder might somehow find its way to a juror and, hence, prejudice them irretrievably. Mrs Justice Rafferty remarked that Mr Boyce was asking for 'pretty Draconian stuff' but, eventually, a form of words was agreed to protect the jury from bias while still allowing proper reporting of proceedings. The order did maintain the ban on publishing Bellfield's photograph; I am still convinced this was much more due to his vanity and unwillingness to be on the front pages than it was to protect any question of the integrity of evidence of identification, of which there was really very little in our case. Boyce then suggested that, as he was intending to revisit the question of cross-admissibility, it might be better to warn the jurors that they were unlikely to be required for the first two weeks. Two weeks? We were looking at legal arguments before the start lasting longer than many entire murder trials. It was clear this was going to be a trial the like of which I had never seen before.

Jury selection was to begin at 11.30am, once the questions to be put to them before they were considered had been agreed. This, too, was aimed at preventing anyone with knowledge of Bellfield's Milly Dowler connection being on the jury. It was clear that the defence were petrified that association with this high-profile case would be fatal to their chances. The questions were framed so that you would be disqualified from the jury if (and there is no shorthand way for me to describe these conditions) you or your parent, child, spouse, partner or sibling were currently, or had been at any time since 2000, resident in the London Boroughs of Richmond, Hounslow or Hillingdon, or in Surrey or Middlesex. Or if you or any of them had ever worked for the Metropolitan Police or Surrey Police. Or if you knew Bellfield or any of his victims. Bearing in mind that the aim was to select twelve good people and true, these stringent conditions were feared to be capable of disbarring so many that a pool of seventy-two people was assembled. Of these, forty-eight were rejected, leaving twenty-four to be empanelled, the group from which the actual twelve would be randomly selected. They were then, at 12.35pm, sent away for two weeks so that the legal arguments could proceed in their absence. So two hours into the 'trial', we had achieved almost precisely nothing . . .

We actually got back before the judge ten days later. She lifted the reporting restrictions on this trial but the prohibition on photographs and reference to the other indictment remained banned and, after a few other esoteric legal points were discussed, at 10.40pm, the potential jury members were summoned. I dwell on jury selection because it illustrates a point which, possibly inevitably, skews the composition of the jury in long trials. Aside from the requirements peculiar to this case, the jurors-in-waiting were, as is usual, told that the case was likely to last upwards of four months. They were, therefore, invited to speak privately with the judge when called forward if they had any special personal circumstances which meant that such a long commitment would cause them real difficulties. Although the factors that would work to excuse them were not put to them openly, presumably for fear of giving them ideas of excuses to invent, the sort of circumstances that would see them relieved of the duty were:

- Holidays booked
- Hospital or similar medical appointments
- Examinations to be taken
- Being a full-time carer for a dependant person
- Being self-employed or running a small business with few employees

Which, of course, is a pretty all-encompassing list. There are not many people, perhaps, who, over a period of four or five months, could not claim that one of those things applied to them. The result of this policy – which I accept is practised for very good reasons so as not to intrude on jurors' ordinary lives – is that students, business people, carers, those who book holidays and those awaiting operations are usually excluded. This means juries in long trials often consist largely of the retired and the unemployed and means the variety in composition that is desirable and often assumed, is absent. That said, by 11pm that day, we had a jury sworn – five men and seven women who, despite the apparent difficulty in passing the eligibility test, had the outward appearance of being a fairly mixed and sensible bunch.

Brian Altman began the opening of the case, a run-through for the jury of the evidence the prosecution would be calling and how it was believed to fit together to prove the case. He started with these words, succinct and leaving the jurors not the tiniest doubt of what the allegations were:

> Between October 2001 and August 2004, five women, four of them young women aged between seventeen and twenty-two, were violently attacked. Two of these young women were brutally murdered by being battered about the head with a blunt instrument. One young woman survived the horrific attack on her when she was driven at and run over. One other woman suffered a nasty injury when she was struck on the head. Another young woman escaped the attack upon her without injury. The prosecution say that this defendant – Levi Bellfield – was the attacker in each case.

The opening continued with the evidence to be called being outlined for three days, relief coming only for a few submissions made by Boyce on behalf of Bellfield, mostly complaining about his treatment in prison – a 'physically disgusting cell' (at which Jo Brunt whispered to me, 'How appropriate for him'), having to get up too early and threats from other prisoners. The judge said she would speak to the governor but whether she did or, indeed, if it made any difference, we never knew. By the end of the week, it was agreed that, henceforth, the court would sit during 'Maxwell Hours', so named after the practice was introduced during the lengthy fraud trial involving Robert Maxwell's sons, Kevin and Ian, in 1996. Aimed at allowing jurors to maintain more of their normal lives, it meant we would start each day at 9.30am and, instead of an hour for lunch, we would have a twenty-minute coffee break after about two hours, sitting then again and finishing the day before 2pm. Which was fine for everybody, we thought. In practice, it meant that, after a quick conference with the lawyers after the court rose, the daily debrief for police tended to be held in the beer garden at Ye Old London pub on Ludgate Hill, where the patio heaters kept everyone happy while the smokers could feed their habit. So the days for us seemed to be longer, not shorter than they would have been had we kept more usual court hours. It was fun, I cannot deny, but it was by no means the most healthy – or cheap – period of my life.

After the two days of scene visits – which presented a difficult security demand on the local police, as Bellfield naturally exercised his right to attend – with the jury on a coach, the judge in a Mercedes and the rest of us tagging along, Brian Altman finished his opening speech and began to call the prosecution evidence at 10am on 19 October 2007, nearly three weeks after the trial had officially commenced. 'No wonder it is going to last for five months,' I thought. Anna-Maria Rennie was the first witness and, although Bellfield was denying being anywhere near the crime, it did not prevent his counsel attacking the veracity of the witnesses, alleging that she had only reported the matter to deflect police from the controlled drugs in her flat and suggesting that what had happened was 'merely horseplay'. A belt-and-braces approach with which we were to become familiar – I wasn't there; if I was, I didn't do anything and, additionally, it probably never happened. Oh, and let's try to discredit the police while we are at it, too – wild and absurd allegations that we fixed the positive identification of Bellfield as the abductor were thrown into the mix; I never understood on what these claims were based.

It was another six days before we began the case relating to Marsha's murder, punctuated at the end of the day by an application by a barrister on behalf of News International for the release of Bellfield's image in the media to be sanctioned. Once again, he opposed this and, once again, the judge erred on the side of caution and upheld her previous ruling. Bellfield was so scared about his photograph being released but it really had little, if any, bearing on the cases we were prosecuting. I am sure it was much more about image and pride to him – he simply didn't want those who knew him by sight but not by name to be aware of his predicament; like so much we had discovered about him, his ego seemed, again, to be his motivation. Or perhaps he was worried others would recognise him as the man who, using one of his many aliases, had assaulted them? And then, for various administrative reasons, the court did not sit for four days. How slowly grind the wheels of justice.

CHAPTER TWENTY-SEVEN

THE CASE UNFOLDS

When we did reconvene, Bellfield's attack on the interpretation of the CCTV from Marsha's bus became apparent. The main suggestion was that, when the Corsa slowed and pulled into the junction as Marsha turned towards her home, it was probably just slowing to turn left. Of course, we could not counter this suggestion from the footage, since the bus had pulled away and the view was lost. But we did have a scale plan of the distances and timings from the CCTV recording, so I furiously began calculations, and checked and rechecked them before passing the result to junior counsel Mark Heywood on a Post-it note. The car had been travelling, as it passed the bus, at an average speed of 9.375 mph. Which was useful not only to counter the argument (for a car travelling so slowly would surely have had no need to brake to make the turn) but also in suggesting that Bellfield was deliberately cruising past the bus at a crawl so that he could look inside for a victim. It was a useful piece of information and, frankly, one which we should have thought of earlier.

William Boyce, QC, then suggested that the traffic conditions were such that the speed was appropriate. It seemed he was making a case that the defendant was driving carefully at the time, while still maintaining that it was not the defendant at all. Cake and eating it sprung once more to mind. There followed our expert evidence regarding the partial view of the registration number of the Corsa and their interpretation of the possibilities. The jury actually got to see the CCTV, in evidence, on 5 November. Two days were spent hearing evidence of the identification of Bellfield's Corsa from it and then, once the jury had gone home for the day, William Boyce engaged on the first of what were to be frequent complaints to the judge about coverage of the case in the press, usually but not exclusively written by Mike Sullivan in the *Sun*. Bellfield's ego, again, would not allow him to let any criticism pass without protest.

By 9 November, we had moved on to Irma Dragoshi's case. A couple of days in, it was her turn to give evidence. She had asked for 'special measures' – the technical term for a witness being allowed to give evidence from behind screens so that the sight of the defendant would not cause discomfort or intimidation. Bellfield, being obstructive as usual, requested his lawyers to oppose this application. When the judge, predictably, agreed to them, the true motivation for Bellfield became apparent, for his counsel then conceded that Irma's statement could be read, that she would not have to give live evidence and, by implication, that they did not challenge any part of it. So it was clear that the opposition to screens was simply a tactic to make things difficult – frightening even – for her. Once that opportunity was denied him, he was happy to have her evidence admitted unchallenged, so it was all about intimidation. However, she was happy to give her evidence if protected by screens, so the prosecution made the tactical decision to call her anyway. The tables had been turned. Bellfield was furious and asked his lawyers to oppose the screens again, to no avail. There is no doubt that, as helpful as screens may be for a timid witness, there is a degree of prejudice in their use – why would they be necessary if the defendant were neither violent nor intimidating? This prejudice explains the caution as to their use, and why permission is needed from the judge. When Mr Boyce started to go through medical reports line by line, I noted, 'Starting to realise that, if WB continues to be so long-winded, we'll be lucky to finish by Christmas '08, let alone '07.'

It made me look back to recall a quote from him during an application at the start of the trial when he said, 'I have a proclivity for traipsing through bogs, usually with reluctant followers.'

This particular excursion was such as to motivate Brian Altman to a rare intervention and objection, to which the judge acceded, and our mystifying journey through pages of medical prose was curtailed. The next witness was Sunil Gharu, Bellfield's friend, who was in the car with him on the day he attacked Irma Dragoshi and so was to give our most vital evidence on that count. After the morning break, Sunil complained that, during his ninety-minute stint in the witness box, he had been subjected to aggressive stares from people in the public gallery – people we knew to be Bellfield's family and friends. The judge assured Sunil she would watch for it;

of course the jury were not present to hear this first of many complaints of intimidation in the court room.

It was 21 November before we started the Kate Sheedy evidence. Bellfield had been ill for a couple of days and then, when we knew he was improved and the court was going to sit, a new challenge presented itself. Media interest in Kate was high; she was the victim who had had a miraculous escape. DCs Gary Cunningham and Helen Rance were looking after her and her family, so we discussed the possibilities. It was relatively easy for us to smuggle her in to court and avoid the reporters, but my fear was that this would merely postpone the problem. And not just to another time but also, very probably, to another place. If we were to avoid the circus troubling her at home, might it be better to give the media one chance? We agreed with Kate and her mother that they would, with the two Family Liaison Officers, make a very public entrance through the front door just once. The press could get their photos and, most importantly, I would make sure, through our media office, that they were aware this opportunity was made available on the condition that they did not trouble the family further. By and large, it succeeded and the journalists kept their word; it was, though, an almighty scrummage outside the Old Bailey that day – an unnerving experience, which the immaculate Kate dealt with in her usual calm, mature and composed manner.

Before the evidence began, we became aware that more smokescreens were to be generated by the defence; we heard questions about two mystery people-carriers, probably mini-cabs, seen outside the Sorting Rooms pub before Kate left it. However, we were to have to wait a few more days for it to unfold as Bellfield claimed a relapse and we were all sent away for a week. Kate gave her evidence-in-chief bravely and then, when cross-examined, it became clear the defence were keeping their options as regards it having been an accident open. Kate's memorable reply to Mr Boyce, when questioned as to why she believed it was a deliberate act, was typically courageous: 'It drove over me twice – I think that's quite enough!'

She was rightly equally dismissive of Mr Boyce's suggestion that her memory of the 'M' or 'N' in the registration number of the vehicle that had mown her down had come to her in a dream. My note after this reads simply, 'Shameful'. As it was.

Kate was unable to bear her ordeal completely unscathed; on two occasions, it all became too much and she wept. Mostly, though, she coped admirably as ridiculous suggestions were made. Especially notable was the notion that the driver had got out of the car to see if she was all right. Again, the defence was hedging its bets – I wasn't there but, if you think I was, it was an accident and I got out to look after her. The basis for this was from what Kate had said during her (recorded) 999 call just after the attack. She had said, 'He stopped . . . to check me out.'

We had always known this was clearly a reference to the car having stopped and watched her walk by before the attack – a meaning confirmed by Kate herself. But the operator at the London Ambulance Control had interpreted it as the driver getting out to look at her and had noted the message to this effect. Of course, Bellfield's preference was to read this simple phrase uttered by a girl clinging to life after a murderous attack in the same way as the ambulance staff. The suggestion was that the driver, so concerned, had left the car to check her condition.

It was as ridiculous as it was desperate and was dealt with conclusively by Kate's firm, eloquent and consistent stating of what she had seen happen.

Her long occupation of the witness box finally ended after more than four hours. We had a few more live and read witnesses, then a moment of some relief from the harrowing events as the *Sun*'s Mike Sullivan was called upon by the judge to explain his piece the previous day, which once again had made Bellfield angry. Sullivan, being more than a hundred miles away, was represented again by counsel for News International, who explained that the headline I WAS RUN OVER TWICE BY BUS-STOP KILLER was not his own work but added to the piece he had written by sub-editors before publication. The piece, he went on, made it clear that they were allegations, which the defendant denied. The judge accepted the apology but did remark that it was the second time the *Sun* had been complained of to her, and she added, to her strict admonishment, that she did not expect there to be a third occasion.

There followed witnesses giving evidence of the CCTV from the County Arms and of Bellfield having been in possession of – and frequently using – the Toyota Previa around the time of Kate's attack. Mr Boyce objected to evidence about the petrol stain on its rear wing, claiming it could not be certain if the smudge on the CCTV pictures was the stain clearly visible in the photographs of the car after it had been seized. The judge ruled it was a matter for the jury to decide.

It was December before we began with Amélie's case. Her parents, though, had been at the trial from the very start. Work was not really an issue for them, as Jean-François had suffered a heart attack shortly after Amélie's death and Dominique, too, had ceased to work. They were staying in a Travelodge in Brentford, the Met eventually picking up the bill on my insistence. It wasn't so much that there was no will to pay – everybody wanted to do as much for these dignified and desolate people as we could. As with many things in the modern police service, it was the bureaucracy. Nobody could, at first, work out which budget the cost ought to come from so there was a reluctance to authorise it until there was an identified person to charge it to. I didn't get involved in the discussions beyond saying that it simply had to happen – and, of course, it eventually did.

Not that the Delagranges' time in London went without hitch. Of course, their very presence in court gave Bellfield a target for his ire and he tried his hardest to make them feel uncomfortable with frequent stares and the occasional outburst of a stage-whispered 'Scum' or 'Vermin'. Always, naturally, when the judge and the jury were safely out of earshot. There was absolutely nothing we could do about it other than protest to his legal team but they, too, were effectively powerless. The danger everyone wanted to avoid was provoking him into a public outburst, which could have resulted in a retrial being ordered. Dominique also suffered a nasty eye infection while she was in London and DC Gary Fuller, their Family Liaison Officer, smoothed the path to a quick resolution – the wonderful staff at Moorfields hospital were only too pleased to help.

Fuller also suggested to me that we should take the Delagranges out for dinner one night; he had noticed that Arthur's bistro, in the former lavatories on Twickenham Green, was holding a Beaujolais Nouveau night. Since this had a French theme and the Delagranges were familiar with the restaurant, it would be a nice idea. I agreed, and so Louise and I went to meet them all there. When we arrived, we found Gary Fuller and DC Jean-Marc Papworth, the interpreter – but no Delagranges. Fuller told me that they had asked that they be allowed, for once, to make their own way, on the bus. I wasn't entirely happy with this; when they appeared almost an hour late, I was sure it had been a bad idea. Yes, they had missed the stop and sailed past us, all the way to 'Ammer-smeeeth', as Jean-François put it. As the irony of their making such a similar mistake to that which had proved so disastrous for their daughter struck us all, I glared at the two detectives as if to say that they should, under no circumstances, mention it. The awkwardness was then heightened several levels as a large party of locals arrived for the evening, the men all resplendent in striped jerseys, berets and with onion-strings about their necks. This was all rapidly going downhill towards what might be the world's worst family-liaison disaster. Thankfully, Dominique went over and managed to express how nice it was to see people dressing up so well, Edith Piaff was put on the vintage record player, excellent food was put out and we had a very pleasant evening.

Much of the early evidence in Amélie's murder was technical, setting the scene, producing CCTV, her background – essential but fairly uncontroversial. Simon Redston, the man on the bike who saw the van drive past at 'crazy speed', was an excellent witness and his testimony was, perhaps, the start of thinking that it sounded like we had a case. As Bellfield's partner, Emma Mills, was lined up as the next witness, we all felt that it was about to get very real. Boyce, as might be expected, opposed special measures, stating that it would be 'particularly prejudicial for a female ex-partner to have screens'.

He also opposed Emma giving evidence of Bellfield's mental-health problems, specifically his admission to hospital and a phone call threatening suicide, which she said took place soon after Amélie's murder, as well as details of his panic attacks beginning in 1999 and getting worse over time. The judge said she was against Mr Boyce on the latter points, even without bothering the prosecution for their arguments. With regard to the screens, she wanted to hear evidence of Emma's story from DC Debbie Ford, who had become Emma's *de facto* liaison officer. Debbie took the witness stand and outlined the terrible catalogue of physical and mental abuse Emma had suffered and, unsurprisingly, the screens were allowed.

It took Emma seven minutes from first entering the court room before she had regained sufficient composure to answer questions. It was clear to everyone that this slight, timid and articulate young woman was finding it an immense strain to tell the world about how the man she had once loved, who had fathered her three children, had made her life an abject misery. She broke out in tears a number of times, first when thinking about the family holiday to Tenerife in 2003 in the wake of the Marsha McDonnell murder and again when Bellfield laughed loudly from the dock as she identified him driving the Courier van in Twickenham, from a bus-lane photograph just two days before he attacked Amélie. He obviously still knew how to get to her. She did, however, confirm the crucial evidence from the evening just prior to Amélie being attacked – the trip to Tesco, the till receipt, his calls and his driving the Courier van and, finally, her calling him at 9.38pm. Despite the difficulties, the fear and his best attempts at intimidation, Emma's courage won through and she delivered.

Experts in videography then gave their conclusive proof that the van in all the various CCTV recordings around Twickenham Green was, indeed, Bellfield's Ford Courier. There was quite a lot of rather turgid and technical detail in this evidence and, when Mr Boyce came to cross-examine the expert witness, Dr Bowie, it became difficult for any of us to follow. The judge intervened, enjoining the defence leader to 'maintain control and direction' and to 'reduce your scattergun approach to cross-examination'. As that cross-examination proceeded, it became clear that Bowie was fully in control of his evidence and the suggestions being put by the defence became increasingly desperate. DS Malcolm Hudson, who had overseen most of the expert work on the CCTV, was sitting next to me and whispered in my ear, 'Bowie's kicking Boyce to death here.'

An unfortunate choice of phrase given the context but no less true for that. Brian Altman, once the jury had been sent out for the day, protested to the judge that the questioning was a little too robust. The judge showed partial agreement by asking, 'Mr Boyce, where exactly *are* we going with this?' but my view was firmly that Dr Bowie needed no such protection. He was clearly a man with absolute confidence in his expertise and ability to express his findings, and nothing was going to shake him.

I passed a note to Altman at the end of the day too. DC Paul Carruth, the exhibits officer, had sidled up to me in a break, saying, 'Hey, Guv'nor, you need to watch that fat bastard. He's looking over your shoulder all the time, reading everything you have on your laptop.'

I was sitting in the back row of benches and so Bellfield in the dock was, indeed, just three feet behind me, slightly raised from me in the dock and separated only by the thick panes of security glass. This meant that he was in the perfect position to shoulder-surf me. However, as the laptop was not connected to any network, it was simply statements and reports he could read, all of which had already been served on the defence and to which he had had access for several months. Anything confidential, like emails and text messages, were on my Blackberry and I was very careful to ensure he could not overlook that. Nevertheless, I knew I did not want Bellfield to think he was getting the better of me so, as well as informing Brian Altman, I jotted in the margin of my notebook, 'Resolve to have some more interesting viewing for him tomorrow.'

Which I did. That night at home, I created a short Powerpoint presentation of full-screen photographs. I chose the best pictures I could find, of Amélie, Marsha, Kate and Milly Dowler. Pictures which showed them for the happy, beautiful, carefree young girls they were before he had interfered in their lives. I set it to loop and, once the court started sitting the next day, left it running on my laptop. I was careful that it was visible only to him in the dock behind me and waited. Of course, I knew it would antagonise him, enough for him to complain about it, which he did, both to his lawyers and, later on the phone from prison, to his family. But I also knew that the response had to be that I was entitled to have whatever I liked on my computer and that, when all was said and done, he ought not to be looking at it anyway. Some might think that was petty of me; I might agree to a degree. But it was much more important for me to make sure he knew that I would not let him take liberties with no response.

CHAPTER TWENTY-EIGHT

THE PROSECUTION CLOSES

There then came a succession of witnesses giving evidence about Bellfield and events, as opposed to experts and technicians. The first was Richard Hughes. Known as 'Yosser' after the much-loved TV character, he was best described as a friend of Bellfield and Emma Mills. Older than both, he was almost a father figure, or at least saw himself as such. He took great pains to try to protect Emma from the worst excesses of Bellfield's chaotic lifestyle and this meant, inevitably, that Bellfield frequently exploited him. However, it was fortunate for us that, not only did Bellfield confide in Hughes in times of crisis but Hughes was willing to talk about it, giving a detailed account of Bellfield's mental issues after he had killed Amélie, most tellingly that on the way to Hillingdon hospital, when the defendant had told him, 'You don't know what I'm capable of!'

Like Emma Mills, Hughes clearly made a huge impact on the

jury. Two ordinary, scared people with no axe to grind, telling the truth because they knew it was the right thing to do.

Mark Petony was called to give evidence of Bellfield using a hammer as a weapon on an unknown occasion, which was probably the attack on Peter Rodrigues. Cue another defence application, on the grounds that this would be prejudicial and was not directly related to the charges being heard. An application that was denied, but not before the judge had pointed out to Mr Boyce the fact he had himself already introduced to Rodrigues's attack in his cross-examination of both Emma Mills and Sunil Gharu. It did, though, pave the way for a serious application on 18 December. After the jury had been dismissed for the day, we were told to reconvene at 2pm for an application from the defence to discharge the jury and order a retrial. This caused consternation, some amongst my team but more amongst the Delagranges and other families. Was there really a chance we would have to start all over again?

Mr Boyce's submission was that there had been a 'highly prejudicial combination of evidence before the jury, which cannot lead to a fair trial'. His argument was that the evidence from Petony and Hughes, when taken together, put the jury in the position of knowing that Bellfield had committed a hammer attack and having to decide whether they were referring to the attack on Peter Rodrigues or on Amélie. He suggested there had been '. . . a consistent push by the Crown, against wise counsel, to lead the Peter Rodrigues evidence [. . .] the defence submit this was a disaster waiting to happen.'

Essentially, the argument was that the prosecution had carelessly or deliberately made sure the details of a similar attack, which was not on the indictment, had been leaked to the jury so as to influence their decision on the cases that had been charged. Strong stuff – and the sort of error or underhand practice that, in truth, we all knew would be the last thing a meticulous and thorough advocate like Brian Altman would entertain.

Altman responded that Boyce had first mentioned the Rodrigues assault on 16 November when he had asked Sunil Gharu if he had 'grassed Bellfield up' for it. He had then also cross-examined Emma Mills on Rodrigues. Boyce countered by suggesting that the Crown make an 'admission' (that is, agree something that the jury can take as fact without hearing evidence) to the effect that Bellfield was not guilty of attacking Rodrigues, which drew a sharp 'Of course *not*' from Altman. Altman continued that the Rodrigues attack was no part of the prosecution case, that it would not be put to Bellfield if he were to give evidence and so it would have no bearing on the jury's deliberations. The judge agreed that she would be careful to direct the jury around this point and that, to our immense relief, the trial could continue.

After Christmas and into 2008, we were still going through the prosecution case. A number of uncontroversial statements from minor witnesses were read to the court, then Mr Boyce asked for DC Neil Jones, the principal CCTV officer in the case, to be recalled in order to question him about the white van in a particular piece of footage. It seemed that the object of this was to determine whether or not the van had stopped at a certain point. It was pretty obvious that the footage was not good enough to prove this point of minor importance one way or the other but, nevertheless, Mr Boyce encountered some difficulty in making

Neil understand exactly what the question was. This happens sometimes when two people with different views of the same incident cannot see what the other is driving at. On this occasion, it did lead to a rather amusing exchange when the judge intervened.

Judge: 'Can you not make this point more simply?'

Mr Boyce: 'I obviously lack the necessary skills . . .'

Judge (to DC Jones): 'Can you see the white van?'

DC Jones: 'No.'

Judge (to Mr Boyce): 'There you are.'

The final act of the prosecution case concerned the elimination of the other 'possibles' for the Corsa on the bus CCTV from Marsha's murder. The defence made the (pretty reasonable) point that, if the actual murderer were one of the other Corsa drivers, he or she would be unlikely to have told us so when we made the inquiries. Of course, there was little else we could have done – we had the list of cars, traced the drivers and asked them if it could have been them in the CCTV. Although we didn't tell them what it was about, if they had been there, they would have known and presumably denied it. I had considered this and concluded that there simply was no other way; no way in which we could take the inquiries further. The defence suggested that, perhaps, we ought to call every Corsa owner or driver who had given us a statement to give live evidence, so that they could be cross-examined and challenged. The judge looked horrified and said that her case-management powers would be used. 'Three hundred and twenty-four people will *not* be paraded before this jury,' she said sharply.

Mr Boyce combined this application with one that there was 'no case to answer' – that is that, if all the prosecution evidence were accepted as true, it still would not convict the defendant. We were confident that both these would fail, as they, in the event, did. So the Corsa statements were read, Clive Grace gave the evidence of how he had eliminated so many with his usual efficiency and clarity and, at 11.40am on 15 January 2008, Brian Altman uttered the words we had been waiting three and a half months to hear: 'That, m'Lady, is the case for the Crown.'

It was now Bellfield's turn.

CHAPTER TWENTY-NINE

'I CALL THE DEFENDANT'

Defendants in English courts are not bound to give evidence in their trial. It is for the prosecution to prove the case; the defendant has to prove nothing. Many notorious criminals have chosen to remain silent at court and we had speculated for some time as to whether Bellfield would join their ranks. My feeling was that he would give evidence. Despite the gravity of what he faced, despite his spending more than three years on remand, despite the weight of the evidence we had uncovered against him, I thought his ego would, as usual, win out. He had spent his adult life talking his way out of trouble, charming and convincing others that he was innocent, the victim, or just plain unlucky. His wit and cunning had always worked for him in the past; why would it not work this time? I knew he had underestimated both my team and our legal team and felt sure he would back himself to beat us here. Mr Boyce confirmed my hunch just one minute after our case had ended when, turning from the judge towards the dock at the rear of the court, he said, 'I call the defendant.'

There was a buzz of whispering from the public gallery and a polite stampede of reporters across the back of the court towards the press box, which quickly became full. Bellfield had, for his big day, ditched his customary golf-club chic attire of open-necked shirt and a Pringle sweater; today, he was clad in a grey suit with a white shirt and a rather insipid pastel-pink tie. It was almost as if he had been briefed to make sure he looked nothing like a bouncer. He certainly did not – more like a salesman or estate agent. Or perhaps, in truth, more like a psychopathic serial murderer trying to look as benign as possible in front of a jury. At least that is what I thought . He strode confidently into the witness box, his nervous blink up towards his relatives in the public gallery making him look, for a second, like a new batsman getting accustomed to the light before taking guard. Then he looked across at the jury and gave a smile – a smirk really – before taking the oath and giving his name.

The judge invited him to sit if he wished. He remained standing while Mr Boyce asked him, in turn, if he had been present at the scene of the five offences of which he stood accused. Which, of course, he denied, save for Irma Dragoshi, when he said he was there but had not done it. Having got the heavy and almost theatrical denials out of the way on his feet, he then sat, as he was invited to go through his previous convictions. Burglary twice, taking a Morris Marina, being drunk and disorderly, taking a Ford Escort, possessing an offensive weapon, theft of a car stereo, fraudulent use of a road-tax licence, assault occasioning ABH three times, theft and deception using a bank card, offensive weapon again and then dangerous driving. Hardly a CV to be proud of but, equally, no real sign of the havoc he was about to wreak on the lives of so many women. Which I suppose is why the defence were content to volunteer it all – in the context of the savage offences he was accused of, Bellfield could almost be presented as a man of good character.

He was then led through the geographical areas where the attacks took place, establishing for the jury that he was very familiar with them. I was dutifully logging every question and reply in my notebook, each A4 page divided into equal lengthwise halves with a hand-drawn line. Just as I used to do all those years ago as a student working for the solicitors in court. But there were a few additional notes; as he was talking about the area, I remarked to myself that he was 'very laid back/cocky'. As if we would have expected it any other way. He did, however, say that he never socialised in Twickenham and never worked as a doorman there – just in West Drayton, Watford, Sunbury and Cobham. He was getting his distance from the scenes of the crimes in early. Then, he went on, he graduated to wheel-clamping, 'providing a service to help sites solve their parking problems'. Boyce then turned on to vehicles, inviting Bellfield to explain how he had many, many different vehicles, that he cherished few of them and would always be open to lending them to his friends, teeing up the 'could have been anybody driving, anybody but me' defence for later, quite nakedly.

Boyce turned to the specific offences. For Anna-Maria Rennie, Bellfield said he had refused willingly to take part in the identification procedure because he thought it would be rigged against him. He said that, when Anna-Maria was attacked, he was in a Chinese restaurant with some friends and relatives, although he 'couldn't be a hundred per cent sure'. He said that, when Marsha was murdered, he was at home with Emma at Little Benty; that he was pretty certain because he remembered watching the Martin Bashir Michael Jackson documentary. This was a bit brazen of him, being a direct lift from the alibi the suspect Sharpe had tried to give for exactly the same offence – and which he had seen in the documents served on the defence prior to the trial. Interesting, though, too, was this remark: 'Emma has a habit of calling me all the time when I am not in.'

Which, of course, was exactly what we were saying enabled us to prove he was at Twickenham Green just before he killed Amélie. It was his first mistake, one borne absolutely from his tendency to over-talk. He would get so caught up in the story he was spinning that he would embroider it with unnecessary detail. While this might not have caused him difficulties in the past, Brian Altman was always going to pick up on the smallest details, just like that one. I realised then that, given enough time and enough freedom to talk, Bellfield was going to dig himself a very deep hole indeed.

The next morning, Bellfield was obviously in good spirits, most incongruously making as if to lick the microphone like a lollipop as he entered the witness box. I looked immediately at the jury and there were sufficient members whispering to each other to tell me this incredibly stupid act had not gone unnoticed. He really was doing himself no favours, I thought. He was led through a whole host of questions about his silver Vauxhall Corsa Y57 RJU. Denying that he was driving it past Marsha's bus was one thing but the way in which he had suddenly thereafter sold it at a massive loss was going to need some explaining. Bellfield claimed that, after an accident, the finance company, which had also arranged the car insurance, had charged him £250 for damage he caused to a courtesy vehicle lent to him while his was being repaired. This had resulted in an argument and he – impulsively and dishonestly, he admitted – stopped paying the finance instalments, sold the car at a cut price and pocketed the proceeds. 'That was how it suddenly disappeared then – it was nothing at all to do with it having been used in the course of a brutal murder and being traceable back to you,' I thought. For good measure, he added that he thought he had sold the car on 1 or 2 February 2003, conveniently a couple of days before Marsha was killed.

Bellfield then gave his explanation of the attack on Irma Dragoshi. He said he was in the car with Sunil Gharu and another, he had got out to visit a business contact and, when he returned towards the car about five minutes later, he saw Gharu attacking the woman. When they got back in the car, he said, 'I was angry, shouting, screaming at what he had done.'

He told the court Gharu had thought the woman was one who had had a bitter dispute with his girlfriend. This was pure invention – but Bellfield had to invent an account for this crime as there was an eye-witness saying he was there and that he did it. Just saying 'It wasn't me' was never going to be enough so he resorted to his favourite Plan B – deflecting the blame on to somebody else. He added, 'Now, looking back, I feel sick. I warned all my employees that, when they used my vehicles, if the police came to my house, I'd just name them.'

Which, of course, is precisely what he did not do in the half-a-dozen or so interviews when given the chance to explain what had happened to Irma.

When asked about Kate Sheedy, Bellfield was back to just simply denying he was there. However, having 'given' Sunil Gharu the Irma attack, Bellfield doubled down and suggested Gharu was also in possession of the Previa at the end of May 2004. But he added in a little gloss just to make sure, pronouncing that the Previa had no interior mirror (it did have), stressing that the driver, therefore, had to rely upon the two perfect and undamaged door mirrors. This was pretty stupid of him, as we had photographs of the car showing the state of the mirrors and were, therefore, easily able to prove his lie. Not that it should have mattered – his explanation of his movements on the night Kate was attacked was convoluted, seemingly designed to fit around a large number of phone calls he had made and received that evening, culminating in meeting Megan and her sister, Emily, at the Crosby Close flat. This had to be the final part of his account, as we had the phone-clip video with the torch, which showed conclusively where he was. The judge had ruled that this should not be shown in evidence because, although we had proved the exact time at which it took place, the events it showed might be misinterpreted and, therefore, be prejudicial. If, however, Bellfield had claimed to be anywhere else, we might have been able to apply to have it admitted, which he obviously wanted to avoid.

Bellfield then turned to Amélie. He started by explaining his history with the Ford Courier van, usefully admitting that the plates on the rear doors, the painted-out windows and the odd front wheel were his handiwork. He repeated that this vehicle, like most of his fleet, was passed around among his friends and employees and so it was impossible to be certain who was driving it on what days. How convenient for him. He said though that he was sure that the last time he ever drove it was on 17 August 2004, just two days before Amélie was murdered. Again, he had little choice but to admit this, the bus-lane photograph from Twickenham showing him clearly in the driving seat. But he had nothing to do with it after that, he said; he had no idea what became of it.

He then admitted that Emma Mills's account of the trip to Tesco and Toys R Us was accurate but for one crucial fact. He said he was using a white Citroen Berlingo van, similar in size, colour and condition to the Ford Courier – and so Emma must have been confused. He even admitted driving to the area of Twickenham Green, saying it was to look at a car he was thinking of buying, and then that Emma had made the call to him from Little Benty. He claimed, though, that he had spoken to her for a while – which the call data refuted, showing that its duration was just one second. He accepted he had the phone and that he was in the area, grudgingly saying, 'If the phone records are saying I was there, I was there.'

For me, this was unexpected; this was a key part of our case and one which I had expected him to fight tooth and nail. He was, it seemed, pinning his hopes on convincing the jury that he was there but in a different van. As we had experts who would confirm that the Courier van was definitely there, too, this meant there had to have been a huge coincidence: on an evening when he drove to Twickenham Green in his Citroen, his Ford van, which he was driving just two days previously, just happened to be in the same area and involved in a murderous attack on an innocent young woman. Detectives often say, 'We don't like coincidences.' The same could also be said of jurors.

He then said he visited his mother's house and then spent less than an hour in a pub in West Drayton, leaving by taxi due to having had a few drinks. The next day, he had driven around the M25 and back (but gave no reason for this) and then decided to go with Emma and the children to stay with a friend, Michelle Wickham, in Kent for a few days. He said he was feeling down – suicidal almost – due to the pressure of debts, relationship problems and feeling that he didn't really want their latest child. He claimed that he had driven there in Richard Hughes's Vauxhall but that, after a few days, had returned this to Hughes, driving back to Kent in the Citroen Berlingo. Michelle Wickham saw the van and had been sure it was a Ford Courier, as was Emma. Michelle had even noticed that the front nearside light was not working. The stay in Kent extended and extended, so much so that the older children missed the beginning of the new school term.

After three days of giving his evidence-in-chief, Bellfield finally faced Brian Altman in cross-examination. This was to last considerably longer. The initial questions were general, dancing around Bellfield's vehicles, his multiple mobile phones and his knowledge of the relevant areas of south-west London. Altman made sure the jury were aware that Bellfield had had access to the case papers for many months prior to the trial, suggesting that this had enabled him to tailor his defence to fit the evidence. Bellfield, naturally, denied this. He said he had replied 'No comment' to most of the questions the police had put to him in interviews only because that was what his lawyers had advised. Bellfield did, though, get irritated enough to snap back, 'I'm not going to bite to your questions,' and, 'You've asked me a trick question,' when being asked again about his ownership of the Ford Courier van. Generally, he was sticking to his guns, always hiding behind the advice of his lawyers when the many opportunities he had missed to explain events in interviews were pointed out to him. Altman frequently accused in passing that the account we had heard was fictional; when he made the outright suggestion that Bellfield had '. . . just been searching through records and back-engineered an account by reference to the phone evidence,' it was met with a testy but brief denial.

As Altman moved on to the Kate Sheedy attack, he repeatedly probed Bellfield's convoluted story that he had lent the Previa to Sunil Gharu that night. Much of the evidence – and, therefore, the questioning – centred on records of phone calls. Altman had the facts and their implications at his fingertips, Bellfield was replying with a version he had clearly made up – and so which was always liable to lead him to forget what he was meant to be saying and utter an inconsistency. There was only ever going to be one winner in this confrontation and it became obvious when Bellfield, flustered and stumbling as he wrestled to make up a version which fitted the evidence, blurted out, 'Give me a chance. I'm fighting for my life here!'

In the context of the charges he was facing, it was a remarkable thing to say. As the thought flashed through my mind that this was a chance he never offered to Amélie or Marsha, I glanced first at the judge and then quickly to the jury to see if the same thought had registered with them. It was clear from the look of Her Ladyship, and by the stares and mumbled whispers in the jury box, that it had. Altman, of course, was not going to miss the opportunity to drive the point home and asked, 'When interviewed on 6 May 2005, you were asked if you still owned the Previa and you said, "No comment." Were you not fighting for your life then, since you were being accused of all sorts of serious crimes then? Or was it just that you hadn't thought of your story back then?'

Bellfield, shortly after, tried to regain some ground with a sickening display of faux sympathy for the girl he had so nearly killed: 'I'm incapable. I couldn't do that. I have children myself. It was bad enough seeing Kate Sheedy give evidence. Senseless.'

Altman made the wry observation, 'You're certainly right about the last bit.'

The rest of Bellfield's cross-examination followed the same pattern – Altman suggesting he was lying, Bellfield saying he was not and that he had not told the story earlier due to legal advice. But over the five days, he had lost something – some sparkle, some of his cockiness. It was apparent he knew he had been battered and that, for once, his charm had failed. I think it was at this point that he first realised he might not make it through this one unscathed.

The defence called Dr Itiel Dror, an expert in cognitive neuroscience. The intention was to try to prove that the expert evidence relating to the interpretation of CCTV recordings – specifically the work done to identify the vehicles – was subject to confirmation bias and, therefore, unreliable. It was the usual story: where there is expert evidence for one side, it is always possible to find other experts to support the opposing point of view. What I was not expecting was for this expert to turn Court 6 at the Old Bailey into something resembling a live version of the puzzle page of the *Mail on Sunday*, as the jury were invited, by way of example, to consider both 'Dingbats' and 'Magic-Eyes'. While Dr Dror was obviously a leader in his field and his theories were plausible, the difficulty for the defence seemed to be in making them plainly applicable to the evidence he was called upon to discredit. Some of the concepts were difficult for the layperson to understand and, while he did his level best to explain and simplify them, I, for one, was left thinking, 'Yes, OK – but so what?' I hoped that the jurors felt the same way; at least those who hadn't found the whole thing just too difficult to consider at all.

The next defence witness was, again, not an eye-witness or somebody able to give evidence of actual events. It was another expert, Michelle Price, a sole-practitioner solicitor specialising in the analysis of unused material. It seems the defence engaged her for the purpose of demonstrating that there were lots of people around Twickenham Green at the time Amélie was murdered who we had, during our investigation, never traced. In thinking about her contribution, it is useful for me to first outline a few basic principles of murder investigation. I view it as a sort of flow-chart or mind-map, although this exists only in my mind and I never actually needed to draw it. Others might do so but I didn't find it necessary. Each bubble or box in the chart represents a piece of known information and that leads to other possibilities or hypotheses, which can be confirmed or rejected when new facts are found. If the investigation goes down the correct route, there will be a path, via several bubbles, which eventually leads to the suspect and a charge. When this route is chosen (and it is by no means always the first choice), there will usually remain little point in following other paths that lead elsewhere – as, by definition, these will not go to the perpetrator. So there are lots of potential lines of inquiry in every successful investigation that do not get pursued.

In Amélie's case, this included the other, unknown, people around the Green when she was attacked. We had followed the van, which led us to Bellfield. We had then investigated him, his movements, his associates, vehicles and phone data and arrived at the evidence proving he was the killer. There was no need, therefore, to go and spend much time and money tracing passers-by who were irrelevant to the case against him.

The defence, however, saw this as an opportunity. I believe they thought that, if they could prove to the jury that there was a significant number of other people around at the time, they might raise a sufficient doubt to help their case. Put simply, they could plant a suggestion that one or more of the unknown could have been responsible. It was a tactic I had never encountered before and one, therefore, of which I was fearful. Perhaps I should not have been; in the event, not only did it not add anything that detracted from the case against Bellfield in any way but also, when in cross-examination, the witness agreed she had '. . . made an assumption which the material did not justify . . .' and that 'I didn't look at the CCTV evidence'.

I was confident that the jury would be thinking exactly the same as me – once again, what was all that about?

CHAPTER THIRTY

VERDICTS AND SENTENCES

The closing speeches from both prosecution and the defence were long, Brian Altman reprising the main points of evidence and giving an accurate and devastating description of Bellfield:

> A man who could hardly give a straight answer to a straight question . . . black became white and white became black . . . behind it all there wasn't a shred of hard evidence to support a word he says. He blamed everyone but himself . . . every witness whose evidence was inconvenient to him was either mistaken or lying . . .

William Boyce concentrated more on explaining his client's demeanour in court and how this ought not to affect their deliberations. I noted that it took him thirty-five minutes of speaking before he even touched on any of the evidence. This did, though, lead him to utter this memorable understatement, with which I wholeheartedly agreed: 'Levi Bellfield is not everyone's cup of tea; you may not be thrilled if your daughter brought him home.'

Indeed.

Mrs Justice Rafferty gave the jury the sort of fair, balanced and comprehensive direction in her summing up that we expected. While she had shown remarkable and unusual empathy with the witnesses who had found giving their evidence such an ordeal, there was never any doubt that she would ensure that she said nothing to give the defendant any cause for complaint in the future. The jury were sent out in the middle of February 2008 and so began two weeks of attending court each day and just sitting around, waiting. Experience had taught me that guessing jury outcomes is a perilous business. I have had murder convictions come back in less than forty minutes and in more than a week. The time they are taking is no guide, nor are any questions they pass to the judge during their deliberations. The only thing to do is wait and hope.

It wasn't until 25 February, after two weeks of nail-biting and a few days after the jury had been told that the court would accept a majority verdict, that we were summoned back into Court 6 and we took our seats, knowing that verdicts were coming – but not what they were. I sat in front of Bellfield, next to Jo Brunt, as we had done for the preceding five months. The foreman reading the verdict was one of those scenes I had visualised in my mind for months, always with him saying, 'Guilty,' naturally. I had decided that I was confident enough that I would look not at him but at Bellfield at that moment, wanting to see if there would at last be some reaction in those cold, unmoving eyes. In the event, I just could not bring myself to do it, knowing that it would be far more than I could bear to see his relief and jubilation if he had, again, won. I just looked at Jo – even found myself holding her arm. I looked across at the families the Delagranges, the McDonnells and the Sheedys, and the detectives who had got us this far – Jayne Farnworth, Clive Grace, Gary Cunningham, Gary Fuller, Debbie Ford, Neil Jones, Paul Carruth and Malcolm Hudson. Just a few of the remarkable bunch of men and women whose talent and tenacity I had been privileged to lead.

The foreman first said that the jury had yet to agree on the Irma Dragoshi and Anna-Marie Rennie counts. This was, I thought, bad news. In those cases, we had an eye-witness and a positive identification, respectively. They were the ones with the hard evidence, not the patchwork of circumstantial facts we had been forced to put together for the other three cases. Of course, we didn't have long to wait. The remaining counts were put in chronological order and so started with Marsha.

Clerk: 'Have you reached a verdict upon which you all agree?'

Foreman: 'No.'

Clerk: 'Have you reached a verdict upon which at least ten of you agree?'

Foreman: 'Yes.'

Clerk: 'Do you find the defendant, Levi Bellfield, guilty or not guilty of murder?'

Foreman: 'Guilty.'

Gasps and hubbub around the court. I should have looked at the McDonnells. I had wanted to look at Bellfield but, in the moment, all I could do was look at Jo and whisper my immediate thought: 'That's the weakest case. We've done it. We're going to get the others, too.'

And, thankfully, I was correct. Ten to two on Marsha, eleven to one on Kate and unanimous on Amélie – they had found him guilty of all three of the most serious offences. The meticulous notes I had taken of the court proceedings in my separate, dedicated book suddenly stopped at this point. As did most of my senses. I am sure there were some sort of administrative things going on in the court, upon which I probably should have been concentrating, but I was oblivious. Relief, joy, pride, disbelief – all were thumping me in turn and demanding my attention. I resolved that I really ought not to cry but I very nearly did, glad that the reflection from my spectacles would probably mask the first hint of tears welling up from Jo. Not that she would have seen them through her own.

The judge said she would be sentencing at 10.30 the next morning and the court rose. The press box emptied in a stampede and I shook hands and hugged so many people that I couldn't begin to recount them all. I was whisked outside by Vish Patel, the media officer, and gave a few interviews to TV and the attending print journalists. I hadn't prepared notes but, like the verdicts, I had rehearsed this a thousand times in my head, making sure that I stressed the dedication of my team and how we had made London a safer place, especially for young women. Once the initial hubbub had died down, I joined the rest of the team, along with a few journalists, in 'our' corner of Ye Old London beer garden. Our celebrations were muted, to a degree, because we knew we had to be back at court in the morning. I think, in truth, the emotional drain had got to most of us; by about 5pm, everyone had started to make for home. I stood on the pavement in Ludgate Hill, still buzzing from the excitement of it all yet wondering what came next. I then remembered that I had an invitation that night to a retirement party for Dave Johnston, the Commander of the Serious Crime Directorate. It was to be held on the *Tattersall Castle*, a boat-bar permanently moored on the Embankment. It was only a short tube ride away. I had appreciated the invitation but, because of the ongoing trial, I had not really intended to go. But perhaps I ought to; perhaps, given the news, which would have reached the attendees, my absence would, this time, be noticed?

As I approached the boat in the gloom of February twilight, I made out the shape of somebody pacing slowly in circles near its entrance, obviously speaking on a mobile phone. As I got closer, I saw it was John Yates, the Assistant Commissioner in charge of crime and an old acquaintance from years ago. He saw me approaching and I heard him say down his mobile, 'Sorry, I've got to go. There's someone here I need to speak to.'

To this day, I don't know who I was more important than at that moment but he thrust the phone into his pocket and shouted, 'Bloody well done!', ignoring the hand I proffered to and going instead for the full-on hug. It was a reaction most unlike an officer of his rank; a genuine expression of joy and affection that moved me. It was a foretaste of what was to come; it seemed that everybody on that boat knew about the verdict and wanted to shake my hand. I felt like pinning a note to my chest saying how lucky I was to have such a wonderful team, so often did I need to say it that evening. Among those offering congratulations was DAC Bill Griffiths, who I was quick to remind of his practical and motivational support during the hunt for the van. My embarrassment became acute when John Yates, at the start of his speech to recount the retiring Commander's long and illustrious career, first spoke of the Bellfield verdict, then of me and prompted a round of applause. It was a fantastic experience to have the adulation of so many of my senior officers and peers – one that I will never forget. But I did feel a bit as if I had hijacked Dave Johnston's do – to his credit, perhaps proving the copper he was, he joined in the applause as much as anyone.

I made it home before midnight and relatively sober; perhaps surprisingly, I slept well. I had arranged for virtually all of my team to come to court to see the sentencing, as well as other victims from the offences we had not been able to charge. 'Your justice is my justice . . .' Even my parents had made the trip into London to sit and watch the final day; both of them had spent much of their working lives in courts and knew what a big day it was for me. It was just, I suppose, a natural extension of the support they had never failed to give me, no matter how old or senior I was.

I took my usual route into the Old Bailey, through the Lord Mayor's entrance at the rear. As I did so, there was a group of ten or so people standing outside chatting and smoking. I immediately recognised some of them as members of our jury. As I walked past, one of them called out, 'Mr Sutton, Mr Sutton!'

I halted and turned towards them and the woman said, 'Are we allowed to talk to you now? Only we want to apologise for taking so long, now that we know . . .'

She stopped in mid-sentence as she realised we had been joined by the foreman. He just looked at her and, shaking his head, softly said, 'I am so, so sorry. I got it wrong. I should have been with you all.'

I wasn't sure what was going on but thought it was a conversation I'd better not have at that time. I told them we should not speak until they were discharged and went into court. What had all that been about? I soon found out – most of the morning's papers had led with the story of the conviction and a few had mentioned the suspicion that Bellfield was a suspect for murdering Milly Dowler, too. The *Sun* had invested heavily in this, under the simple but devastating front-page splash, 'HE KILLED MILLY TOO.'

The problem with this was immediately apparent to me. The jury were still, at least technically, deliberating on the cases they had as yet failed to agree upon. This publicity was clearly prejudicial to their doing so fairly – and I had first-hand evidence of this. Obviously, Mr Foreman had been reluctant to convict but what they had all read in the papers on their way in had convinced him – and them – that he was wrong. Instantly, I knew that the jury could not continue and that Irma's and Anna-Maria's cases must be left to lie on file, undecided. Even if the defence had not so applied, I would have made sure the court was aware of what I had heard from the jurors. Not that this would make any practical difference to the defendant: Bellfield was going to get life imprisonment and I was confident that, in his case, it would be a whole-life tariff – he would never be released.

In the event, Mr Boyce did make the expected submission that the outstanding cases should not be proceeded with due to 'the welter of overnight adverse publicity' the defendant had received.

Brian Altman did not oppose, and the jury was discharged. Then Mr Boyce explained the absence of Bellfield from the dock. He had decided he did not want to be there to face his sentence in person and was refusing to come up from his cell. There being no legal power to force him to do so, Mrs Justice Rafferty got on with passing sentence in the absence of Bellfield, who, by this act, showed his cowardice to the last for all to see.

'You have reduced three families to unimagined grief. What dreadful feelings went through your head as you attacked them and, in two cases, snuffed out a young life is beyond understanding,' she said, sentencing him to life imprisonment on each of the three counts and recommending that he should, on all three counts, never be eligible to apply for parole but would spend his whole life in prison. The judge then surprised me by calling, 'Detective Chief Inspector Sutton, please,' smiling at me and motioning with her eyes towards the witness box. I felt like I had borrowed somebody else's legs. Somebody who was very drunk. I knew that what was coming was nothing bad; it was probably going to be most pleasant. But it was so public. And I knew that I would struggle – really struggle – to keep my emotions in check. I stood in the witness box and the judge looked me straight in the eye. I had seen over the past five months that she was able to be quite severe, that her tongue could be as sharp as her mind, but also that she was very human, expressive in her looks and capable of undoubted warmth too. I was certainly getting warmth.

'A rocky road?' she asked.

'Yes, it was m'Lady,' I replied, realising that my voice was already starting to tremble.

'And one which was travelled successfully by a team which took their lead from you, your firm, determined motivating hand on the tiller leading your officers to heroic instances of redoubled labour . . .'

Having it put like that, by somebody of such stature, was too much for me. Choke as I might, the tears were going to come. But she went on: '. . . Grand pronouncements do not lead to convictions. Dogged, well-directed, painstaking, unglamorous police work does and, in this case, did.'

I think I said, 'Thank you.' I think she probably formally said she was commending me. But all I really remember was blustering another mumbled reply through a tightened throat and that, as I stepped down, first the public gallery and then those in the well of the court broke out in a ripple of applause. Another first, I looked back at the judge and, with a beaming smile and a theatrical shake of the head, she said, 'Er, not in a court of law!' but her tone and expression spoke volumes. She had said what she knew she ought to say but everybody could see she really didn't mind the spontaneous expression of thanks and relief.

I then went up to the City Police station at Snow Hill, where we did a press conference with DCS Andy Murphy, the Delagranges and Marsha's mother Ute and her uncle. After that, there were a few more TV interviews I did alone and so I was the last to arrive at the inevitable celebratory drink. Although our plan had been to go to the All Bar One on the corner near the court, it was still only just after 11.30am and it was shut. I looked around and saw, across Ludgate Hill, that La Grande Marque wine bar was open and looked unusually busy. I strolled across, saw Gary Cunningham puffing away at a cigarette outside and so joined him. After a few minutes, Jo Brunt came out and exhorted me: 'Are you going to come in here or what?'

So I entered. I've seen those scenes in TV dramas scores of times. You know the one, where the successful SIO goes back into the office to a rapturous round of applause from the team. Well, this time it was for real and here I was in the middle of it. I looked around – my whole team, most of the victims or families, most of the jury and both prosecution counsel, clapping, cheering. I wasn't vain enough to take it as being all for me. It was much more of a release, a celebration, an acknowledgement that, despite all the difficulties and obstacles, we had done it. Together.

After an hour or two, I was at the bar with Brian Altman. I joked with him, 'Brian, despite the fact for every pound I earn you earn ten, I really feel I ought to buy you a drink.'

He smiled. 'That's very kind of you Mr Sutton – I'll have a Peroni, please.'

I asked the barman for two Peronis. He looked at me apologetically and said, 'I am very sorry, sir. We have no more beer left.'

Even with the cost of my round now increasing to two large glasses of Sancerre, nothing could spoil this moment. Gaining the attention of all by the time-honoured method of banging on a glass with a knife and yelling, I gave my only speech of the day: 'OK, I need to say a few words here. To my team, the people here I have grown to love and respect so much. And to the lawyers as well . . . Thank you for all you have achieved today and over the past three and a half years. Your dedication, your ability and your resilience have been amazing and I am so truly grateful to you all. You have all done so much, so many things of which I am proud, but today, you have exceeded my wildest hopes and dreams. Today, ladies and gentlemen, Major Investigation Team Seven of the Homicide and Serious Crime Command, with a little bit of help from the CPS, counsel and jurors, and with the support of our friends, has achieved something very special. We have drunk a pub completely dry of beer. And for that, I will always salute you!'

CHAPTER THIRTY-ONE

WHAT NEXT?

February 2008 was much colder than August 2004 had been, so my introspection that night was in the living room, rather than the garden. But I sat there alone as the clock ticked into the next day, thinking how, three and a half years ago, I had sat and doubted myself – and how I had battled on and pulled it off. Whatever misgivings I or others had had, in the event, I had been up to it. I knew that the case would, in many ways, define my career, perhaps even me as a man – and I decided there were certainly many worse ways to be remembered. I was forty-seven years old, I still had nearly three years to serve until I could retire with a full pension and, while I was more than happy to continue leading the team and investigating murders, I did worry that 'ordinary' investigations would appear somewhat anti-climactic given what we had all been through. I knew though that there was no other role within the police to which I could move and be happy, let alone effective.

I remembered shortly after I joined the police in 1981, when I was voraciously reading as much non-fiction about my chosen profession as I could lay my hands upon, I had read a book that was an in-depth account of Operation Julie. This was a vast and sprawling operation taking place over nearly three years in the mid-1970s using many undercover officers, which led to two LSD-production rings being brought down. The fact from this which I remembered above all others was that none of the six or seven officers who were at the heart of the operation completed thirty years' service. Each of them, once Julie had been resolved, had realised that it had been their peak, that nothing would ever compare with it in the future and so their motivation, their job satisfaction, had gone forever. I had found this strange back then but was now starting to understand it. Had I reached my peak? Could I still raise my interest, my passion for whatever investigations were to come? Because I knew that, if I could not, I might be better to give up like them, for, once my passion and desire to succeed were diminished, so, too, would be my effectiveness. Had the Bellfield conviction come three years too early?

Back at Putney the next morning, my doubts were further fuelled by Gary Cunningham suggesting to me exactly that – it would have been a great time to retire. But the mood in the office was, of course, still generally buoyant. Steve Kinchington, a detective sergeant who had replaced Norman Griffiths as my office manager, had gone to great pains to cover every mention of my name on notices and signs around the place with the word 'Sleuth' – a reference to the caption to a photograph of me used in that morning's *Metro* free newspaper. Kinch, as he was known, was an interesting character. Six-feet seven tall and always immaculately and slightly flamboyantly attired, he was famous for his eccentric behaviour and jokes. His gentle teasing of me was, in some part, payback for an amusing bit of interaction we had had several months previously. While we had been preparing the case papers, he had complained that he was walking miles each day during repeated trips from his desk at one end of our floor to the photocopier at the other. His creative but rather dangerous solution was to use a micro-scooter for the journeys. I had a short discussion with him, explaining that, while I did find it funny, there was a danger he would run into somebody and cause an injury and so he had to stop. He said he understood and I thought that was the end of it. The next day, I was at my desk when I heard the unmistakable sound of a bicycle bell. I was furious as he said, 'There we are, Guv'nor – no danger now!' scooting away up the aisle between the desks, bell trilling. But I said nothing, went home that day and thought about it and how I could respond in kind. I borrowed my son Joe's micro-scooter to gauge the size, disappeared down to my garage and put my metalworking skills to use. After an hour or so of cutting, bending, welding and spraying, I had manufactured a bright-yellow wheel clamp – a perfect replica of those used by Bellfield – sized for a micro-scooter and secured with the padlock from a suitcase. For possibly the first time ever, I then got into the office before everybody else the next morning and applied the clamp to Kinch's scooter. I could have had a lie in actually, because he was off for a few days, but this at least gave everyone else the chance to see it. When he returned, he admitted it was funny.

And that he had been beaten and, once the clamp was removed, the scooter was never used again.

One of the joys of the return to my desk that day were the congratulatory emails that kept arriving in my inbox. Many from my colleagues, the other SIOs and Detective Inspectors on our Command, some from people I had never met and others – the special ones – from people I had worked with in the past. One that was particularly touching was from Chris Binns, a lovely man and excellent copper who I had the pleasure of working with during my time in West Yorkshire. Not knowing how to contact me, he had called the switchboard at Scotland Yard and insisted that the operator took down his message and emailed it to me. Although I had an email with glowing praise from Chief Superintendent Neil Basu, the Staff Officer to Commissioner Sir Ian Blair, nothing at all was forthcoming from the top man himself. Indeed, a few weeks later, I was to find out that not only was Sir Ian silent after the verdict but that he wasn't very keen on passing on any praise received from elsewhere. I was speaking on the phone to Wendy, a delightfully friendly and helpful staff member in the Command HR department, about something unrelated to Bellfield.

'Wasn't that a lovely letter from the judge I put on your personal file last week?' she said casually and in passing as she looked up the information I was asking for.

'I don't know. I haven't seen it,' I replied, it then not being clear whether she or I was the most shocked. She agreed to fax me a copy immediately; to this day, the only copy of the letter I have ever seen. It was sent by Mrs Justice Rafferty, to Sir Ian Blair, on 13 March 2008, about two weeks after the verdict. Over a page and a half, she lavishes praise on me and the team and, at the end, lists another seven officers who, in her opinion, were worthy of commendation. This was dealt with by means of copies being silently added to our personal files; in my view, a shameful failure by the Commissioner, both in terms of adequately recognising officers who had given so much and of his ignoring the wishes and opinion of a senior judge.

Throughout the last three years of the Bellfield investigation, my team had been fulfilling its usual role in the day-to-day work of the Command, being on call one week in nine and taking on other, less complicated investigations to run alongside Yeaddiss. One of these, picked up on-call and solved over the Easter weekend in 2007, was the senseless and tragic murder of Krystal Hart. Krystal, who was just twenty-two years old, was shot by her neighbour's boyfriend, Thomas Hughes, on her own doorstep. Her unborn child, of course, died with her. Hughes had been arrested quite quickly and the case, being relatively simple, came up for trial just a couple of weeks after Bellfield's case finished. Hughes was sentenced to life with a minimum of thirty years and we then became aware that he and Bellfield had, on remand, become prison friends. I guess they at least had me in common – a fact which became obvious when we played a recording of Bellfield calling his brother, Richard, from prison just after Hughes had been sentenced. Bellfield had clearly spoken about Hughes before, as the conversation went like this.

Bellfield: 'Y'see Tom got thirty then?'

Richard: 'Who?'

Bellfield: 'Tom! . . . Shot the bird . . .'

Richard: 'Oh, yeah . . . fuckin' hell . . .'

Bellfield: 'Sutton an' all, that was.'

Richard : 'Yeah, I know. I see the cunt outside the court on telly.'

Bellfield: 'Yeah, fucking scumbag. I 'ope 'e 'as an 'eart attack, the cunt . . . Anyway, Mum's not in so tell 'er I rung . . .'

Far from being offended by this, I was quite proud that I had done so much to curb the activities of this vile man. How enlightening was his attitude towards Krystal and his effortless ability to slide from horrible insults to speaking about his Mum not being in to receive his call? And they called me a 'scumbag'?

I should, perhaps, point out that all prisoners know that their calls are liable to be monitored by both prison staff and police. This was, though, not the funniest excerpt from the Bellfield tapes. We stopped monitoring his calls shortly after that one, but Surrey Police continued in support of their ongoing efforts to make a case against him for murdering Milly and one of their officers told me about the following conversation. I never heard it first-hand but can reconstruct it reasonably accurately. Bellfield had an aged aunt who owned a valuable house in south-west London. I forget her name but let's call her Betty. Speaking to his mother, Jean, Bellfield learned of her passing and we knew he would immediately be interested in what would happen to her not inconsiderable estate. The conversation was something like this.

Jean: 'Ooh, Lee, Aunt Betty's dead, you know.'

Bellfield: 'Oh, no, Mum, that's such a shame. She was a lovely old girl . . .'

Bellfield: '. . . so, what about the will then, Mum?'

Jean: 'Ooh, they've read the will, Lee . . . Yeah . . . We're all getting a ninth.'

Bellfield: 'A ninth?'

Jean: 'Yeah, a ninth.'

Bellfield: 'How many's that between then?'

Jean: 'I dunno . . . Five or six of us, I think.'

Both of these passages became part of my 'routine' as I was called upon to talk about the case to various conferences and audiences. The National Family Liaison conference and National Intelligence Analysts conference were two big gigs, but I also spoke regularly to SIO courses at Hendon and at the quarterly SIOs conference at the Yard. I even, towards the end of my career, gave the usual Bellfield presentation to a group of officers from the Potsdam Police; after years of wishing I had learned French because of Amélie, my German finally became of use in the Bellfield context. I also had a recurring slot at the start of the 'Media Management' course at the National Police College, Bramshill. The way in which we had engaged with the media and influenced the reporting was viewed as a model for others to emulate – at that time. This, of course, was before the Filkin report and Operation Elveden looked at the police-media relationship and concluded – wrongly, in my view – that it was better for police to withdraw and say nothing. Hence, we now have a generation of journalists who have a default position to be critical of police because they have no opportunity to learn how issues appear from the police side. My point back then was that, if police refuse to engage, the media will get the information from other sources, which may be less accurate, and police will have no opportunity to influence the reporting. We are now seeing the result of this entrenched and inward-looking policy every day in our news streams.

CHAPTER THIRTY-TWO

OTHER OFFENCES?

One of the pieces of work I had prepared during the latter part of the Bellfield investigation was a rescan of intelligence and crime reports, to see what additional offences he might have committed. One thing was certain – his offending was so prolific it was impossible that there were none. Going back as far as 1994, there was a blitz attack with a 'truncheon-like weapon' on a twenty-nine-year-old woman in Hinchley Wood, in the familiar territory of the London/Surrey border and at a time when we knew Bellfield was working as a doorman just over a mile away. The assailant was wearing a balaclava but matched Bellfield's description. The victim had just left a railway station, was attacked while using a public telephone and, despite sustaining serious wounds to her head from several blows, managed to fight him off by firmly grabbing his genitals. It was noted that there was no property stolen. The motive was suggested by the investigating officer as 'a determined attempt to either murder or rape this victim. The blows were delivered with extreme force.' In other words, exactly the (unusual) type of attack that we knew Bellfield carried out.

In 2000, a nurse was found unconscious on the pavement in Wellington Road, Twickenham, a few short yards from Fulwell bus garage where Amélie had begun her fateful walk home. She had a head wound requiring forty stitches and had lost four front teeth. Perhaps because she had been drinking quite heavily, the incident had been dismissed by her as a fall, despite the surgeon who treated her remarking that the wound was consistent with being hit by a bottle or similar instrument. Like Bellfield's other victims, there was no reason to suspect robbery – her handbag lay by her side, untouched. She had come forward to us after seeing the publicity around Amélie's murder; it seemed, once more to me, that the location and the nature of her injuries were identical to other victims of Bellfield – nobody else was committing that sort of crime on that sort of victim in that sort of area.

Another crime we found in our intelligence trawl. In the late afternoon of New Year's Day 2003, Dr Kieron Coghlan, ironically perhaps a reconstructive surgeon, was depositing rubbish from the Christmas festivities at a recycling site near the library in Whitton. As the crow flies, this was about a kilometre from both where Bellfield attacked Kate Sheedy and, in the other direction, the bus stop where he had tried to abduct Anna-Maria Rennie. Dr Coghlan had heard somebody approaching him and turned to see a man with a hammer who, without warning, had hit him on the head. He fell and the assailant tried again; despite the pain, Dr Coughlan managed to parry the second blow with the palm of his hand. The suspect then calmly placed the hammer in the inside of his jacket and walked off. Not a word was exchanged between the men. Dr Coghlan received nine stiches in his head wound, together with bruising and swelling to his head and hands. He was unable to give a meaningful description of the attacker but the location and method, added to the absence of a robbery motive, pointed to the possibility of Bellfield's involvement. One might ask why – but then that question might be posed about all of his offences.

Two offences which came to notice from our national research took place in Sussex in January 2004 when, on the same evening, in separate incidents, two young women were struck on the head from behind, out of nowhere, while walking on the street. Initially, we had shelved any work on these; we had been told about them in the very early stages of the investigation and had no reason to suspect they were connected to the offences in Twickenham and Hampton. This changed once we identified Bellfield as our suspect, as we realised that, at that time, he was fulfilling a clamping contract in Sussex, at an out-of-town shopping park near Chichester. Although this was more than sixty miles away from the locations of the attacks, which were near Hastings, it was the same county so worth an inquiry. Sussex Police told us that the offences had been investigated as forming part of a series of robberies, and their records showed that a man had been convicted after pleading guilty. So that took them back off the agenda again but it was not the end of the story. As our knowledge of Bellfield's movements and habits increased, we discovered more detail about his time in Sussex. He had stayed in a cheap hotel near to Chichester for the few weeks in early 2004 that his contract survived. However, the number of complaints the management company were receiving about his intimidating and unreasonable attitude led them to cancel the agreement and he had returned to London. However, we were told that, while working away, Bellfield had discovered that an old friend who had worked in a pub in West Drayton had taken up a position managing a pub in Hastings. As it wasn't so far away and he was, in any case, bored in the hotel during the evenings, Bellfield had begun to visit Hasting a couple of times a week to see the friend. Armed with this information, I asked Clive Grace to check with Sussex again – it seemed too much of a coincidence that these attacks should have been committed by somebody else when Bellfield was definitely very close to them. A more detailed conversation with the officer who had dealt with the Sussex case was revealing. Yes, these attacks had been investigated as part of a series and, yes, a man had admitted the string of robberies that made up most of the series. But he had not admitted these two attacks; actually, he had specifically excluded them from his admissions. And in neither of them was there any suggestion of property having been stolen.

So we delved further. The first victim, Sarah Spurrell, was walking to a friend's house at about 7.15pm on Sunday, 11 January 2004. She felt a hard blow to the back of her head and saw blood spatter on her sleeve. She turned to see her attacker and he struck two further blows to her head, although she managed to get her hands up on to her scalp, thus shielding her skull from the impacts. A car approached and the assailant turned and ran; she noticed that he was carrying something large in his left hand (Bellfield, as we know, is left-handed and the pathologist's opinion was that both Amélie and Marsha were struck with a weapon held in the left hand). About a mile away and nearly three hours later, another young woman was walking home when she noticed a car parked in the street with somebody sitting in the driving seat. As she got nearer, she saw that the driver was wearing a balaclava. The car's engine and lights were off. She thought the car was a small hatchback, similar to a Peugeot 205 in size, and she thought it was medium blue in colour, although it was dark and the sodium street lighting would naturally distort the colour somewhat. She walked past the car and, shortly afterwards, felt a heavy blow across the back of her head. She shouted, turned and saw a figure in a balaclava who hit her over the head again. This caused her to stumble to the ground and she saw her attacker run off, back in the direction of the car she had passed, removing his balaclava as he did so.

In addition to these specific, previously reported offences, I had expected new ones to come to our attention in the wake of the trial. Bellfield's image was now very much in the public domain, the prohibition on its publication having been lifted on the day of his conviction. We knew that he had used in excess of thirty aliases, so there might have been many victims unable to connect his name with their crime until they saw his picture. Also, there might have been other 'stranger' attacks where sight of that distinctive face and frame would jog some horrific memories. As it turned out, we had fewer calls like this than I had imagined; one lady who was drugged and raped by what she took, by his size and clothing, to be a doorman in Kingston and a couple more teenagers alleging Bellfield had drug-raped them too. Not the flood I had perhaps expected but, nevertheless, very grave offences in their own right and, added these to what we already knew, a substantial series of further serious assaults and sexual offences which, in ordinary circumstances, would merit thorough investigation.

However, I was very aware that these were not usual circumstances. Here we had a man who was already serving three whole-life sentences, who would never be released from prison. So there was no future threat to the community – we could be assured that our successful case had seen to that. Moreover, there were already two series of horrific offences of which we were aware but where prosecution had been stalled – the indictment for nine offences against his former partners, the 'holding' charges that had seen him remanded into custody in November 2004 had been ordered to be 'left on file', a sort of legal limbo whereby they could only be reactivated in peculiar circumstances (if, for example, he were successfully to appeal his conviction or sentence for the murders and was likely to be released) – and then only if authorised by leave of the Court of Appeal. The two undecided charges involving Irma Dragoshi and Anna-Maria Rennie had also been placed into this category. Then there was the series of drug-assisted rapes on teenagers, which the CPS had 'tactically' declined to prosecute back in 2006. If strings of offences of their severity could be put on ice, what point might there be in investigating other, similar series? The issue was simply one of public interest – that is, was the time, money and resources necessary to complete the required investigations and prosecutions justified by the 'best case' outcome? My view was genuinely one of indecision – I could see both sides of the argument. I would have been absolutely happy for Bellfield to be prosecuted for each and every violent and depraved act he had ever committed – and this was the attitude, it seemed, of every member of my team. They, too, pointed out that the many victims of his violence and perversion deserved their day in court to see justice. I couldn't disagree with that either. I was, though, equally aware that police managers, as well as the CPS, had a duty to use the limited public funds available to them to the best effect, to make sure it was wisely spent to maximise not only a sense of justice but also the ongoing safety of the community. Bellfield, for all he had done, was locked up and incapable of causing more physical harm. The neutral, impassionate and probably responsible decision was to move on and use our talents and resources to fight those who posed a threat in the future. I did the honourable thing, pushed the decision upstairs and awaited directions from those who managed me. As I expected, their view was that we ought to draw a line under Bellfield and move on to the new challenges of other cases.

CHAPTER THIRTY-THREE

BACK TO NORMAL?

Almost without me noticing it, investigating Bellfield had changed the way I led my team. I had always been pretty hands on, leading from the front some might say, involved in every facet and detail of the investigations for which I was responsible. This suited me – I had said many times that, despite the pressure, the long hours and the disrupted private life, the SIO role was the best in the force, allowing as it did for a Chief Inspector to escape from behind the desk most days, to be operational, to keep on being a copper. But the scale and breadth of the Bellfield case was such that I had to delegate much more; not only in breaking the vast investigations into strands under a Detective Inspector but also with the other, unrelated, less complex cases we had taken on along the way. Most of these were effectively managed by one of my excellent Detective Inspectors – Tony McKeown, Joe Farrell and, later, Andy Perrott – and some of the easier cases by the experienced and very capable detective sergeants like Kevin McSharry, Mick Snowden and Steve Kinchington. I was simply too busy getting myself fully immersed in Bellfield, reading and rereading every single piece of paper, determined that I knew every last detail just in case I could pick up on a crucial snippet.

When we returned to normal and were engaged in investigations into more routine, 'one-off' murders, it was difficult for me to return to the old ways. There was a degree of the feelings of anti-climax I had feared but I also felt it would be disrespectful to the great work these talented officers had performed when I needed them to if I were to step back in and reduce their influence. I didn't realise that this had an impact on how the constables – the troops who did the bulk of the work – saw me. They saw it as disinterest on my part; an understandable conclusion but one which I honestly don't think was true. The situation on the team was complicated by yet another change of MIT Manager, the Superintendent who was my immediate boss. At the start of the Bellfield case, it had been Sue Hill. She had been replaced by the Chief Superintendent Andy Murphy, who had taken direct line responsibility for a couple of months at the end of 2004. He then had to perform other duties and I had reported to Julian Worker and then, finally, for the last year of the investigation and all through the trial, to John Sweeney. John was an absolute gentleman, much loved by all who worked for him. He trusted me, encouraged me and, although he was always there if I needed him, he let me get on with my job. I had become his ad-hoc deputy, acting as Superintendent when he was away from work, attending meetings for him and fulfilling the on-call MIT manager role.

BACK TO NORMAL?

John was replaced, due to yet another series of moves and promotions, in 2008 by Colin Lee. Colin was an affable man but very much driven by processes and systems. For some reason, he and I just didn't get on. I don't know why but it wasn't for lack of trying on my part. He was, I thought, over-intrusive in his supervision of administrative things that didn't really matter that much and far less enthusiastic in providing the practical support and encouragement that actually helped his teams succeed in solving murders. Which, when all was said and done, was what we were really there for. It is ironic, therefore, that he made a decision that caused me to get back to my old self somewhat.

In February 2009, seventeen-year-old Michael Wright was stabbed to death near Maryland Point, Stratford, in east London. It was a more senseless than usual slaying, being the outcome of a dispute over a nightclub entrance ticket to the value of £15. It took place during a time when there was much debate around knife crime in general and knife crime among young black men in street gangs, in particular. Colin Lee was the on-call Detective Superintendent and, therefore, responsible for allocating the crime to an investigation team. Its location was diametrically opposite across London from our base in Putney and, of course, firmly in the centre of the East Murder Command, just about three miles from their offices in Barking. Nevertheless, it was to us that Colin Lee turned. He was honest – it wasn't that the East teams were too busy, which would have been the usual reason for us being asked to operate so far from our own patch. It was, he said, because it was going to be a heavily political and public investigation and that it needed to be dealt with well and solved quickly. He thought we were the best team for the job. The thought went through my mind that he might actually much prefer for me and my team to be the ones that failed in such a case, but that just made me more determined. I had thought – said, on many occasions – that my team was the best and there was nothing I wouldn't take on with them. It was time to prove it.

We went over to Barking and received the handover briefing from the on-call team, just like it was all those years previously at Twickenham when we first assumed responsibility for Amélie. And, without realising it, I was just as engaged, just as keen. We then broke out to another room, where I discussed what there was with my team, what we needed to do, who would do it, when we would regroup for another briefing, firing out suggestions, firmly directing what needed to be done. I just thought I was doing my job in the same way I always had, until the meeting broke up and DC Helen Rance came up to me and smiled, saying, 'Welcome back, Guv'nor.'

I realised what she meant immediately. It was really just like it always had been, something had rekindled my fire and it was actually what they wanted me to be like.

Thanks to some brilliant and determined work, especially by Steve Kinchington and Mick Snowden in persuading young witnesses to give us statements, we had the murderer, sixteen-year-old Bradley Walters-Stewart in custody the next day and charged within a further forty-eight hours. He was subsequently sentenced to life with a minimum of fourteen years for the murder and the tragic case never became the political hot potato it had been feared to be. Once again, we had delivered, I was back in the saddle and all was well. The team truly was back to normal. Except it wasn't . . . the team was going to be disrupted, whether we liked it or not.

Detective Chief Superintendent Hamish Campbell was the new leader of the murder command when, in April 2009, he went out to visit all his teams. I was on holiday and missed him coming to Putney. He therefore invited me to go to have a chat with him at his office in New Scotland Yard, which I did. During this meeting, he explained that he wanted a review done of Operation Minstead, which was a very long-running investigation based at Lewisham, into a string of burglaries and rapes committed against the elderly in their own homes in south-east London over more than seventeen years. The media had, over the years, become accustomed to referring to the unknown suspect as 'The Night Stalker'. It was to be just a review; I was to go over and spend a couple of weeks looking through the case, applying, as Hamish put it, 'your investigative acumen', and then report my findings. There was, as far as I was concerned, no question of it being anything other than a temporary, one-off task for me to carry out before returning to my team at Putney.

I returned to Putney and asked Clive Grace to prepare me some of the most recent Minstead crime reports and to keep it quiet as I didn't want to upset the team by any suggestion that I was about to be bailing out. Within a couple of days, though, the bush telegraph was up and running or, as it was often put in Met-speak, 'Rumour Control was open.' Well and truly open. It seemed that the entire murder command had heard that I was being moved and was going permanently to Minstead. Andy Perrott was to be appointed acting DCI and take charge of my team and I would never be returning to Putney. I laughed this off and said it would never happen but, when I asked Hamish about it, he just said that we would have to see how things progressed. As is often sadly the case, the rumour and tittle-tattle proved to be more accurate than the situation as it was officially portrayed to me. I left for Lewisham in late May and never did return. Gradually, the Bellfield team went on to other things, one by one, so that, by the end of 2010, just a handful of the greatest, most dedicated, most talented, most successful team I was ever lucky enough to be a part of remained at Putney.

Gary Cunningham, as perceptive and honest as ever, spoke to me over a pint in the Boat House shortly after I left.

'You've been done up like a kipper, Boss. They've smashed up the team. All because we were so successful, we had such a reputation and they thought we were untouchable. But not only that, got you moved over to the biggest crock of shit in existence, where you've got no chance of succeeding. I told you after the trial [nobody ever needed to say the Bellfield trial; it was always just "the trial"] it was a shame you couldn't retire on a high then.'

I smiled at his analysis, which, for all I could know or make out, was pretty much spot on, but I realised then the desire was still burning in me.

'Don't write me off yet, Gary,' I said. 'It is a shame we can't all do it together as a team again, but I think I'm a bit like George Foreman or Joe Bugner. An ageing heavyweight who everyone thinks is past it – but I'm pretty sure I've still got one more fight left in me.'

Which I then knew I would have to back up with action, so off I went to do it. And that is another story altogether.

EPILOGUE

Lewisham Police station, a huge monolith at the north end of Lewisham High Street, handy for the overground and DLR, home to the Borough Police, Murder Squads and the Mounted Branch, soulless and modern – even boasting its own multi-storey car park – and all paid for by a PFI scheme, which meant even a light-bulb change cost hundreds. It had a nice canteen, though – good food, smiling staff and proper coffee. Despite this, as I strode in on the morning of 30 March 2010, my mind was not on breakfast but on the large television set fixed to the wall in the corner of the lounge area. Three PCSOs were on the sofas. The fact that they were all riveted to their smartphones didn't, these days, actually mean they would not claim to be watching as Jeremy Kyle refereed the usual tale of urban domestic strife but I decided it was reasonable, at least, to ask.

'Do you mind at all if I change the channel? There's something on Sky News I especially need to see.'

Two of the young community support officers didn't even stir from their Angry Birds, Facebook, Match.com or whatever it was that was holding their attention captive. The other looked up at me. I am sure he decided in an instant that this old bloke in a suit and a Murder Squad lanyard was probably the sort of person with a special need to whom it was a good idea to defer. And why not, I thought – we are still a disciplined service, aren't we?

'Yes, of course, Guv. We're not really watching this crap,' he said, showing both excellent taste in television and that he had enough experience to have learned to spot a senior officer. Or at least such keenness of vision to be able to read a hanging warrant card from three metres. 'Either way, he'll go far,' I thought. I thanked him as he handed me the remote control and I punched '132' into the Freeview box while still walking to a good vantage point.

The press conference I wanted to see had just begun. Centre stage was Nigel Pilkington, the Crown Prosecution Service lawyer dealing with the Milly Dowler case being investigated by Surrey Police, flanked by Maria Woodall, the Surrey SIO still leading the investigation eight years after Milly was taken and murdered and she had begun to work on it, two promotions ago. I wanted to remark how odd it seemed to see the CPS grandstanding like this. They had traditionally worked very much in the background, making their important contributions to our prosecutions quietly yet decisively. All that seemed to have changed since Keir Starmer had become the Director of Public Prosecutions (DPP). Now it seemed they wanted to grab a piece of the limelight at every opportunity. 'Just so long as they do the same when it all goes pear-shaped, eh?' I stopped short of articulating this out loud, though. I wasn't sure the PCSOs were particularly interested, especially the one who had just zoomed in to a photo of a young lady and was eagerly showing it to his colleague. How I wished I was there with Brunty or Clive or Cunningham or Carruth or all of them – any of the old team that would have understood. But there was just me, alone yet in a room of twenty people, fixated on a screen depicting real and momentous events.

The previous evening, I had received a phone call, by a circuitous route, telling me that the CPS were going to announce the charging decision on the Milly Dowler case at 11am the following morning. Live, at a televised press conference. Not for Surrey colleagues either the thrill or the privacy of gathering around the fax machine as it churned out the message of such great import. Live TV, where your reaction and expression would be there for all to see. 'Surely, they must know what is happening?' I thought. I had called Maria Woodall and she had assured me she did not know what Pilkington was going to say. I made the reasonable point that 'my' families needed to know but she said that all she had been able to tell the Dowlers was that the decision would be announced, not what its substance was, so that was the most I could tell mine. CPS grandstanding is one thing, I remarked, but I really didn't expect them to try to milk it with the audience. Maria muttered something, but it was clear to me that she was being truthful and really didn't know.

I was going to have to watch the television like everyone else and so it came that I was settled down in the Lewisham canteen as Pilkington began his address. He was very keen on stressing it was *his* decision, *he* requested further enquiries, *he* then considered them and *he* had now reached *his* decision. I had never met the man but instantly decided he was quite pompous, not in the plummy, verbose and caricatured lawyerly fashion but more self-centred, egotistical and self-promotional. Still, I guess even organisations as large as the CPS soon begin to take on the traits of their leader. He told us there was sufficient evidence and that it was in the public interest to charge Levi Bellfield with three offences. Hang on a minute, three offences? This was going to be interesting. Kidnapping Milly and murdering her, I expected. I wondered what the third was? I didn't have long to wait. He outlined the charges chronologically and so it was with the unexpected offence he started:

'First, that he attempted to kidnap Rachel Cowles on 20 March 2002; second, that he kidnapped Milly Dowler on 21 March 2002; third, that he murdered Milly Dowler on 21 March 2002.'

Maria Woodall put in a sterling performance, keeping a completely straight face during what must have been a very emotional moment for her. Doubly so since, I later found out, she had absolutely no idea that the Rachel Cowles offence was going to be mentioned, let alone authorised. Which, of course, meant that they had no opportunity whatsoever to prepare Rachel and her family for what was coming. Her father was watching the media conference. Of course, he had more than the general public interest in it given how closely his daughter was involved with the case or, indeed, how close Rachel had come to being another of Bellfield's victims. Once again, he would have thought that he and Rachel had been forgotten, that the system had failed them as they had to find out important information from the media, rather from those who should have been talking to him. This was true but, on this occasion, Surrey Police were completely blameless. His unfortunate situation was entirely due to the CPS and their desire to grab the headlines, coupled with their naivety and inexperience in dealing with the tricky issues involved in family liaison.

For my part, I was thrilled that Surrey had finally got their man 'on the sheet', as the Met slang went, from the days when charges were laboriously written longhand on to A3-sized pieces of self-copying paper (the northern forces' equivalent was 'Fingers in the ink', referencing the old way of taking 'wet' fingerprints after charge. I actually preferred it but never used it once back in the Met. When in Rome . . .). There had been many things during the whole Milly Dowler investigation for which Surrey Police might justly be criticised but one could never knock their determination and tenacity. Much of this towards the end of the investigation I am sure was due to Maria Woodall possessing those qualities in spades; whether the Operation Ruby inquiry would actually have got anywhere at all without our intervention and the information we were able to pass them regarding Bellfield is debatable – Bellfield was just not on their radar at all. I am sure though that, even if they had got there in the end, we certainly made their path easier and probably quicker.

What remained of my team – principally Clive Grace – continued to assist Surrey with any information from our supersized database, but I had little more to do with it. I was completely tied up in Operation Minstead and then, in January 2011, completed my thirty years' service and retired. Bellfield's second trial, for the Surrey offences, took place a couple of months later. I had passed up the opportunity to attend it, every day, as a national newspaper invited me to have one of their press passes so that I could cover it for them. While I was most definitely keen to do it, I had a serious reservation. Given the hostility that had existed between Bellfield and me right from the day he was arrested, would my obvious presence upset him? Of course, I cared nothing for his feelings but I was determined that I should not cause a disruption; a sideshow which would make the trial more difficult for everybody to manage. And I certainly didn't want to be on the receiving end of a ruling from the judge removing me from the court, which was a real fear as I knew Bellfield would kick up a fuss. So I did the responsible thing, I think, and called Brian Altman. He agreed that my misgivings were real and his view was that it would be better if I declined. Naturally, I took his advice and turned them down, glad that I had thought about it and made the correct choice.

Many words have been written about the second trial; I was not there so I will not add much to them. That Milly's parents and sister were subjected to a further horrific ordeal at the hands of Bellfield's lawyers brings only shame on him and them. Doubtless the lawyers were correct in principle by protesting that they had no choice but to put the defence as they were instructed; it is a pity that other more common principles – those of decency and humanity – appeared to be completely absent in what they did.

Then after he was convicted, the media showed they had learned nothing from the first trial. Once again, they went overboard overnight, so much bad publicity being printed that the Rachel Cowles case – upon which the jury had still not decided– had to be abandoned. Just as with Anna-Maria Rennie and Irma Dragoshi, she was denied her justice simply by the excesses of the media. At least this time there were repercussions; both Mirror Group Newspapers and Associated Newspapers were, in 2012, fined for pieces in the *Daily Mirror* and *Daily Mail*, respectively, which were held to be in contempt of court.

Reading the reports and seeing the utterly devastated Dowlers on television sickened me. It served only to reinforce the decision I made all those years ago, that I could never live with myself if I had aligned with people like Bellfield and those who worked so hard, ruthlessly, to represent and defend them.

Joining the good guys might have made me poorer, too often very tired and stressed, have interfered with my relationships and personal life and have taken me to some dark places. But it had also given me the funniest, most touching, most terrifying, most satisfying and most memorable experiences of my life, in the company of courageous and dedicated men and women who were worth a thousand of Bellfield or his lawyers.

At the end of it all, I had emerged relatively unscathed, smiling and with the wonderful warm glow that only comes from knowing that you did the right thing.

Another old Met saying sprang to mind: 'At the end of the day, we did some good.'

ACKNOWLEDGEMENTS

Thanks to every one of the scores of amazingly dedicated officers who contributed in any way to make these investigations a success. It was my absolute privilege to know you and to lead you. My special personal thanks go to Ed Whitmore for his encouragement – without which I would never have completed this book.